The Benedict Proposal

The Benedict Proposal

*Church as Creative Minority
in the Thought of Pope Benedict XVI*

JOSHUA BRUMFIELD

◈PICKWICK *Publications* · Eugene, Oregon

THE BENEDICT PROPOSAL
Church as Creative Minority in the Thought of Pope Benedict XVI

Copyright © 2020 Joshua Brumfield. All rights reserved. Except for brief quotations in critical publications or reviews, no part of this book may be reproduced in any manner without prior written permission from the publisher. Write: Permissions, Wipf and Stock Publishers, 199 W. 8th Ave., Suite 3, Eugene, OR 97401.

Pickwick Publications
An Imprint of Wipf and Stock Publishers
199 W. 8th Ave., Suite 3
Eugene, OR 97401

www.wipfandstock.com

PAPERBACK ISBN: 978-1-5326-7313-9
HARDCOVER ISBN: 978-1-5326-7314-6
EBOOK ISBN: 978-1-5326-7315-3

Cataloguing-in-Publication data:

Names: Brumfield, Joshua, author.

Title: The Benedict proposal : church as creative minority in the thought of Pope Benedict XVI / Joshua Brumfield.

Description: Eugene, OR: Pickwick Publications, 2020 | Includes bibliographical references and index.

Identifiers: ISBN 978-1-5326-7313-9 (paperback) | ISBN 978-1-5326-7314-6 (hardcover) | ISBN 978-1-5326-7315-3 (ebook)

Subjects: LCSH: Benedict—XVI,—Pope,—1927-. | Catholic Church—Doctrines—History—20th century. | Catholic Church—Doctrines—History—21st century.

Classification: BX1378.6 .B77 2020 (print) | BX1378.6 .B77 (ebook)

Manufactured in the U.S.A.　　　　　　　　　　　　　　　　APRIL 29, 2020

Unless otherwise noted, Scripture quotations are taken from Revised Standard Version of the Bible—Second Catholic Edition (Ignatius Edition) Copyright © 2006 National Council of the Churches of Christ in the United States of America. Used by permission. All rights reserved worldwide.

To Ashley, my wife

Contents

Introduction | 1

Part 1
1. From Metaphysics to Modernity | 13
2. Post-Conciliar Crisis and Ratzinger's Response | 27

Part 2
3. Being as Relation: Communion in the Trinity | 61
4. *Communio* Ecclesiology | 76
5. Eucharist and Mission | 90

Part 3
6. Questions and Critiques | 117
7. Response and Analysis | 138
8. Communion and Mission Made Concrete in the Movements | 158
9. Conclusion | 181

Bibliography | 185

Index | 195

Introduction

WHEN POPE ST. JOHN XXIII convoked the Second Vatican Council, he desired for it to present the faith in a new way. He hoped for an *aggiornamento* to enable the church to preach the Gospel more effectively to the modern world. He wanted the council to better equip the church to carry out her mission as the universal sacrament of salvation.[1] The council proved to be a momentous event, perhaps even "the most important event within the Church in the past 400 years."[2] Most of the ecumenical councils were called to address major theological or pastoral crises facing the church, but the crisis facing the church during John XXIII's pontificate was perhaps not as obvious. Nevertheless, in retrospect one can surmise that in the council the church received the gifts necessary to weather the coming crises.

Pope Paul VI's *Evangelii nuntiandi* and John Paul II's *Redemptoris missio* have echoed John XXIII's call, inviting the church to "renew her missionary commitment."[3] Pope John Paul II repeated his call in *Novo millennio ineunte*, writing of the Jubilee Year as "a providential opportunity during which the Church . . . would examine how far she had renewed herself in order to be able to take up her evangelizing mission with fresh enthusiasm."[4] In short, the popes perceived the purpose of the council to have been to inaugurate a renewal of ecclesial life, which would equip her for mission. Since the 1985 extraordinary synod of bishops taught that communion was the main theme of the council, one may say in retrospect that one way in which the council sought to accomplish the renewal of the church was through the theme of communion. After all, as John Paul II explained, "Communion and mission are deeply connected . . . to the point that communion

---

1. John XXIII, *Humanae salutis*, 1.
2. Hitchcock, *Catholicism and Modernity*, 75.
3. Paul VI, *Evangelii nuntiandi*.
4. John Paul II, *Novo millennio ineunte*.

represents both the source and the outcome of mission."[5] However, despite the recent emphasis on communion ecclesiology and the longstanding missionary mandate of Christ echoed in the teachings of the council, Catholics do not often experience parish life as life in communion, and the missionary impulse of the majority of Catholics remains rather muted. Indeed, the so-called New Evangelization has yet to make any significant and noticeable headway in its attempts to re-evangelize the post-Christian West.

One of the great Catholic philosophers of the last century, Alasdair MacIntyre, recognized some of the foundational problems of this modern era and indicated an approach to imagining how the church might engage the modern world. MacIntyre famously concluded his *After Virtue* with a call for a new Saint Benedict, but the overall context of that call is worth recalling:

> It is always dangerous to draw too precise parallels between one historical period and another; and among the most misleading of such parallels are those which have been drawn between our own age in Europe and North America and the epoch in which the Roman empire declined into the Dark Ages. Nonetheless certain parallels there are. A crucial turning point in that earlier history occurred when men and women of good will turned aside from the task of shoring up the *imperium* and ceased to identify a continuation of civility and moral community with the maintenance of that *imperium*. What they set themselves to achieve instead—often not recognizing fully what they were doing—was the construction of new forms of community within which the moral life could be sustained so that both morality and civility might survive the coming ages of barbarism and darkness. . . . We ought also to include that for some time now we too have reached that turning point. What matters at this stage is the construction of local forms of community within which civility and the intellectual and moral life can be sustained through the new dark ages which are already upon us. . . . This time however the barbarians are not waiting beyond the frontiers; they have already been governing us for quite some time. And it is our lack of consciousness of this that constitutes part of our predicament. We are waiting . . . for another—doubtless very different—St. Benedict.[6]

---

5. John Paul II, *Christifidelis laici*, 32.
6. MacIntyre, *After Virtue*, 263.

This "Benedict Option"[7] therefore places its hope in the foundation of stable and local communities not only to sustain authentic Christian communion but to evangelize the world precisely through that communion. Here I will argue that Joseph Ratzinger's eucharistic ecclesiology provides a model for living the relation between communion and mission, a model that provides a sound image for conceiving of and imagining the church's engagement with modernity and the embodiment of the missionary communion called for by the post-conciliar popes. Ratzinger's vision is deeply influenced by St. Benedict's own response to the problems of his day, therefore, a brief exposition of "Ratzinger's Benedict"—Benedictine themes underlining Ratzinger's ecclesiology—will help to introduce the main contours of the argument.

First, Ratzinger, like MacIntyre, draws a comparison[8] between the late stages of the Roman Empire and the current state of the Western world. Ratzinger perceives Europe and the West to be exhibiting similar symptoms. He identifies a few key characteristics of this "secular age."[9] I explore Ratzinger's analysis in more detail in the first and second chapters. We must first recognize that for Ratzinger the modern era is characterized by a technological, rationalistic culture and logic, which reduces the "world" to the merely observable and "truth" to the empirically verifiable. "In the wake of this form of rationality, Europe has developed a culture that, in a manner hitherto unknown to mankind, excludes God from public awareness. His existence may be denied altogether where considered unprovable and uncertain and, hence, as something of belonging to the spirit of subjective choices. In either case, God is irrelevant to public life."[10] Second, he proposes that one major reason for this devolution of culture is the impotence of the church: "Here what we are actually addressing, in my opinion, is the decisive reason for the abandonment of Christianity: its model for life is apparently unconvincing. It seems to place too many restraints on humankind that stifle its *joie de vivre*, that limit its precious freedom."[11]

Ratzinger compares the current situation to that of the early church during the time of Julian the Apostate, who attempted to turn the religious practice of his citizens back to paganism by imitating Christian charity and emphasizing the "joy" of pagan religious activities. Ratzinger explains that Christians, in response to this, "were able to demonstrate persuasively how

---

7. MacIntyre's call has been popularized as the "Benedict Option" in Dreher, *Benedict Option*.
8. Ratzinger and Pera, *Without Roots*, 66–67.
9. See Taylor, *Secular Age*.
10. Ratzinger, *Christianity and the Crisis of Cultures*, 30.
11. Ratzinger and Pera, *Without Roots*, 125.

empty and base were the entertainments of paganism, and how sublime the gift of faith in the God who suffers with us and leads us to the road of true greatness."[12] For this reason, "Today it is a matter of the greatest urgency to show a Christian model of life that offers a livable alternative to the increasingly vacuous entertainments"[13] of our secular age.

What might this look like? Ratzinger offers St. Benedict as a model for responding to the needs of our time: For example, before being elected pope he reflected, "Time and again, our world could so easily find its corrective in the Benedictine Rule."[14] He continued, "We need men like Benedict of Nursia, who, in an age of dissipation and decadence, immersed himself in the uttermost solitude. Then, after all the purification he had to undergo, he succeeded in rising again to the light . . . where he assembled the forces from which a new world was formed."[15] Thus the key themes of Benedict's proposal, of his vision for how the church might embody missionary communion, can be gleaned from his reflection on the example of Benedict of Nursia. First, there must be an initial purification, which often comes about through some form of withdrawal from "the world" or those parts of it which threaten purity of heart. St. Benedict's response to his experience of the corruption and moral decay of Rome—his retreat to hermetic life—indicates he saw the church, or the monastery as it may have been, as a society standing in contrast to "the world." Thus, in response to the debauchery of Rome, he did not seek to find the movement of the Spirit active within the crumbling Roman society. Rather, he withdrew to the desert to turn to the Lord.[16] One could rightly say that the original monastic impulse was to be counter-cultural, to separate oneself from the distractions of the world in order to be single-mindedly devoted to God—and to become single-mindedly devoted to God for the sake of the world.

Second, in forming his monasteries, St. Benedict emphasized personal conversion and commitment to the Gospel. The first word of Benedict's Rule is "listen,"[17] from the start exhorting his monks to be attentive to God's Word. Indeed, St. Benedict attempted to encourage radical conversion to Christ through prayer and the spiritual reading of the scriptures. Thus, the

---

12. Ratzinger and Pera, *Without Roots*, 125.
13. Ratzinger and Pera, *Without Roots*, 125–26.
14. Ratzinger, *God and the World*, 392.
15. Ratzinger, *God and the World*, 392.
16. Note that the *telos* of the withdrawal is not escapism or quietism but conversion. It is turning to the Lord. It is seeking that "purity of heart" demanded of disciples of Christ which is also a prerequisite of evangelization.
17. Benedict, *Rule of Saint Benedict*, 3.

Rule calls the monks to "prefer nothing whatever to Christ,"[18] a phrase that Pope Benedict quoted in his very first general audience.[19] This life of listening literally ordered by the divine office was intended to cultivate humility, receptivity, and obedience in the monks and to help them to acquire a thoroughly biblical imagination and to develop virtuous habits grounded in service to the Lord. The monasteries offered stability—a setting where God's Word more easily could be heard, encountered, and embodied. St. Benedict thought that praising God and living that praise in community was the best medicine for a flawed, depraved, poverty-stricken world.

Third, the radical orientation to Christ demanded by the *Rule* implies a counter-cultural approach to the church's relationship to the world. Thus, monastic communities ultimately developed into stable contrast-societies. In Benedict's monasteries, the monks shared a liturgically-ordered life, centered on prayer and work—*ora et labora*—in which worship was the most important work to be done. This shared life gradually developed into a rich, biblically-based culture. Over time, monasteries became centers of learning that were particularly important during the Middle Ages. The primary goal was not to minister to the wider church or to evangelize but to establish a community of Christians devoted to helping each other live out the Gospel. It was precisely because they lived and breathed in this liturgical milieu that the monks were able to bring Christ to the Western world, which happened slowly, organically.

It is this Benedictine model that Ratzinger has in mind when, reflecting upon the founding principles of the Christian culture that once characterized Europe, he argues that "throughout the great upheavals of history [monasticism] has continued to be the indispensable bearer not only of cultural continuity but above all of fundamental religious and moral values, the ultimate guidance of humankind. As a pre-political and supra-political force, monasticism was also the harbinger of ever welcome and necessary rebirths of culture and civilization."[20] So, following the analysis and argument of Arnold Toynbee,[21] Ratzinger calls for the church to develop "creative minori-

18. Benedict, *Rule of Saint Benedict* 72.11.
19. Benedict XVI, "General Audience."
20. Ratzinger and Pera, *Without Roots*, 55.
21. Toynbee, *Study of History*, 276. Ratzinger explains, "[Arnold] Toynbee emphasized the difference between technological-material progress and true progress, which he defined as spiritual realization. He recognized that the Western world was indeed undergoing a crisis, which he attributed to the abandonment of religion for the cult of technology, nationalism, and militarism. For him this crisis has a name: secularism. . . . If you know the cause of an illness, you can also find a cure: the religious heritage and all its forms need to be reintroduced. . . . Rather than a biologistic vision, [Toynbee] offers a voluntaristic one focused on the energy of creative minorities and exceptional individuals" (Ratzinger and Pera, *Without Roots*, 67–68).

ties" that might leaven a crumbling culture: "we must agree with Toynbee that the fate of a society always depends on its creative minorities. Christian believers should look upon themselves as just such a creative minority, and help Europe to reclaim the best of its heritage and to thereby place itself at the service of all humankind."[22] To this end, he articulates three theses which convey his model of today's "creative minorities,"[23] which offer that urgently needed "convincing model of life" precisely "through their persuasive capacity and their joy."[24]

First, Ratzinger argues that in order for Christian communities to function as "creative minorities," leavening society as did the monasteries of old, they must be formed by "human beings who in their encounters with Christ have discovered the precious pearl that gives value to all life (Matt 13:45ff)."[25] Such formation enables them to bear eloquent witness to the "joy of the Gospel," to live a convincing and persuasive Christian life. In other words, people must be able to encounter these communities concretely and to experience their shared life as convincing and attractive.

Second, while these communities can rightly be called "creative *minorities*," which implies they do not explicitly encompass the whole of the world or even of the church, nevertheless "we all need forms of belonging or of reference to these communities."[26] After all, St. Benedict's monasteries would not have shaped the culture of Europe so pervasively if only monks had had contact with them. Instead, the "monastic communities knew forms of belonging or of reference to the monastic family that enabled their energies to renew the Church and society as a whole. Meeting places that become 'yeast' (Matt 13:33)—a persuasive force that acts beyond the more closed sphere until it reaches everybody—should therefore be formed around the minorities that have been touched by faith."[27] This requires that churches, parishes, or Christian communities rediscover monastic

---

22. Ratzinger and Pera, *Without Roots*, 80.

23. Ratzinger is here dialoguing with Marcello Pera, former professor of the philosophy of science at the University of Pisa and one-time President of the Italian Senate, about the current state and future of Europe. In this context he argues for "creative minorities" to help Europe regain a kind of "civil religion," which cross denomination and religious boundaries and still perform the function of leavening the whole. For our purpose it is sufficient to imagine these communities as Catholic (or catholic, if you prefer) communities with ecumenical membership and universal scope, which is to say concern for all and rejection of none in the local community.

24. Ratzinger and Pera, *Without Roots*, 121.

25. Ratzinger and Pera, *Without Roots*, 120–21.

26. Ratzinger and Pera, *Without Roots*, 121.

27. Ratzinger and Pera, *Without Roots*, 122.

hospitality and again become places of solace, of peace, and of belonging.[28] There is a public character to authentic Christian community. Further, creative minorities cannot be creative if they are merely withdrawn minorities. After all, the Quakers and Amish, despite their fervent faith and consistent form of life, do not qualify as "creative" in this sense. They have not evangelized American society. In Benedict's proposal, creative minorities must do so.

Third, these "creative minorities" cannot be merely self-sufficient religious clubs, however, good their intentions may be. Rather they can only remain stable and vital if they "live naturally from the fact that the Church as a whole remains and that it lives in and can stand by the faith in its divine origins."[29] Thus, the creative minority exists in a reciprocal relationship: on the one hand relying on the whole church, receiving from her the living tradition, the grace of the sacraments, the life in Christ, and on the other hand, giving new life to the church as a whole with its own creativity and vitality, joy and love—just as the monasteries of old existed within and from the church and simultaneously revitalized the church and the broader world by their presence. This reciprocal relationship ultimately points to the givenness of the church who can only ever receive herself from above. Only if creative minorities are visibly not self-sufficient clubs, can they function as pointers to the transcendent, to God.

Sharing St. Benedict's counter-cultural inclinations, christocentrism, and logic of indirection, Ratzinger awaits in patient hope for "creative minorities" to grow within the shell of Christendom, thereby bringing renewal

---

28. John Henry Newman once described the patient, hope-filled, world-restoring work of Benedict and his monks and the ways in which society as whole developed in contact with and in reference to them as follows: "[Benedict] found the world, physical and social, in ruins, and his mission was to restore it in the way, not of science, but of nature, not as if setting about to do it, not professing to do it, by any set time or by any rare specific or by any series of strokes, but so quietly, patiently, gradually, that often, till the work was done, it was not known to be doing. It was a restoration rather than a visitation, correction, or conversion. The new world which he helped to create was a growth rather than a structure. Silent men were observed about the country, or discovered in the forest, digging, clearing, and building; and other silent men, men not seen, were sitting in the cold cloister, trying their eyes, and keeping their attention on the stretch, while they painfully deciphered and copied and re-copied the manuscripts which they had saved. There was no one that 'contended or cried out,' or drew attention to what was going on; but by degrees the woody swamp became a hermitage, a religious house, a farm, an abbey, a village, a seminary, a school of learning, and a city. Roads and bridges connected it with other abbeys and cities, which had similarly grown up; and what the haughty Alaric or fierce Attila had broken to pieces, these patient meditative men had brought together and made to live again" (Newman, *Historical Sketches II*, 410).

29. Ratzinger and Pera, *Without Roots*, 122.

and restoration to the church and the world. He shares the Benedictine vision of the church as a contrast-society, an image which itself demands and implies an insistence on personal conversion to the Gospel and an emphasis on the stability of the ecclesial community. Conversion is conversion-into-communion with God and the church. In other words, just as St. Benedict's monasteries were not mere aggregates of more-or-less holy individuals but were liturgical communities, which modeled to the world a way of living that witnessed to truth and love, so Ratzinger believes that the eucharistic liturgy is the heart of the church, forming Christians into a spiritual and moral communion. The current times call for dioceses and parishes to be transformed from sacramental dispensaries into creative minorities—small communities capable of bearing credible witness to the presence of God in history, indeed, to his presence in the here and now. Like St. Benedict, Ratzinger takes the long, patient view, grounded in eschatological hope, which waits for the Spirit organically to build up communities capable of bringing Christ to the world. John XXIII wanted the council to enable the church again to become a culture-shaping force in the world. Ratzinger shares this desire, and he believes that it can be achieved only in God's time, through the work of the Spirit, through listening to the Word, worshiping the Lord, and being gathered in communion around him. In this way, Christian communities become "creative minorities."

In what follows I argue that Ratzinger's thoroughly liturgical and eucharistic ecclesiology of communion provides a theological basis for properly understanding the relation of communion and mission and thus articulates an effective model of how the church might once again fulfill her mission as the universal sacrament of salvation. To this end, I have divided the book into three parts. Part one consists of two chapters: In chapter 1 I explore Ratzinger's analysis of the roots of modernity, the initial defensive response of the church, and the conciliar attempt at *aggiornamento*. The second chapter explores Ratzinger's understanding of, and response to, the post-conciliar crisis through the lens of his Bonaventurean understanding of the *analogia entis*.

In part two, I explore the theological depths of Ratzinger's ecclesiological view of communion and mission in three chapters. Since his ecclesiology is properly theological, articulated with reference to the Trinity, chapter 3 is an analysis of his trinitarian theology and his understanding of person as relation. In chapter 4, I articulate his communion ecclesiology with regard to the origins of the church, the sacramentality of the church, and the eucharistic nature of the church. I tie Ratzinger's ecclesiology to his missiology in chapter 5 by examining his thoroughly eucharistic and liturgical notion of the relation between communion and mission.

In part three, I offer my own tentative contribution in three chapters. Chapter 6 recognizes the trinitarian criticism articulated by Miroslav Volf, the ecclesiological criticism of Joseph Komonchak, and the missiological critique of Mary Ehle. In chapter 7 I expound a Ratzingerian response to each of these critiques of his ecclesiology. In chapter 8 I explain how Ratzinger's eucharistic ecclesiology provides the theological foundation for "creative minorities" and suggest one of the new ecclesial movements as a possible model embodying the relation of communion and mission in Ratzinger's ecclesiology.

Part 1

1

From Metaphysics to Modernity

BEFORE DEVELOPING RATZINGER'S ECCLESIOLOGICAL notion of, and call for creative minorities, accounting for the particular challenges with which the modern era presents the church and to which any adequate ecclesiology must respond is in order. To this end, I first briefly trace the philosophical, theological, and societal developments which shaped the context for the ecclesiological renewal formally inaugurated at the Second Vatican Council.[1] It would be beyond the task of this study to attempt such a survey comprehensively. Thus, I limit myself primarily to Ratzinger's own diagnoses and supplement his observations with other notable perspectives in order to place his view in a broader context. This chapter examines Ratzinger's perception of some trends which led up to the Second Vatican Council by first considering the modern shift from ontological considerations to more utilitarian concerns. Next, I explore the implications of the church's response to the encroachments of modernity. Finally, I close this chapter with an introduction to the response of the church as embodied in two key documents of Vatican II.

---

1. For more on Vatican II's history and theology, see O'Malley, *What Happened at Vatican II*, which offers a comprehensive overview of the pertinent events and issues in reasonably balanced fashion. Also, Alberigo and Komonchak, *History of Vatican II*, a five-volume project, is the most extensive and detailed compilation of Vatican II information. Both of the above assume a hermeneutic of rupture in interpreting the conciliar events and documents as marking significant change from prior church councils and documents. In contrast, Lamb and Levering, *Vatican II*, propose a hermeneutic of reform and renewal, understanding the council as a renewal by returning to tradition. Other important resources include Latourelle, *Vatican II*; Rush, *Still Interpreting Vatican II*; Vorgrimler, *Commentary on the Documents of Vatican II*, a major resource in which most of the commentaries were written by those who helped compose the documents themselves.

1.1 From Metaphysics to Facts, and from Facts to Progress

As early as 1873, Cardinal Newman had identified the presence in modernity of a crisis of faith: "You will find," he writes, "certainly in the future, nay more, even now, even now, that the writers and thinkers of the day do not even believe there is a God."[2] For his part, Joseph Ratzinger traces the origins of modernity and thus of the present crises back even further, to Giambattista Vico (1668-1744) and the birth of the historical approach.[3] In Vico's axiom *verum quia factum*, Ratzinger detects a significant and devastating departure from the traditional, which is to say metaphysical, view of the scholastics who thought of being itself as convertible with the truth. According to Ratzinger, the scholastics took up and christologically transformed the ancient Greek notions of ontology. Since, the biblical concept of God is bivalent—on the one hand God is personal and relative, "the God of Abraham, Isaac, and Jacob," and on the other hand, God is transcendent, is being itself[4]—the early church was able to adopt critically the Greek notion of *logos* in order to emphasize the idea of being over and against any mythological conception of the world and of worship. It attempted to integrate the God recognized in the faith of Abraham and the God made flesh in Jesus Christ with the God of the philosophers.[5] In opting against *religio* and myth in favor of *logos*, "Christianity thus resolutely put itself on the side of truth."[6] The cosmos comes from the being that is *logos*, truth. Any rejection of this resolution is ultimately a metaphysical decision to the contrary which leads to the necessary separation of religion from truth and undermines the claims of reason itself. This is because "it is an obvious fact that the rational character of the universe cannot be explained *rationally* on the basis of something irrational."[7] Such a rejection is precisely what Ratzinger interprets Vico to be proclaiming in his *verum quia factum*: we can truly only know that which we ourselves have made.

Since the scholastics viewed human reasoning to be a real but incomplete participation in the *logos*, they "took the view that knowledge of human things could only be merely *techne*, manual skill, but never real cognition and, hence, never real science."[8] In other words, a properly Christian

---

2. Newman, "Infidelity of the Future," 124.
3. Ratzinger, *Introduction to Christianity*, 59.
4. Ratzinger, *Introduction to Christianity*, 135.
5. Cf. Ratzinger, *Introduction to Christianity*, 138.
6. Ratzinger, *Introduction to Christianity*, 141.
7. Ratzinger, *Christianity and the Crisis of Cultures*, 199.
8. Ratzinger, *Introduction to Christianity*, 60.

metaphysics sees an analogous relation between *logos* as the immanent rationality of the world and human knowledge;[9] humanity's thought has a real relation to God's thinking of the world, but human thought and our creativity are always logic mixed with a-logic and are simultaneously always passing away and lacking presence. But in Vico, "the old equation of truth and being is replaced by the new one of truth and factuality; all that can be known is the *factum*, that which we have made ourselves."[10] This effectively blurs the distinction between God and man, equating the perfect knowledge which God has of creation with the knowledge man has of that which he makes. Whereas for God, creation is "made" by *logos*, by God's reason or thought, our human thoughts have no creative capabilities in themselves. Vico's axiom completely subverts this position by stating humans can only really know their own artifacts, their products. Thus, his axiom "denotes the real end of the old metaphysics and the beginning of the specifically modern attitude of mind. The revolutionary character of modern thinking in comparison with all that preceded it is here expressed with absolutely inimitable precision."[11] After all, if humanity can truly know only that which we have made, then why should one attend to metaphysical thought, to God? Thus began the modern obsession with the "fact" and the subsequent reduction of humanity from the pinnacle of creation to "a chance occurrence" of history and evolution. Indeed, because modernity has largely accepted Vico's argument, "We have given up seeking the hidden 'initselfness' of things and sounding the nature of being itself. We have . . . limited ourselves to our own perspective, to the visible in the widest sense, to what can be seized in our measuring grasp."[12] Reason has been limited to the *factum*. Truth is no longer pursued. Natural science is seen as the only reputable and sufficient knowledge.[13] The human person no longer remembers—or consciously refuses—to ask himself or herself the great existential questions.

But Vico's focus on historical facticity was not sustainable on its own. History cannot fully be determined or reconstructed. It cannot be empirically verified repeatably. If man is the author of truth, he cannot be satisfied with interpreting the past but must focus his energies on making the future.

---

9. Cf. Benedict XVI, "Faith, Reason, and the University": "The faith of the Church has always insisted that between God and us, between his eternal Creator Spirit and our created reason there exists a real analogy, in which—as the Fourth Lateran Council in 1215 stated—unlikeness remains infinitely greater than likeness, yet not to the point of abolishing analogy and its language."
10. Ratzinger, *Introduction to Christianity*, 61.
11. Ratzinger, *Introduction to Christianity*, 31.
12. Ratzinger, *Introduction to Christianity*, 58.
13. Ratzinger, *Introduction to Christianity*, 62.

Thus, Vico's *verum quia factum* was transformed by Marxist ideology into *verum quia faciendum*. This new formulation was exciting and persuasive. "In the final analysis all that man could really know was what was repeatable, what he could put before his eyes at any time in an experiment. . . . [Thus], the fact has set free the *faciendum*, the 'made' has set free the 'makeable,' the repeatable, the provable, and only exists for the sake of the latter."[14] No longer is creation perceived to be received as given by God with a nature and purpose. No longer does creation lead to contemplation of the creator. Now creation is raw matter which demands not stewardship but domination. "To put it another way: the truth with which man is concerned is neither the truth of being, nor even in the last resort that of his accomplished deeds, but the truth of changing the world—a truth centered on future and actions."[15]

Now humanity has the obligation to create the world in its image, indeed to re-create itself in its own indeterminate image. "Now wherever [man] comes from, he can look his future in the eye with the determination to make himself into whatever he wishes; he does not need to regard it as impossible to make himself into the God who now stands at the end as *faciendum*, as something makeable, not at the beginning as *logos*, meaning."[16]

For the modern consciousness, in Ratzinger's view, dependence on a creator as implied by acceptance of creation as given is an intolerable threat to the notion of human freedom assumed by modernity.[17] If humanity is to be truly free, it must be entirely autonomous, liberated from the restrictions that accompany createdness. "Since creation equals dependence and dependence is the anti-thesis of freedom, the doctrine of creation"[18] must be opposed, rejected, and concealed. Cardinal Newman described the rejection of faith as follows: "Seeing and proving is the only ground for believing. . . . Since proof admits of degrees, a demonstration can hardly be had except in mathematics; we never can have simple knowledge; truths are only probably such. So that faith is a mistake in two ways. First, because it usurps the place of reason, and secondly because it implies an absolute assent to doctrines, and is dogmatic, which absolute assent is irrational."[19] Therefore, in place of creation and dependence upon a creator, the modern mind enthrones chance and probability.[20]

---

14. Ratzinger, *Introduction to Christianity*, 64–65.
15. Ratzinger, *Introduction to Christianity*, 63.
16. Ratzinger, *Introduction to Christianity*, 66.
17. Ratzinger, *In the Beginning*, 84.
18. Ratzinger, *In the Beginning*, 91.
19. Newman, "Infidelity of the Future," 124.
20. Ratzinger, *In the Beginning*, 52–53.

Thus we see that the move from scholastic thought to the modern approach has limited reason in such a way that, for the modern mind, faith "was felt to be of no use for new times, for a humanity come of age, proud of its rationality and anxious to explore the future in novel ways."[21] God and truth are left out of the equation. God is irrelevant. "Slowly but surely, however, it would become evident that the light of autonomous reason is not enough to illumine the future; ultimately the future remains shadowy and fraught with fear of the unknown,"[22] leading humanity to renounce "the search for a great light, Truth itself, in order to be content with smaller lights."[23] The resulting timidity of reason has had far-reaching consequences, which, for Ratzinger, have culminated in the present "dictatorship of relativism,"[24] because "in the absence of light everything becomes confused; it is impossible to tell good from evil, or the road to our destination from other roads which take us in endless circles."[25] Furthermore, the atomistic scientism of modernity coupled with its philosophical trends has led to a certain individualism, which often results in a community of strangers. Ironically, people are isolated and alone in the midst of being constantly engaged in some form of communication. The creative minorities of Benedict's proposal must once again proclaim Christ and the church as relevant while offering people the sense of belonging that can overcome digital isolation.

1.2 An Anti-Modern Modern Church

Of course, all of this was not immediately apparent. The developments were slow and gradual. Not only were the philosophical sands shifting, but so were the political and cultural. Indeed, from the Reformation through the French Revolution and on into the Enlightenment, the church perceived itself to be under attack. Christendom was crumbling in the face of a new rationalism. With the Reformation and the French Revolution the "spiritual framework provided by the Holy Roman Empire—without which Europe could not have been formed—shattered in a formal sense."[26] The ensuing cultural and political changes rocked Christendom more visibly and

---

21. Francis, *Lumen fidei*, 2. While Pope Francis is technically the author, Pope Benedict had begun writing it before stepping down from his role as pope. Much of his language and thought can be detected in portions of *Lumen fidei*.

22. Francis, *Lumen fidei*, 3.

23. Francis, *Lumen fidei*, 3.

24. Ratzinger, "Homily for Mass."

25. Francis, *Lumen fidei*, 3.

26. Ratzinger and Pera, *Without Roots*, 62.

violently than philosophical developments alone could have. But these were all woven from the same rationalistic cloth. "This rationalism was the great enemy of the Church and of faith. Its essence was the repudiation of authority and of tradition, the self-proclaimed independence or autonomy believed to be enshrined in Luther's private judgment or in Kant's definition of the Enlightenment."[27] In response to the concealment of creation, the privatization of religion, and the sequestration of God to an irrelevant first cause, the church adopted apocalyptic language[28] and spoke of medieval Christendom as an ideal of integrated Christianity to be regained.[29] Thus, the church grew increasingly alienated from modern culture and society. Since the church perceived itself to be engaged in a cultural war, "clarity of command and unity of response" received greater emphasis and resulted in increased centralization.[30] Thus Rome played a greater role in the ecclesiastical functioning of the various churches and attempted to "not only oversee but also to direct theological developments."[31] These attempts to solidify the church's position in society culminated in the First Vatican Council and the teaching on papal infallibility. Altogether the church quite consciously became ghettoized, a sub-culture. Komonchak describes the change as follows:

> The Church has long since lost its monopoly as the ultimate inspirer and guarantor of western meanings and values. In the course of the nineteenth century, it further lost the political and social supports to its own activity which the State had once provided. Unwilling to abandon the right to an overarching and final interpretation and legitimation of culture meanings which it had enjoyed under the regime of Christendom, unable to share the basic philosophy of which first liberalism and then its competitors, socialism and communism, were built, and largely either unwilling or unable to winnow the wheat from the chaff in the modern developments, the Church constructed another world of meaning and value, a distinct social body within the larger society, a culture distinct from that which directed the ruling and planning classes.[32]

---

27. Komonchak, "Modernity," 358.
28. Cf. Pius X, *E supremi*, in Komonchak, "Modernity," 360.
29. Komonchak, "Modernity," 361–63.
30. Komonchak, "Modernity," 371.
31. Komonchak, "Modernity," 374.
32. Komonchak, "Modernity," 378.

While the development of a Catholic sub-culture was deemed necessary to protect the faith and the church itself from the heresies of modernism,[33] from "civilization without Christianity,"[34] it inevitably left the church irrelevant and impotent, voiceless in the conversations about the direction of modernity.

Thus, while the sub-culture of Roman Catholicism itself may have seemed stable and without crisis on the outside, without a problem analogous to Arianism or the Reformation with which to contend, the fortress mentality of a church perceiving itself to be under siege from all sides led to a hierarchical pyramid-structured conception of the church with a strong emphasis on juridical obedience. This external view of the church tended to streamline the "chain of command," as it were, and to distinguish clearly insiders from outsiders. However, it also diminished the self-understanding of the church as a sacramental entity, rather than merely structural, and as evangelical, rather than interested in self-preservation.

Additionally, despite the church's attempts to protect herself and the faithful from the influence of modernity, theologians adopted both the historical framework of the *factum* and in time the progressive and revolutionary framework of the *faciendum*, of the desire to change the world. In attempting to adjust to the former, the move from the metaphysical to the historical, theology began to present faith as centered on history, with reference to the Incarnation as the center of all history.[35] After all, "Christian belief really is concerned with the *factum*; it lives in a specific way on the place of history, and it is no accident that history and that historical approach grew up precisely in the atmosphere of Christian belief."[36] However, theology's move to the historical approach backfired on two counts.

First and most fundamentally, theologians adopted the historical-critical method to evaluate better the historical claims of the faith, of the scriptures. However, this method, adopting as it does the philosophical preconceptions of modernity "in the shape of positivism and phenomenalism . . . invites us to confine ourselves to the 'visible' the 'apparent' in the widest sense of the terms; to extend the basic methodology to which natural science is indebted for its successes to the totality of our relationship with reality."[37] Thus, there was an attempt to distinguish the Jesus of history from

---

33. Here "modernism" indicates not merely the work of Tyrrell and Loisy but also more broadly refers to the tendency to elevate human reason over and against scripture, faith, and tradition.

34. Manning, "On Progress," 313, in Komonchak, "Modernity," 380.

35. Ratzinger, *Introduction to Christianity*, 66–67.

36. Ratzinger, *Introduction to Christianity*, 67.

37. Ratzinger, *Introduction to Christianity*, 74.

the Christ of faith. However, while the positivism of the historical-critical method allowed for greater accuracy with regard to historical claims about the man Jesus, it was necessarily agnostic about the claims of faith, about his being the incarnate Son.[38] Therefore, research tended to vacillate between those who focused on the so-called historical Jesus and those who tended to emphasize the Christ of faith. The view of the Jesus Christ of the creed, quite predictably, became muddled and confused. As a result, "The man of today no longer understands the Christian doctrine of redemption.... He simply cannot imagine what vicarious atonement and satisfaction are. What was meant by the word Christ, Messiah, does not occur in his life and thus remains an empty formula. In this way the profession of Jesus as the Christ vanishes quite automatically."[39]

Furthermore, the individualism of modernity began to influence the way Catholics perceived faith and salvation. In the preface to his *Catholicisme*, Henri de Lubac quoted an accurate depiction of this individualistic corruption in action: "Should I have found joy? No . . . only my joy, and that is something wildly different. . . . The joy of Jesus can be personal. It can belong to a single man and he is saved. He is at peace . . . now and always, but he is alone. The isolation of this joy does not trouble him. On the contrary: he is the chosen one! In his blessedness he passes through the battlefields with a rose in his hand."[40] Ratzinger shares de Lubac's distaste for such an individualistic soteriology, describing it as a "caricature of Christianity that, in the nineteenth and twentieth centuries, made possible the rise of atheism."[41] In addition to the loss of the metaphysical worldview and the weakening of reason that accompanied it, this individualism, which also signaled a depletion of an ecclesial consciousness among Catholics, was symptomatic of a church that was still learning how to be herself after the loss of Christendom. In the face of this crisis, the Second Vatican Council intended to "endow Christianity once more with the power to shape history. . . . Christianity—at least from the viewpoint of the Catholic Church—was trying to emerge again from the ghetto to which it had been relegated since the nineteenth century and to become involved once more in the world at large."[42]

---

38. Ratzinger, *Introduction to Christianity*, 196.

39. Ratzinger, "Probleme von Glaubens und Sittenlehre," 10, in Heim, *Joseph Ratzinger*, 264.

40. Giono, *Les vraies richesses*, v, viii, in de Lubac, *Catholicism*, 13; Benedict XVI, *Spe salvi*, 13.

41. Ratzinger, *Principles of Catholic Theology*, 49. Hereafter, *Principles*.

42. Ratzinger, *Introduction to Christianity*, 13.

1.3 The Council's Response: Coming Out of the Ghetto

The centuries prior to the Second Vatican Council led to a decapitation of reason. Its reach was now limited to only the material and empirically verifiable, often rendering people incapable or unwilling to strive for truth itself, leaving the idea of God absent and irrelevant. The councils of Trent and Vatican I attempted to defend the church's positions against the rationalism of modernity and the attacks of the Reformation and the French Revolution. They tried to strengthen and fortify the church's already existing structures, which eventually resulted in a buttressed but impotent church unable or unwilling to engage the secular world. The initial schemata of the Vatican II documents, which were penned by men closely connected to the Roman Curia and sent off to the bishops prior to the council, attempted a similarly defensive approach. However, many of the bishops sharply criticized and rejected them. The German bishops and their *periti*, Joseph Ratzinger among them, were leaders of this "progressive"[43] majority, which rejected the dominant and defensive neo-scholasticism favored by the curial minority. Thus, the fathers of Vatican II chose to knock down the walls and open the church so that she might once again be a culture-shaping force, a sacrament of salvation. Indeed, they hoped "to restore the primacy of God in Christ to the centre of our lives . . . enabl[ing] the light of faith to illumine our human experience from within."[44]

Since Ratzinger perceives *Lumen Gentium* to be the central document of the council and since the church is among our key subjects, it makes sense to focus our brief examination of the council's response to modernity in *Lumen Gentium*, the dogmatic constitution on the church. We shall also refer to *Gaudium et Spes*, the pastoral constitution on the church in the modern world, the constitution around which the theological differences within the "progressive" majority most clearly came to the fore, leading to a splintering of the reform-minded theologians of which Ratzinger was a part.

Upon promulgating *Lumen Gentium*, Paul VI explained its import and the council's hopes for its relevance to the evangelical mission of the church: "Henceforth it will be possible to have a fuller understanding of the thought of God in relation to the Mystical Body of Christ, and we shall be able to draw therefrom clearer and surer norms for the life of the Church,

---

43. Admittedly, to label the sides progressive and conservative or curial is to oversimplify matters. This work shall attempt to move beyond, what is in Ratzinger's words, "the elementary and rough opposition that people like to make between a curial tendency and a progressive tendency" below. See Ratzinger, "Catholicism after the Council," 18.

44. Francis, *Lumen fidei*, 6.

greater strength in order to lead men to salvation, better hopes for the reign of Christ in the world."[45] Indeed the opening lines of the document emphasize the mystical, sacramental, christological, and missional dimensions of the church, which the church's defensive responses to the Reformation, the Enlightenment, and modernity had obscured in some ways. The first sentences of *Lumen Gentium* teach:

> Christ is the Light of nations. Because this is so, this Sacred Synod gathered together in the Holy Spirit eagerly desires, by proclaiming the Gospel to every creature, to bring the light of Christ to all men. . . . Since the Church is in Christ like a sacrament or as a sign and instrument both of a very closely knit union with God and of the unity of the whole human race, it desires now to unfold more fully to the faithful of the Church and to the whole world its own inner nature and universal mission.[46]

Accordingly, for Ratzinger, "to understand Vatican II correctly one must always and repeatedly begin with this first sentence."[47] In part, this is because in contrast to most prior official ecclesiological treatises, the fathers of the council chose not to begin with the visible or hierarchical structures of the church but rather to consider the church's nature and mission from a thoroughly christological and theological perspective. The second, third, and fourth paragraphs of the constitution indicate that the triune life of God functions as the proper basis for contemplation of the church's nature. The fifth paragraph further emphasizes and specifies this theological nature with reference to the kingdom of God. After all the church "receives the mission to proclaim and to spread among all peoples the Kingdom of Christ and of God"[48] from Christ himself. Reflecting upon the ecclesiological writings that started appearing in the 1920s, Ratzinger wrote:

> It is difficult to communicate the enthusiasm and the joy that was involved in that kind of insight at that time. In the age of liberal thought, up to the first world war, the Catholic Church was regarded as a fossilized machine that persistently opposed the achievements of the modern age . . . the Church appeared essentially as a centrally directed institution which one was dogged in defending but which only encountered one externally. What now became visible once again was that the Church is much more, that in faith we all share in living responsibility for it just

---

45. Paul VI in Anderson, *Council Daybook*, 299.
46. Second Vatican Council, *Lumen Gentium* 1. Hereafter, LG.
47. Ratzinger, *Church, Ecumenism, and Politics*, 15.
48. LG 5.

as it supports us. . . . It had become clear that through it the mystery of the incarnation remains present and contemporary.[49]

The statements of the council can be interpreted as the fulfillment of this joy. Indeed, following the lead of these earlier writings, the council fathers no longer insisted upon self-referential definitions of the church but described and defined her christologically and theologically.

The document went on to describe the church according to various biblical images, central among them were the "people of God" and the "body of Christ." The term "people of God" emphasizes the pilgrim nature of the church and pushes against a certain clericalism that sometimes accompanies the structural emphases of the anti-modern church. For Ratzinger, "discourse about the Body of Christ moved the Church out of all those mere legalities and externals and into the realm of mystery with Christ as the center."[50] Furthermore, it stresses the sacramental aspect of the church, denying the possibility of the "people" being reduced to a mere sociological reality.

While the aforementioned paragraph and other early chapters on episcopal collegiality tend to get the most attention, any consideration of conciliar ecclesiology must not ignore the concluding chapters of the constitution that discuss the lay faithful, the universal call to holiness, religious life, and the Marian and eschatological dimensions of the church. "In these chapters the inner reason for the church's existence, what is essential in her life, once more makes its appearance: they are concerned with holiness, that is, with what is fitting for God—in order that space may be made in the world for God, so that he may dwell therein and the world may thus become his 'Kingdom.'"[51] Correcting an emphasis on the structural nature and individualist mission that came to mark the church's response to modernity, the fathers of Vatican II highlighted both her nature as a people gathered in mystery by the triune God in the body of Christ and her communal pilgrim mission as the sacrament of salvation.

While *Lumen Gentium* primarily focused on the church *ad intra*, the final constitution promulgated by the council, *Gaudium et Spes*, concentrated on the church *ad extra*, on clarifying her relation to the modern world. For many, *Gaudium et Spes* is the document of the council that most clearly signifies both the new winds that were blowing during the council and the controversy that was to ensue.

---

49. Ratzinger, *Church, Ecumenism, and Politics*, 4.
50. Ratzinger, *Volk und Haus Gottes*, xi.
51. Ratzinger, *Pilgrim Fellowship of Faith*, 149.

Before moving on to the debate surrounding *Gaudium et Spes*, let us briefly examine its contributions to the church's response to modernity. The tenor of *Gaudium et Spes* can best be described with reference to its title. *Gaudium et Spes* is unique in that it is the first and only "pastoral" constitution promulgated by an ecumenical council. Through it, the bishops tried to speak not only to the church but also to the broader world. By choosing the preposition "in" as the relational term connecting "church" and "modern world" in the title, the bishops chose to articulate their vision of the church's role and presence not vis-à-vis the world but within the world. In doing so, they moved past the fortress mentality, the view that saw the church as a *societas perfecta* standing opposite secular society. This move is echoed poetically and anthropologically in the first paragraph, which states,

> The joys and the hopes, the griefs and the anxieties of the men of this age, especially those who are poor or in any way afflicted, these are the joys and hopes, the griefs and anxieties of the followers of Christ. Indeed, nothing genuinely human fails to raise an echo in their hearts. For theirs is a community composed of men. . . . That is why this community realizes that it is truly linked with mankind and its history by the deepest of bonds.[52]

Not only is the church not a separate society standing against the world, but Christian life is not a separate existence. Rather, it is a particular form of human existence.

The remainder of the preface accents the divine origin and end shared by the church and world and calls for the church to engage the entire human family in conversation aimed at progress.[53] The first chapter, *On the Dignity of the Human Person*, again corrects the individualistic soteriology, which had influenced Catholic thought in the nineteenth and early-twentieth centuries by highlighting the communal nature of human existence[54] and its christological foundations.[55] The following chapters, *On the Community of Mankind* and *Man's Activity in the Universe* respectively, deepen this anthropology with reference to humanity's trinitarian source and goal and to its relationship to the cosmos.

In contrast to the judgmental and defensive rhetoric which marked the church's early responses to modernity, notions of dialogue and reciprocity mark the key fourth chapter of *Gaudium et Spes*. Because the church "goes forward together with humanity and experiences the same earthly lot

---

52. Second Vatican Council, *Gaudium et Spes* 1. Hereafter, GS.
53. GS 2–3.
54. GS 12, 23–24.
55. GS 22.

which the world does. She serves as a leaven and as a kind of soul for human society."⁵⁶ The church and world run along parallel paths in history and have a perichoretic existence. Therefore, the church does not exist to defend the faithful from the corrupting influence of a secular world. Rather,

> Pursuing the saving purpose which is proper to her, the Church does not only communicate divine life to men but in some way casts the reflected light of that life over the entire earth, most of all by its healing and elevating impact on the dignity of the person, by the way in which it strengthens the seams of human society and imbues the everyday activity of men with a deeper meaning and importance. Thus through her individual matters and her whole community, the Church believes she can contribute greatly toward making the family of man and its history more human.⁵⁷

Having thus described the church's mission in terms of humanization and cognizant of a "mutual exchange" with the positive elements of secular society, the document proceeds to elucidate principles for fostering such an exchange. The principles focus on the ways in which "the world" can contribute to the church and in which the church can aid the world, in other words, on the mutual reciprocity necessary for authentic human development. Here, in contrast to the clericalism which sometimes marked church life in the preceding centuries, the council fathers stressed the responsibility of the laity as living and acting in the world.⁵⁸

After discussing some specific problems which the bishops felt they ought to address, including family life, culture, economics, politics, and international peace, the pastoral constitution concludes by returning to the sacramental mission of the church, which "stands forth as a sign of that brotherhood which allows honest dialogue and gives it vigor."⁵⁹ This mission calls the church to conversion, to strive for Christian unity, and to fulfill all her tasks in the spirit of love.

In short, the Second Vatican Council marks the end of the dominance of officially sanctioned neo-scholastic theology and of the mentality of the church as the *societas perfecta*, as a fortress fending off the attacks of the world. In the place of condemnations are elucidations and invitations to dialogue. In the place of a church defined by extrinsic structures are definitions in accord with the church's christological and trinitarian foundations

56. GS 40.
57. GS 40.
58. GS 43.
59. GS 92.

using biblical and sacramental imagery. Instead of *anathemas*, we read of calls to conversion and the responsibility, which comes with the church's sacramental mission. Indeed, although formally and dogmatically speaking the council may have taught nothing new, it nevertheless marks a new era in the history of the church. Yet despite the needed reforms, the subtle crises that lurked below the surface prior to Vatican II manifested themselves more fully after the council. Instead of becoming once again a culture shaping force in the world, the church descended into varying degrees of chaos as the splintering of conciliar theologians led to various groups vying for the power to put into practice their interpretation of the council.

Ratzinger narrates the end of the scholastic period and the rise of modernity with reference to Vico's axiom, *verum quia factum*, which eventually gave way to the *faciendum*, thus cutting off reason from the pursuit of truth, rendering God irrelevant, faith irrational, and the church impotent in the world. The Second Vatican Council attempted to reinvigorate the faith of the church. The next chapter shall study the fundamental theological ideas of Joseph Ratzinger in the context of the debate, which surrounded *Gaudium et Spes* during the council as well as the cultural and ecclesial crises which followed the council. Such a study will lay the theological and contextual groundwork for what follows, which will explore and analyze Ratzinger's own ecclesiological suggestions for authentic and evangelical ecclesial reform.

2

Post-Conciliar Crisis and Ratzinger's Response

2.1 The Controversy of Gaudium et Spes

IN ADDITION TO ITS unique status as a "pastoral constitution," *Gaudium et Spes* is also unique among the major conciliar documents because it alone was not developed or re-worked from one of the "preparatory schema" issued before the council. The idea for the document grew out of John XXIII's desire for the council to address "modern man" and out of the realization that the document that became *Lumen Gentium* focused primarily on issues pertaining to the inner life of the church, rather than to its relationship to the world. Thus, "the preparatory work was unsatisfactory, and the Council rejected the extant texts. But the question at this point was: What now?"[1] The attempt to answer "what now" in the context of the church's relation to the modern world acutely raised the more complex theological divisions that had previously been hidden by the majority's shared rejection of the dominant and largely curial neo-scholastic theology. Ratzinger criticized the text with a surprising sharpness: "The text and, even more, the deliberations from which it evolved breathe an astonishing optimism. Nothing seems impossible if humanity and the Church work together."[2] However, some like M. D. Chenu were quite pleased with the text and defended it fiercely, arguing that the "optimism" of the text comes not from some self-sufficient anthropology, but from the intrinsic potential for God built within human nature:

> Grace is grace, and secular history is not a source of salvation. Evangelization is of another order than civilization. . . . To promote culture is not to convert to faith. . . . But this insuperable transcendence, both in initiative and in content, does not eliminate nature and history but on the contrary calls for . . . a

---

1. Ratzinger, *Theological Highlights of Vatican II*, 148.
2. Ratzinger, *Principles*, 380. See also Ratzinger, "Introductory Article," 115–63.

> real encounter with an interiority open to the divine love which offers itself, an effective (though not "active") capacity to understand it and to respond to it. Human undertakings, the mastery of nature, the rising awareness of peoples, the development of minds, the haunting desire for peace, the universal solidarity of the human race, these are not some incidental matter, a condition quite extrinsic to the individual and collective life of grace. As ambiguous as they are, these are so many building blocks.³

Shortly after the council, he explained further:

> It is not as if grace were built on top of nature, as if the kingdom of God were built on top of the world as the scaffolding of a city to come. As points of contact with the Gospel, all terrestrial goods develop man's capacity to open up to the divine life, for in the strongest sense of the word, man is the "subject" of grace. He is *capax dei*, not only in his essential nature, but in this nature as it develops through time, not only in his person but in his character as a social being. . . . There is a social dimension to obediential potency. This is a very important point to note in a period when socialization is the major and universal phenomenon of the human race.⁴

Chenu's defense of the document highlights the key theological points over which the controversy raged: the relation of nature and grace in Christian anthropology. The differing assessments of *Gaudium et Spes* might be said to be products of whether given theologians emphasized the natural good and freedom of creation or the deleterious impact of sin on human engagement with creation. Thus, while Chenu defended the "created autonomy and intelligibility of the world of nature,"⁵ others, like Ratzinger, rejected this view. The latter argued that the former "had so stressed the autonomy of the world and of human reason that the first constituted a separate world capable of being understood by the second, with the result that the world disclosed by revelation and accepted by faith appeared to be a more-or-less arbitrarily imposed alternative."⁶ This rift brought to light by the debate

---

3. Chenu, "Les signes des temps," 222, in Komonchak, "Redaction and Reception," 6.

4. Chenu, "Signs of the Times," 56–57, in Komonchak, "Redaction and Reception," 7.

5. Komonchak, "Redaction and Reception," 19.

6. Komonchak, "Redaction and Reception," 19. Komonchak identifies the former groups as Thomists and the latter as Augustinians. However, Bauerschmidt shows that such tropes are misleading and inadequate on several levels (Bauerschmidt, "Augustine and Aquinas"). First, there is no consensus Augustinianism or Thomism. Second, the

over *Gaudium et Spes* became more sharply articulated in the post-conciliar theological climate, as illustrated by the history between the two theological journals *Concilium* and *Communio*. Throughout, the deeper theological rift remained a debate about the analogy of being, or put another way, the relation between nature and grace, between faith and reason.

In what follows, I examine in depth Ratzinger's approach to this fundamental issue in order to lay the philosophical groundwork of his diagnosis of the crisis of our time. After all, Ratzinger's position on these fundamental issues will determine in large part the manner in which he proposes that the church ought to engage the world so as fulfill her mission as the universal sacrament of salvation.

2.2 Ratzinger and the Analogy of Being

While Ratzinger has been critiqued for changing his stance sometime during or immediately following the council, his position on this most fundamental of issues was already set well before the council by his engagement with the debate between Karl Barth and Erich Przywara over the *analogia entis*.[7]

Before getting into Ratzinger's thought as it pertains to the debate, the question must be asked: why this issue? What is it about the *analogia entis* that has caused such a flurry of theological activity and controversy? Why might Karl Barth have responded to Przywara's description of the *analogia entis* as a formal principle of Catholicism[8] by calling the doctrine "the invention of the anti-Christ"?[9] Ratzinger once defined the analogy of being as "simply a term for the ontological option of Catholic theology, for its synthesis of the philosophical idea of being and the biblical conception of God."[10] One could also rightly say, as John Betz does, that it is "the doctrine of the relation between God and creation."[11] In short the analogy of being touches on the most fundamental of topics: one's perception of the relation

---

positions said to be associated with the tropes do not either adequately or accurately reflect the depth and nuance of Augustine and Aquinas, nor the degree to which Aquinas is depending upon Augustine. Third, any attempt to map the theological tropics of a given age simply and neatly into two groups like Augustinians and Thomists or optimists and pessimists is necessarily an oversimplification, which fails to do justice to the complexity and inter-reliance of the various theologians being implicated.

7. See Betz, "After Barth," 35.
8. Przywara, *Analogia Entis*, 120.
9. Barth, *KD* I/I:viii.
10. Ratzinger, *Nature and Mission*, 19.
11. Betz, "After Barth," 36.

between God and humanity will have implications for metaphysics, anthropology, liturgy, eschatology, the relation between philosophy and theology, and most relevant to this study, the relation between the church and the world. Anyone aware of the sweeping implications of such a doctrine will have little difficulty finding something upon which the *analogia entis* impinges that excites or agitates her sensibilities. So, where does Ratzinger fall in this debate and how does it affect his response to the present ecclesiological crisis?

Ratzinger only directly addressed the debate once, in a contribution to a *Festschrift* in honor of his mentor Gottlieb Söhngen.[12] However, due to the wide range of topics impacted by this doctrine and the impressive integrity, consistency, and systematization of Ratzinger's thought, his own stakes in the debate can be discerned via his numerous writings throughout his career. I contend that the young Ratzinger displays a general acceptance of the analogy of being as understood by Erich Przywara and a close affinity to Söhngen's Bonaventurian approach, which reflects Söhngen's ecumenical concerns, his christological emphases, and his doubt concerning a perceived optimistic notion of nature. In short, Ratzinger's early influences profoundly shape the way he has approached and responded to the debates surrounding *Gaudium et Spes* and the various forms of secularism, which he perceives as attacks on the fundamentals of the faith. In support of this contention, I start with a brief consideration of Przywara's *analogia entis* in addition to Söhngen's use of Bonaventure as a prototype of the *analogia fidei*, before offering an examination of Ratzinger's contribution to the *Festschrift*, entitled "*Gratia Presupponit Naturam*," and his habilitation on *The Theology of History in Bonaventure*. This will provide a baseline of Ratzinger's thought on the relevant issues as they are manifested and developed in the context of present crises. Second, I will contend that Ratzinger maintains these foundations in his encounters with modernity and post-modernity through his defense of creation, his notion of the relation between the analogy of faith and the analogy of being, and his concept of God as *agape* and *caritas* which reveals the inherent relationality of man.

2.2.1 Early Influences

Przywara

Although scholars do not often associate Joseph Ratzinger in any explicit or direct way with Erich Przywara, the German Jesuit who taught Hans Urs

---

12. Ratzinger, "*Gratia Praesupponit Naturam*."

von Balthasar also seems to have had a noteworthy influence on the young Ratzinger. Ratzinger's writings on the relation between God and the world have much in common with Przywara's *analogia entis*, which represents a certain codifying of Aquinas's analogical *via media* between univocity and equivocity. Thomas wanted to affirm that we cannot predicate anything of God univocally but added that, when we do speak of God, we are not merely equivocating. Aquinas explained that the usage of analogy in reference to God is "the case of the same word used of two things because of some relation that one has to the other . . . and so whatever is said both of God and creatures is said in virtue of the order that creatures have to God as to their source in which the perfections of all things pre-exist transcendentally."[13] For Thomas, this analogical mode of reference was the appropriate and the actual way in which we speak of and think of God.

Thomas proceeded to make a further distinction: analogy requires knowledge of a central thing, and this central thing must be understood before it can be applied to something else in the analogy. Since we understand creatures, which we know through our perceptive powers more fully and immediately than we understand God, "all words used metaphorically of God apply primarily to creatures and secondarily to God. When used of God they signify a certain parallelism between God and the creature."[14] Further, for Thomas, analogical predication reflects analogy in ontology. Likewise, for Przywara, the *analogia entis* is not merely a grammatical rule. He considers it a "formal principle,"[15] which relates to metaphysics as such and governs both ontics and noetics.[16] Przywara interprets Thomas's analogy to be a concept which applies to being as it is.[17] Thomas's analogy represents the form of an adequate metaphysics, which is dynamically

---

13. Aquinas, *Knowing and Naming God*, 1a.13.5.

14. Aquinas, *Knowing and Naming God*, 1a.13.6.

15. Przywara, *Analogia Entis*, 117.

16. Przywara, *Analogia Entis*, 121.

17. "This is what characterizes Thomas's doctrine of analogy as it applies to the most important determinations of things: *ens et bonum et huiusmodi*. There is the *prius* of an ascending analogy of 'positive naming,' rising from the creature to God (*prius fuerunt creaturis imposita, et ex his ad divinam praedicationem translata*),—but subject to the *prius* of the descending analogy of a 'antecedent validity (and thus one that can only be discovered),' descending from God to the creature (*quamvis esse et bonum prius inveniantur in Deo*).—But we see this relation in our formal configuration of the middle, secondly, in the special concreteness of the relationship that between the 'natural' mode of ascent to God (rising from man and going beyond the angels) and the 'supernatural' mode of descent from God (in the 'mediator'). The concrete form of Thomas's concept of analogy is revealed in a familiar maxim, one that is rooted in Thomas's thought: *gratia (fides) non destruit, sed supponit et perficit naturam (rationem)*" (Przywara, *Analogia Entis*, 303).

balanced, a metaphysics of "pure logic" and one of dialectic, or "identity in contradiction."[18]

However, Schenk detects already in Przywara, before Söhngen or Barth enter the discussion, a move away from Thomas.[19] According to Schenk, Przywara's exposition fails to remain faithful to the autonomy to which Thomas attributed philosophy,[20] since "Przywara's philosophy finds its fulfillment and its end in theology, from where it alone learns of its limitations and the need for its replacement by the 'One Metaphysics.'"[21] Schenk's perceptions find support in the words of Przywara:

> *Analogy* is established *as a participatory being-related-above-and-beyond.* As a genuine consequence of such an "above-and-beyond," however, one must ultimately grant at least an objective priority to the "from-above." If the sphere of eternal movement (noetically and ontically) *is* by virtue of a movement produced by the eternal mover, then (ontically) the former "is" properly speaking "in the latter," and not "in itself."[22]

In other words, for Przywara, although the analogy of being appears to start from the immanent—that is, from nature—the creaturely knower, that is man, reveals himself as being from the divine. Without the gifts of revelation and grace, man cannot make abstractions from creation in order to reason to the Christian God, and even if reason can reach all the way to faith in the transcendent, this *ratio* has no salvific efficacy, although it could play a role in one's journey to faith. "Thus analogy, as a participatory being-related-above-and-beyond, has as its profounder premise an *analogy as the self-imparting-relation-from-above* of the divine identity of the Is (Truth, etc.)."[23]

Notably, however, Betz sees this as a strength, for in his mind, it effectively negates any just accusations that Barth could make against the analogy of being as a claim to pure natural knowledge of God. Betz explains:

> In no sense, therefore, can the *analogia entis* be said to establish an immediate ontological or epistemological connection between God and creatures, as Barth seems to have feared. On

---

18. Przywara, *Analogia Entis,* 195–97.

19. Przywara later explained that by "*analogia entis*" he did not mean the more specific doctrine about which Aquinas and Scotus differed, but rather something broader. See Przywara, *Gott Geheimis der Welt,* in Schenk, "Analogy," 171.

20. Przywara "asserts a dynamism from below" (Schenk, "Analogy," 177).

21. Schenk, "Analogy," 177.

22. Przywara, *Analogia Entis,* 213.

23. Przywara, *Analogia Entis,* 214.

the contrary, for Przywara, the *analogia entis* prohibits any such immediacy, whether ontological or noetic, precisely by virtue of this fundamental, dynamic, even explosive rhythm of the "in-and-beyond," which militates against every form of pantheism, every secular doctrine of pure immanence, and every form of titanic human presumption.[24]

Thus, in Betz's view, Przywara's "formal principle" effectively safeguards the transcendence of God without negating the autonomy of creation. Przywara attempts to express a "dynamic polarity"[25] in order to respect both God's transcendence and his presence to creation. In order to deal with this polarity Przywara envisions the *analogia entis* as the intersection of an "immanent analogy," "which emphasizes a participatory 'sharing' . . . of creaturely being in the divine,"[26] with a "theological analogy" that "emphasizes that being 'is' only *as* the 'im-parting' of a gift; moreover, the creature only 'is' insofar as it is between nothing and the 'Creator *ex nihilo*.'"[27] Thus for Przywara, the *analogia entis* represents the convergence of philosophy and theology, of nature and grace. Further, Przywara rightly sees the existence of God and man, or all created beings, as fundamentally different: only in God does there exist an identity between essence and existence, while for the creature there is a "unity-in-tension" between essence and existence, which itself is only participatory.[28] Additionally, and significantly, this "principle" is not to be understood as something

> originally static, "from which" everything else could be deduced or "to which" everything else could be reduced. On the contrary, it is essentially the primordial dynamic: defining the swaying of the intra-creaturely, the in-between-God-and-the-creaturely, and the intra-divine itself, the hyper-transcendent expression of which is the theologoumenon of the intra-divine "relations" (*relationes*), which *are* the Father, Son, and Holy Spirit.[29]

---

24. Betz, "After Barth," 53.
25. Betz, "After Barth," 54, referencing Przywara, *Gottgeheimnis der Welt*.
26. Betz, "After Barth," 64.
27. Betz, "After Barth," 64.
28. Betz, "After Barth," 69, citing Przywara, *Schriften*, 2:403.
29. Przywara, *Analogia Entis*, 314.

Söhngen: Bonaventure as Klassiker der Analogia Fidei

Karl Barth famously responded to Przywara's work by calling the analogy of being the "invention of the anti-Christ."[30] Gottlieb Söhngen, Ratzinger's mentor, engaged in his own ecumenically motivated discussion of analogy with Barth.[31] As Schenk explains, Söhngen's understanding of a properly Catholic approach to issues of nature and grace was more palatable to Barth, who wrote that "Söhngen has presented in his two essays on *analogia fidei* . . . a teaching in this matter that marks a significant shift from the previous position, according to which now the knowledge of being and the *analogia entis* are subordinated to, rather than placed above, the knowledge of God's deeds and thus the *analogia fidei* in theology."[32] Barth perceived this shift in Söhngen because Söhngen, having a certain suspicion toward the account of nature posited by some "optimists"[33]—not unlike that which we later encounter in Chenu and in parts of *Gaudium et* Spes itself—adopted a biblical focus on the *theologica crucis* and the *discrimen legis et evangelii* in order to more fully relativize Przywara's analogy of being and to highlight the priority of the *analogia fidei* vis-à-vis the *analogia entis*.[34] Söhngen also recognized the dangers of Neoplatonism: "from the perspective of Christian theology, the Neoplatonic philosopher seems to me to be like the philosopher's monkey, who apes theology (as *scientia Dei et beatorum*) by mimicking the state of being adopted by God."[35] In other words, platonic idealism,

---

30. Barth, *KD* I/I:xiii.

31. Schenk, "Analogy," 180.

32. Barth, *KD* II/I:89–90, in Schenk, "Analogy," 181.

33. Due to space, I cannot explore in depth the anthropological or eschatological optimism of Söhngen's interlocutors, nor can I give Chenu the detailed attention his thought is due. There is some unfortunate oversimplification here. Nevertheless, it is true that (1) Söhngen and Ratzinger were reacting similarly to similar tendencies they perceived in their respective interlocutors; (2) the "progressive" opposition to previously dominant neo-scholasticism was divided approximately along these lines during the debate surrounding *Gaudium et Spes*; and (3) Ratzinger and Chenu were indeed in opposing camps on this issue.

34. Ratzinger, "Gratia praesupponit aturam," 143; Schenk, "Analogy," 180. Despite his preference for Bonaventure, Söhngen knew Thomas well. "Gottlieb Söhngen, by the way, is picked out in Otto-Herman Pesch's masterly survey of the place of Thomas Aquinas in modern German theology (see *Contemplating Aquinas*, 201). He picks him out, indeed, as the pioneer who transformed Thomas from being 'the dogmatically binding head of the Thomist school' to 'the most significant medieval impulse to modern theology.' Pesch is thinking of Söhngen's remarkable essay in the collective volume *Mysterium Salutis* . . . on theology as wisdom reached by way of scholarship, in which Söhngen heralded the kind of readings of Thomas Aquinas which are becoming common now, forty years later" (Kerr, "Recent Thomistica IV," 654).

35. Söhngen, "Analogia fidei," 202, in Balthasar, *Theology of Karl Barth*, 275n15.

into which Ratzinger has been accused of falling,[36] obfuscates the great distinction and difference between worldly universals discovered through the light of reason and divine revelation, which can only be received via grace. Therefore, Söhngen not only wished to offer a tradition of Catholic theology, which might be more appealing to Barth, but also hoped to offer a corrective to Barth by maintaining the Catholic "yes" to creation's ontological goodness.[37] For example, in one of a series of important articles entitled "Analogia fidei," Söhngen explains:

> God's revelation in nature is communication by the positing of an individual sphere of being that is, primordially and to its very depths, dependent upon God inasmuch as God created it and maintains it. The sphere of nature stands and moves within its own being and essence, or at least in the being and essence given to it. In the natural knowledge of the Creator from his works (Rom 1:20) the human is therefore directed to himself, to his human nature, and to the whole sphere of nature and being in which he himself stands. . . . The metaphysical analogy of being . . . is thus a genuine analogy of *being*, from humanity to the God spoken in the being of nature. . . . God's revelation in nature is not a sharing of himself. . . . God lives in nature according to his external life, not his internal life. . . . God shows himself in nature, which means he shows only his external side. . . . According to Thomas's concept of metaphysics, God is not the *subjectum* of metaphysics (as God is in sacred theology), but only the *objectum* or *praedictum*, which we must understand according to the antique account of the subject/object distinction. The *subjectum* of metaphysical statements in the *ens commune*, and because metaphysics as a science searches for the first cause, God falls within its horizon as the first cause of beings insofar as they exist.[38]

For Söhngen, contra Barth, the revelation of God in creation allows humanity's "philosophical" knowledge to ascend to an acknowledgment of God as first cause, but only as cause. Thus, what is at stake here is Barth's denial of any usefulness to natural theology. Accordingly, one of Söhngen's key contributions is his insight that even with Barth's analogy of faith in mind, "there can be no *analogia fidei* without the 'external ground' of an *analogia entis*,"[39]—or put another way, "the analogy of faith requires the analogy of

---

36. For example, Kasper, "On the Church."
37. Ratzinger, "*Gratia praesupponit naturam*," 143.
38. Söhngen, "Analogy of Faith," 187–88.
39. Söhngen, "Wesen und Akt," 650, in Betz, "Beyond the Sublime," 8.

being in order to be meaningful."[40] In this regard, he did not have a problem with the analogy of being itself, as Barth did; therefore, he disputed Barth's setting the analogy of faith over against the analogy of being. On the other hand, Söhngen differed from Przywara in holding that one can only truly speak of an analogy of being within the context of the analogy of faith.[41] Outside of the context of an analogy of faith, there is little cause for the so-called optimism about the world and human nature exhibited by Chenu.

Söhngen's most lasting and influential contribution to the extended discussion has probably been his introduction of Bonaventure's thought on the nature-grace axioms into the dialogue. Under the perception that Bonaventure avoids the apparent difficulty that Thomas's view of analogy was (mis)perceived to have with incorporating a *theologica crucis*, he hoped Bonaventure might offer the possibility of a rapprochement between Catholic and Reformed thought.[42] Accordingly, he intended to propose the theology of the Franciscan master as a middle position between a neo-Thomist "understanding of God based on an autonomous 'natural' understanding of the world" and a Barthian view based on a "revealed grasp of God and the world that would be largely unencumbered by historical and worldly constraints."[43]

Why might Bonaventure have been an attractive choice for Söhngen? In the first place, Söhngen and Barth both agree with Bonaventure in accepting Saint Anselm's so-called ontological argument.[44] Thus, Bonaventure can be seen to take up Anselm's "rationality based upon faith," and therefore Söhngen can refer to him as "Klassiker der analogia fidei," a counter-claim to Pryzwara's citation of Thomas as a "classic of the *analogia entis*." Additionally, though he never comes close to Barth's radical subordination of

---

40. Oakes, "Nature and Grace in Barth," 604–5, referencing Söhngen, "Analogia Fidei: Gottähnlichkeit allein aus Glauben?," 113–36; "Analogia Fidei: Die Einheit in der Glaubenswissenschaft," 176–208.

41. However, as Betz notes, "What is meant by 'analogy of faith,' however, is itself a matter of dispute. Strictly speaking, the phrase refers to Romans 12:6, where Paul says that the 'analogy of faith' must hold for the prophets; in other words, what prophets say must be 'proportionate' to the rule of faith. This is the primary sense in which Przywara understands the term, though, following Augustine, he also speaks of the *analogia fidei* in terms of the analogy between Old and New Testaments. In Barth, however, it tends to mean either that there is no analogy between God and creatures apart from the analogy that God himself causes in the creature by faith—whereby alone we are made like God—or it refers to the self-correspondence of God in Christ. See Barth, *KD* I/I:251ff." (Betz, "After Barth," 87).

42. Schenk, "Analogy," 183.

43. Schenk, "Epilogue," 415.

44. On Söhngen, see his *Die Einheit in der Theologie*, 24–35, referenced in Schenk, "Analogy," 183. On Bonaventure, see his *Disputed Questions* 1.1.response (117).

creation to redemption in Christ, Bonaventure frequently speaks of the need of nature to be not merely elevated, but healed and reformed. Thus, "Grace is the perfection of nature not only in as far as it equips nature but also in as far as it both reforms and elevates it. But in reforming and elevating it, grace does not destroy nature itself nor any part thereof, but only the defects surrounding nature."[45] As we shall see, this inclusion of nature's need not only for elevation but also for healing or conversion is one of the key themes Ratzinger perceived to be lacking in *Gaudium et Spes*. Bonaventure's real appeal to Söhngen as a means for dialogue with Barth becomes more fully clear in Ratzinger's habilitation.

The Role of Bonaventure: Ratzinger's Habilitation

Ratzinger was disinclined from the start to adopt a thomistic program of study. He explains, "I had difficulties in penetrating the thought of Thomas Aquinas, whose crystal-clear logic seemed to me to be too closed in on itself, too impersonal and ready-made."[46] Thus, it should come as no surprise, that Söhngen, the ecumenically-minded Bonaventurian, eventually became his mentor.

> The investigations presented in Ratzinger's doctoral and habilitation theses were inspired to a large degree by the ecumenical program of his academic mentor, Gottlieb Söhngen, whose appeal to Bonaventure (rather than to the Thomism of the day) and to the Augustinian ideal of the unitive wisdom of faith (as opposed to autonomous disciplines in philosophy, theology, and the positive sciences) was understood as an attempt to work out a Catholic sense of the *analogia fidei* with a corresponding distinction of law and gospel that could mediate between Protestants and Catholics (represented notably by K. Barth and E. Przywara).[47]

Accordingly, Söhngen's own ecumenism and approach to the relation between God and the world remain relevant to this study of Ratzinger. Additionally, Ratzinger's study of Bonaventure as well as his contribution to a *Festschrift* in honor of Söhngen remain particularly relevant to a discussion of his proposal for an ecclesiology of communion that successfully evangelizes the modern world. After all, whether the world can be accepted and

---

45. Bonaventure, *Disputed Questions* 1.2 (134).
46. Ratzinger, *Milestones*, 44.
47. Schenk, "Unsundered Net," 93.

cooperated with as is or whether it first requires healing, purification, and *metanoia* determines to a large degree the tenor and tactics of the church's performance as the universal sacrament of salvation.

Ratzinger states that the real theme of his study on Bonaventure is the Franciscan master's "anti-Aristotelianism," which makes Bonaventure particularly useful for a critique of neo-Thomistic accounts of creation. Ratzinger identifies two strands of Bonaventure's anti-Aristotelianism.[48] The first relates to Bonaventure's rejection of an objective-metaphysical position, which he traces back to Aristotle: the doctrine of the eternity of the world. "The root of the matter is that St. Bonaventure's Christian universe differs from the pagan universe of Aristotle in that it has a history,"[49] which Bonaventure sees as an egress from God and a regress to God. The center of this circle—formerly dislocated due to sin—has been re-located in the cross of Christ. To protect the unicity of the Christ-event, Bonaventure adapts the image of the circle to maintain the unrepeatability of history, which might fit the image of an ascending spiral.[50] Bonaventure associates the "doctrine of the eternal circle" of the philosopher with the apocalyptic sign of the beast. He considers it "the sum of all heresies,"[51] leading to the denial of the unrepeatable character of history as highlighted by the Christ event. The second strand of Bonaventure's anti-Aristotelianism grew out of the emergence of Latin Averroism. Bonaventure perceived in the latter an attempt to grant too much to philosophers, who, in fact, were not capable of discerning the most important truth about man, because they were unaware of "man's sickness and it's cause."[52] This second strand of anti-Aristotelianism is not so much directed specifically at Aristotle but at philosophers who assume the self-sufficiency of their philosophy, which nevertheless lacks what is finally necessary—an infused light.[53] Consequently, Bonaventure issues a warning against too optimistic an appraisal of the abilities of the intellect. "He who loves Scripture, loves philosophy as well; for with it he can strengthen his faith. But philosophy is the tree of knowledge of good and evil since truth and falsehood are mixed together in it. If, however, you are a fanatic of philosophy, then you say: How can Aristotle be mistaken? Then you do not love

---

48. Ratzinger, *Theology of History in Bonaventure*, 148.

49. Ratzinger, *Theology of History in Bonaventure*, 142, quoting Gilson, *Philosophy of St. Bonaventure*, 174.

50. Ratzinger, *Theology of History in Bonaventure*, 147.

51. Ratzinger, *Theology of History in Bonaventure*, 148.

52. Ratzinger, *Theology of History in Bonaventure*, 150.

53. Bonaventure, *Disputed Questions* 1.2.response, referenced in Ratzinger, *Theology of History in Bonaventure*, 130–31.

Scripture and you necessarily fall from the faith."⁵⁴ Thus Bonaventure does not reject philosophy *in toto*. In fact, according to Ratzinger, Bonaventure does not direct this warning against any already existing Christian philosophies, but against "the rise of a philosophy,"⁵⁵ perhaps not unlike many modern philosophies that reject the givenness of creation and the existence of a creator. Bonaventure's intent is not to excoriate those who use Aristotle in good order, but rather those who reject Christian *sophia* for the harlot of reason.

Ratzinger concludes his habilitation by re-emphasizing that despite his strong disagreement with Aristotle on the eternity of the world, Bonaventure continues to hold the philosopher in high regard. With the dawn of Latin Averroism, Bonaventure fights back against self-sufficing philosophy, believing that "Philosophy must be integrated into the truth coming from Revelation."⁵⁶ However, even this rational theology is only transient and will be transcended by loving obedience to *auctoritas*.

Ratzinger in the Festschrift

Joseph Ratzinger most directly contributed to the debates a few years later in his 1962 article "*Gratia praesupponit naturam*: Erwägungen über Sinn und Grenze eines scholastischen Axioms," in which the young professor closely followed his mentor's lead in adopting Bonaventure—rather than Thomas—as his scholastic point of contact from which to discuss issues of nature and grace in an ecumenical key. Note that Ratzinger composed this essay well before the debates surrounding *Gaudium et Spes* began to heat up. Here I offer a summary of Ratzinger's claims and use of Bonaventure before attempting to analyze Ratzinger's purpose and argument. This lays the foundation for a broader discussion of the development of his position in response to the various issues with which he has engaged throughout his career.

The young Ratzinger's work reflects Söhngen's wariness of a neo-Thomistic approach towards nature while also attempting to "defend the right of 'nature' in faith against Barth's one-sidedness."⁵⁷ For the young Ratzinger, as for the old, the concern with protecting the goodness of creation is not merely an argument against Barth, but is also an attempt to counter the rejection of creation by modernity powerfully present in Marxist

---

54. Bonaventure quoted in Ratzinger, *Theology of History in Bonaventure*, 153.
55. Ratzinger, *Theology of History in Bonaventure*, 154.
56. Ratzinger, *Theology of History in Bonaventure*, 160.
57. Ratzinger, "*Gratia praesupponit naturam*," 143.

eschatology and the existential nihilism of Sartre.[58] Additionally, he argues that "the naturalism that melts grace into nature leads to the same result as the supranaturalism that disputes the existence of nature, and by denying creation, makes grace meaningless as well."[59] Ratzinger is interested in both defending nature and defending grace, and he believes both are in danger of being obfuscated or denied by various intellectual and societal trends. Nevertheless, he will stress the impact of sin on nature.

The problem, as Ratzinger sees it, is that original sin and concupiscence turn that which was unnatural to man into his natural state.[60] Grace, then, cannot be merely a continuation and fulfillment of this (fallen) natural state (as he perceives neo-Thomism to teach), but can only mean "disruption, paradox, thwarting,"[61] which has everything to do with the requirements of an adequate ecclesiology and missiology. The presence of sin indicates that the acceptance of grace requires the embracing of one's cross, of accepting a death to self. To illuminate a portion of the ecumenical difficulty key to the debate, Ratzinger explains that while Catholics speak of sins in the plural as transgressions against God's will, for Protestants sin in the singular refers to humanity's self-centeredness, our lack of freedom for God-centeredness. In this view, man is "by nature a sinner."[62] In accord with this difference on the meaning of sin, is a difference on the meaning of "nature." Ratzinger explains that for those who speak of the *analogia entis*, "nature" refers to that which is not artificial, to that which is originally in accord with creation. For Barth, human nature refers to the essence of humans, which we encounter and experience in history as fallen. Accordingly, any reference to a "pure nature" unaffected by sin is ultimately irrelevant for historical humanity.

In this context, Ratzinger discerns that "originally" the scholastics understood *natura* of the nature-grace axioms to mean "the formal definiteness of what is human" or to refer to "the particular man in his humanness as such, which is to be the point of reference for the grace event."[63] This also means that in using the axioms, the scholastics did not intend to say anything about our "constitution in view of grace." Ratzinger explores this more deeply in the specific example of Bonaventure for whom, "man's personhood is not included in the general concept of nature."[64] Human person-

---

58. Ratzinger, "*Gratia praesupponit naturam*," 144.
59. Ratzinger, "*Gratia praesupponit naturam*," 144.
60. Ratzinger, "*Gratia praesupponit naturam*," 147.
61. Ratzinger, "*Gratia praesupponit naturam*," 147.
62. Ratzinger, "*Gratia praesupponit naturam*," 149.
63. Ratzinger, "*Gratia praesupponit naturam*," 151.
64. Ratzinger, "*Gratia praesupponit naturam*," 152.

hood implies a human will, which is not "merely natural," but spirit. While bodily nature can heal itself in overcoming sickness, the will cannot "raise itself out of guilt without grace." This is because, for Bonaventure, "A merely natural soul is inconceivable; an essential feature of the soul is that it cannot subsist in itself alone. It must be preserved by something that is greater than itself, by something 'supernatural.'"[65] The human spirit remains fallen and in need of repair, which cannot come about naturally but only from without, supernaturally, from the divine physician.

Ratzinger concludes his exposition of Bonaventure's approach by adding that the Seraphic Doctor "calls original sin a *'culpa non personalis, sed naturalis'* [a guilt that is not personal but natural] and logically speaks then about man's *natura corrupta*."[66] Ratzinger's point here seems to be that while Barth, or at least Protestant thought more generally, rejected the formulations of neo-scholastic Thomism, they, in fact, fall in line with another strand of Catholic tradition. After all, they, like Bonaventure, see "the nature of man as marked by its history,"[67] a marked nature, which Ratzinger believes is inadequately reflected in portions of *Gaudium et Spes*. This marked nature becomes the site of the Incarnation. Thus, Ratzinger reasons, "if we observe nature from its true point of reference, from God's perspective, it becomes evident that in the end all nature is 'grace,'"[68] since creation itself is a result of the divine will. Therefore, human nature is constituted in the double freedom of God's will and its own will.

After concluding his excursus on Bonaventure, Ratzinger finds a congruent answer in scripture via a brief examination of a series of relevant Pauline texts. He concludes that for Paul, humanity's "being" can most clearly be seen in relation to Christ, not in "nature," since nature speaks of man as both an object of God's creation and an expression of a sinful history.[69] Thus for Ratzinger in scripture "once again we find, as in Bonaventure's writing, the nature of man in tension between two freedoms: God's and man's."[70] Human nature exists in an analogical relation to the divine.

Based upon his survey of Bonaventure and of scripture, Ratzinger concludes that the (human) nature, which grace does not destroy but saves and fulfills, cannot be found undistorted by concupiscent "second nature" in any

---

65. Ratzinger, "*Gratia praesupponit naturam*," 153.

66. Ratzinger, "*Gratia praesupponit naturam*," 154, citing Bonaventure, *Breviloquium*.

67. Ratzinger, "*Gratia praesupponit naturam*," 154.

68. Ratzinger, "*Gratia praesupponit naturam*," 154, citing Bonaventure's commentary: "*hoc totum quod fecit, fuit gratia*" [all this that he made was grace].

69. Ratzinger, "*Gratia praesupponit naturam*," 153–54.

70. Ratzinger, "*Gratia praesupponit naturam*," 158.

man. Accordingly, "the way grace travels to reach man has to pass through the 'second nature,' breaking open the hard shell of vainglory that covers the divine glory within it. And that means that there is no grace without the cross."[71] The restoration and perfection of nature by grace requires a purging, a being freed from one's merely natural inclinations and habits. Accordingly, any merely "natural" humanism can only result in the self-assertion of man at the expense of the true worship of God. The true worship of God is precisely what is at stake for him in *Gaudium et Spes* and is the theological cornerstone for his conception of the necessity of personal and communal conversion as a prerequisite for both authentic ecclesial reform and evangelization. There is within man a "yearning cry" for something beyond the natural. Thus, the cross does not destroy man but frees him for true worship. "The Cross is not the destruction of man but, rather, the foundation of true humanity. . . . The humanity of God—this is indeed the true humanity of man, the grace that fulfills nature."[72]

Ratzinger's contribution to the *Festschrift* in honor of Söhngen's seventieth birthday attempts to show that our human nature does not merely need to be fulfilled by grace but first must be healed. Accordingly, a *theologica crucis*, which he perceives to be lacking in the pastoral constitution, is needed. Grace certainly does not violate nature and eliminate the freedom of the will, yet it does break-in from without in order to restore intrinsically to nature what has been lost and to elevate it for what it has been made. His utilization of Bonaventure attempts to situate Barth's concerns within a Catholic theological tradition "parallel" to Thomism and has a largely apologetic character. While he says that "the Creator and his creation must be defended"[73] against both a supernaturalism in which grace destroys nature and a nihilistic materialism, the brunt of his argument here seems concerned less with defending creation and instead seeks to "overcome the facile optimism of a shallow concept of nature as innocence."[74]

In sum, following the lead of Bonaventure and Söhngen, the early Ratzinger admits of a need to defend creation and the creator, but chooses here to defend them from neo-Thomism's inadequate recognition of humanity's marked nature rather than from the materialism and domination of creation characteristic of Marxism. He sees human nature as spirit that is intrinsically open to relation with God, but which suffers the wounds of sin and stands in need of healing. This healing and elevation comes about

---

71. Ratzinger, "*Gratia praesupponit naturam*," 159.
72. Ratzinger, "*Gratia praesupponit naturam*," 161.
73. Ratzinger, "*Gratia praesupponit naturam*," 144.
74. Schenk, "Analogy," 182n28.

through the cross via an extrinsic infusion of grace, a second gift. The young professor seems to agree with Bonaventure's skeptical outlook towards any philosophy that claims self-sufficiency but maintains the importance of philosophy for theology. These initial impulses will form the foundation of his response to constructivism, positivism, and secularism, and more to the point, will influence his reaction to *Gaudium et Spes*, a reaction, which is further reflected in the Benedictine themes that undergird his eucharistic ecclesiology and communion missiology.

2.2.2 Ratzinger's Appraisal of Gaudium et Spes

As a *peritus* who contributed to several of the key conciliar documents and who was among those who recognized the need for church reform, "the spirit of Vatican II" raised warning flags for Ratzinger. He was wary of the anthropological and theological approach of *Gaudium et Spes* from the start. "This way of speaking of the Church involves no small danger of sinking once more into a purely sociological and even ideological view of the Church through ignoring the essential insights of the Constitution on the liturgy and the Constitution on the Church and by oversimplifying, externalizing and making a catchword of a term which can only keep its meaning if it is used in a genuinely theological context."[75] He perceived the preface of the pastoral constitution to have used the term "world" "in a pretheological" manner, as something distinct from the church.[76] It did not reflect, in his Bonaventurian view, the true historical situation of humanity as fallen and in need of redemption. Following from this relationship of distinction is the notion of humanization through dialogue, but for Ratzinger the essence of the church's mission involves preaching not dialog. "The kerygma remains in this sense the distinctive linguistic form of the Church, for which it is responsible before others. ... This distinctive gift she cannot make an object of negotiation; she can only offer it for the decision of faith."[77] The church never exists for dialog with the world, but rather as a creative minority within a world in need of conversion.

Vorgrimler and others have argued this represents a departure from Ratzinger's earlier insistence upon the need for reform, the importance of moving beyond the neo-scholastic manuals. Did he not flip from a

---

75. Ratzinger, "Introductory Article," 118–19.

76. Ratzinger, *Principles*, 379–81.

77. Ratzinger, *Das neue Volk Gottes*, 294, in Komonchak, "Redaction and Reception," 7–8.

progressive reformer to a conservative traditionalist somewhere in the course of the council and the time immediately following it?

To this Ratzinger answers, "My basic impulse, precisely during the Council, was always to free up the kernel of the faith from encrustations and to give this kernel strength and dynamism. This impulse is the constant of my life. It would also have ruled out my withdrawing into an anti-Church opposition."[78] Reform was needed. The bastions needed to be razed.[79] But, this reform, for Ratzinger, must always be a return to Christ "who is our origin as well as our Future."[80] Reform must take the form of a re-orientation to the Lord, of a *ressourcement* rather than a modernization. Because, "When reform is dissociated from the hard work of repentance, and seeks salvation merely by changing others, by creating ever fresh forms, and by accommodation to the times, then despite many useful innovations it will be a caricature of itself. Such reform can touch only things of secondary importance in the Church."[81]

Ratzinger perceived that many of the voices pushing for further *aggiornamento* were moving beyond the council, pushing for modernization and dialogue, which was not authentic ecclesial reform. The council is not a new beginning to be surpassed but a cornerstone to be built around in continuity with tradition. Thus, the newness of the council does indeed involve an "openness to the world" which had been neglected in the nineteenth and early-twentieth centuries, but this openness ought to be a "desecularizing opening-up of the world."[82] It requires the cross. Whereas the prior fortress mentality had closed off the world from the church and covered up, as it were, the saving light of the Gospel, the council calls for the church to once again open her gates to world, not to let the world in, but to bring Christ to the world. "Real 'reform' is to strive to let what is ours disappear as much as possible so what belongs to Christ may become more visible."[83]

In other words,

> One could say that the Council marks the transition from a conservationist to a missionary attitude, and the conciliar alternative to "conservative" is not "progressive," but rather "missionary." In this antithesis is found basically the precise meaning of what the conciliar "opening-up to the world" means and what

---

78. Ratzinger, *Salt of the Earth*, 79.
79. See Balthasar, *Razing the Bastions*.
80. Ratzinger, *Das neue Volk Gottes*, 70, in Heim, *Joseph Ratzinger*, 197.
81. Balthasar and Ratzinger, *Two Say Why*, 70.
82. Ratzinger, *Das neue Volk Gottes*, 126–28, in Heim, *Joseph Ratzinger*, 196.
83. Ratzinger and Messori, *Ratzinger Report*, 53.

it does not mean. It does not provide the Christian with greater comfort by setting him free to conform to the world in a fashionable mass culture—the Council could never do that, because as a Christian event it was bound to the nonconformism of the Bible: "Do not be conformed to this world" (Rom 12:2).[84]

For Ratzinger a new openness to the world was indeed needed, and he pushed to end the mentality that had closed the church within itself. However, the openness, which was being declared and promoted following the council in the name of *Gaudium et Spes* and the "Spirit of Vatican II," was in his view more accommodation to the world than witness to the world. It failed to reflect adequately the need for conversion and the cross—as pointed out by Bonaventure and Söhngen—in every authentic event of reform and evangelization.

Post-Conciliar Crisis

In Ratzinger's view, this witnessing did not happen. Thus far, the church has not become once again the culture-shaping force that John XXIII had hoped. "The faith would really have come out of the ghetto only if it had brought its most distinctive features with it into the public arena: the God who judges and suffers, the God who sets limits and standards for us; the God from whom we come and to whom we are going. But as it was, it really remained in the ghetto, having by now absolutely nothing to do."[85] What's more, "the post-conciliar crisis in the Catholic Church coincided with a global spiritual crisis of humanity itself, or, at least, of the Western world."[86] The tumult of the late 1960s and the increasing popularity of Marxism in the West deeply influenced a church, which had not yet found its post-conciliar footing.

Therefore, at the same time as the theological turn to history was muddying the very christological core of the faith, modernity was moving on from the *factum* to the *faciendum*. Ratzinger describes Marxism as possessing "something of the primordial potency of Old Testament messianism, now gone anti-theistic and demanding an un-conditional commitment through its claims that here at last all reality can become scientifically knowable, the past, present, and future of humankind receiving their exact

---

84. Ratzinger, *Das neue Volk Gottes*, 128, in Heim, *Joseph Ratzinger*, 196.
85. Ratzinger, *Introduction to Christianity*, 17.
86. Ratzinger, *Principles*, 370.

interpretation."[87] This potency was appealing to theology. It gave theology the opportunity to feel relevant, practical once again—an eschatology with concrete content and action, but also an eschatology without God. Reflecting on this, Ratzinger associates Marxism with Barth: "It is curious, and yet, in the light of Barth's violent separation of faith and religion, also understandable that when theology is thus placed before the alternatives of faith in God and a religious pathos directed to futurity, it is willing to choose religion over against God."[88] Accordingly, many theologians were convinced by the claims of self-sufficiency put forward by Marxist ideology. If the "initselfness" of things has no meaning, and if the basis of truth has been transferred from the *factum* to the *faciendum*, then all that matters has been pushed into the future. A faith which speaks of the God who *is* and who came into the world some two-thousand years ago no longer has anything meaningful to say. However, "these messianic goals in which Marxism's fascination lies rest upon a faulty underlying synthesis of relation and reason."[89] Its goals are well beyond the reach of its means. (This is because Marx, despite all his genius, fails to account for humanity's fallenness, or else presumes that the party can be humanity's redemption. Marxism suffers from modern materialism and his own brand of naïve optimism).[90] Thus, "both the goal and planning suffer shipwreck,"[91] and humanity continues to suffer.

Now the theological question became, "How can the church change the world?" This question led to the politicization of theology and to the adoption of certain Marxist ideas aimed at empowering the Gospel once again to be a liberating force for people in the world. The adoption of Marxism would be the way in which the church would come out of ghetto. The church would once again shape culture by baptizing certain Marxist principles. Nevertheless, the modern worship of progress for progress's sake combined with the Marxist notion of the need to change the world necessarily leads to tyranny. "The scientific facade hides a dogmatic intolerance that views the spirit as produced by matter, and morals as produced by circumstances."[92] While members of the church were trying to adopt modern ideas to bring Christ to world, those very ideas and the reduction of reason to mere facts and of ethics to mere chance neutered the Gospel of its force. The Christian difference was slipping through the fingers of the post-conciliar church.

87. Ratzinger, *Eschatology*, 3.
88. Ratzinger, *Eschatology*, 3–4.
89. Ratzinger, *Eschatology*, 212.
90. See Benedict XVI, *Spe salvi*, 21.
91. Ratzinger, *Eschatology*, 212.
92. Ratzinger and Pera, *Without Roots*, 72.

A Christian revolution aimed at liberating the poor and oppressed by somehow mingling the Gospel with Marxist ideology inevitably had to choose whether it would worship the God of freedom or the god of progress. Any revolution that does not have the patience to wait for men and women to choose to join the revolution in their own freedom will eventually deny the freedom of these persons and turn to tyranny. Indeed, in secular revolutions the social overthrow often occurs rapidly by means of open and direct violence precisely because the present generation, the generation which desires the revolution, cannot afford to wait forever. The revolution that often begins with a demand for one's own freedom and dignity to be respected ends with the violent suppression of the freedom and dignity of the other. God's revolution is always different. From the beginning God desires to overthrow the reign of sin and violence; he desires a revolution of love, which respects the freedom of the persons whom he created free precisely so they might choose love. The revolution "can spread abroad, but not through persuasion, not through indoctrination, not through violence,"[93] since each person must be given the opportunity to accept or reject the revolution being offered.

Despite the fall of the Berlin Wall and the decline of Marxist influence, "the essential problem of our times, for Europe and for the world, is that although the fallacy of the communist economy has been recognized ... the moral and religious question that it used to address has been almost totally repressed. The unresolved issue of Marxism lives on: the crumbling of man's original uncertainties about God, himself, and the universe."[94] The crisis has not been avoided or resolved.

Indeed, "the arc of modernity leads to the absence of transcendence, to rampant individualism, the eclipse of the other, and ultimately the destruction of the self."[95] If there is no *logos* from which the cosmos comes, there is nothing that is finally true or good. The weakening of reason leads to the loss of morals. Humanity has sold its soul for autonomy, for the power to define itself and the world as it wishes, without reference to the providential plan of its creator.[96] Put another way, the decline of Marxism has not led to a resolution of the modern crisis because all of modernity—Communists, Democrats, Socialists, Fascists, etc.—share its most fundamental philosophical flaws. "The most opposite modern views of the world share the same starting point: the denial of the natural ethical law and the reduction

---

93. Lohfink, *Does God Need the Church?*, 27.
94. Ratzinger and Pera, *Without Roots*, 73–74.
95. Norris, *Fractured Relationship*, 31.
96. See Ratzinger and Pera, *Without Roots*, 34.

of the world to 'mere' facts. The measure of what they illogically retain of the old values is variable, but they are threatened by the same danger in their central point."[97]

In this regard, Ratzinger expresses agreement with Bonaventure's assessment. Philosophy can never be self-sufficient as modern philosophy attempts to be. Any merely natural philosophy does not provide firm ground on which to stand. The young professor writes, "Of course, this temptation is present in every age. Thus in the thirteenth century the great Franciscan theologian Bonaventure felt obliged to reproach his colleagues of the philosophical faculty at Paris with having learned how to measure the world but having forgotten how to measure themselves."[98] Ratzinger translates Bonaventure's concern with the self-sufficiency of Latin Averroism to his own critique of modernity. After all, in modernity's rejection of creation, man also rejects his own givenness and finitude, aims to redeem himself by remaking the world. However, "No man can pull himself up out of the bog of uncertainty . . . as Descartes still thought we could, by a *cogito ergo sum*, by a series of intellectual deductions. Meaning that is self-made is in the last analysis no meaning."[99] Meaning, our meaning, must be received. Otherwise, we are left with no ground on which to stand.

In short, Ratzinger agrees with Przywara. Created beings exist in an analogical relation to the God who is. For although it is proper to speak both of human reason and God's reason, this similarity only exists within the infinite difference between the *Logos* who created the world and is the ground upon which existence stands and the *logos* that can only work with that which it has been given. "This is in accordance with the thought of Przywara who maintains that the inner order (ἀνά) of creation is always 'in-and-beyond history' due to truth being 'above and beyond.' As described by Ratzinger, the inner order and truth of reality is like the ground that man does not create."[100] Humans can speak of truth with meaning because the cosmos has been bestowed with intelligibility by its creator who is the *Logos*.

Therefore, any adequate response to the crisis, any attempt at a New Evangelization, must somehow point the world beyond itself and back to God. After all, "the existence of value that cannot be modified by anyone is the true guarantee of our freedom and of human greatness; in this fact, the

---

97. Ratzinger and Pera, *Without Roots*, 34.
98. Ratzinger, *Introduction to Christianity*, 71.
99. Ratzinger, *Introduction to Christianity*, 73.
100. Kucer, *Truth and Politics*, 51.

Christian faith sees the mystery of the Creator and the condition of man, who was made in God's image."[101]

Human freedom, in its full depth and dignity will continue to be violated until the church can again communicate the Gospel to the world. However, because of the positivism of the historical turn, lost was the very idea of God as the personal force gathering the church in love, as the end for which we are made. Therefore, the church was now viewed as a human institution whose structures and core principles became quite arbitrary. If the church is not the people *of God* but just a people, if the church was not historically and actually called and gathered by Jesus, if the notion of the church as the body of Christ is not more than a mere metaphor, then how is the church different from any other historical and human institution? And,

> If the Church ... is viewed as a human construction, the product of our own efforts, even the contents of the faith end up assuming an arbitrary character: the faith, in fact, no longer has an authentic, guaranteed instrument through which to express itself. Thus, without a view of the mystery of the Church that is also supernatural and not only sociological, Christology itself loses its reference to the divine. . . . The Gospel becomes the *Jesus-project*, the social-liberation project or other merely historical, immanent project that can still seem religious in appearance, but which are atheistic in substance.[102]

This is precisely what happens when God is left behind and emptied of relevance. Moreover, "a Church that is there only for her own sake is superfluous. And people notice that straightaway."[103] To paraphrase Flannery O'Connor, if the church is not the body of Christ, then to hell with it. Thus, the church, the Gospel, and Jesus himself are no longer credible to modern man.

The experience of life in Christian community no longer communicates the reality of the original experience of the presence of God in Christ. For Ratzinger, this reduction of Christian life from communal participation in and worship of the triune God to an empty moralism "is the decisive reason for the abandonment of Christianity: its model for life is apparently unconvincing."[104] Since Christianity has been reduced in large part to a pious moralism, it is no longer seen as salvific, as a reason for joy and hope. Rather it is perceived to sap the joy out of life with overly strict moral codes

---

101. Ratzinger and Pera, *Without Roots*, 75.
102. Ratzinger and Messori, *Ratzinger Report*, 46.
103. Ratzinger, *Pilgrim Fellowship of Faith*, 128–29.
104. Ratzinger and Pera, *Without Roots*, 125.

that do not comport with the relativistic and utilitarian ethical norms of our times. As Ratzinger explains, "it seems to place too many constraints on humankind that stifle its *joie de vivre*, that limit its precious freedom, and that do not lead it to open pastures—in the language of the Psalms—but rather into want, into deprivation."[105] Ratzinger reflects that similar claims were made against the church by Julian the Apostate, "but the Christians were able to demonstrate persuasively how empty and base were the entertainments of paganism, and how sublime the gift of faith in the God who suffers with us."[106] There is an urgent need for the church once again to expose the vacuity of secular life and pleasures by making a space for people to experience the depth and fulfillment that accompanies the joy in loving. When Christians once again live the life of communion in a concrete way, only then can non-believers enter "that space of grace" and "find the fullness of life, not as a theory, but as an experience, not as a burden but as a gift, not as a law but as an adventure."[107] Only when communion with God can be experienced concretely in the church will the church's missionary efforts, will the New Evangelization, begin to bear a bountiful harvest. This can only happen if the church is distinguishable from the world, is a minority, which creatively calls the world back to God.

Two questions remain: how does Ratzinger envision reform of a church that has come to be perceived as merely a sociological institution, and how does Ratzinger foresee that reformed church evangelizing the modern world?

Analogia Entis and Analogia Fidei

The issue of the church's place within and relation to the modern world is an analog of the relationship between the *analogia fidei* and the *analogia entis*. While there is no clear agreement among scholars on how Ratzinger perceives the relationship between the analogy of faith and the analogy of being, I explore his perception below in order to grasp the fundamental theological roots of Ratzinger's ecclesiological position, which will be explored in some detail later. To start with, there is an issue with defining the term "*analogia fidei*." As noted earlier, John Betz explains,

> What is meant by "analogy of faith," however, is itself a matter of dispute. Strictly speaking, the phrase refers to Romans 12:6,

---

105. Ratzinger and Pera, *Without Roots*, 125.
106. Ratzinger and Pera, *Without Roots*, 125.
107. Norris, *Fractured Relationship*, 42.

where Paul says that the "analogy of faith" must hold for the prophets; in other words, what prophets say must be "proportionate" to the rule of faith. This is the primary sense in which Przywara understands the term, though, following Augustine, he also speaks of the *analogia fidei* in terms of the analogy between Old and New Testaments. In Barth, however, it tends to mean either that there is no analogy between God and creatures apart from the analogy that God himself causes in the creature by faith—whereby alone we are made like God—or it refers to the self-correspondence of God in Christ.[108]

On the other hand, for Gottlieb Söhngen, the analogy of being fits within and is grounded by the *analogia fidei*, understood as something similar to what White expressed as the "ontological resemblances between creatures and God that are known to us uniquely by virtue of the supernatural revelation of God in Christ."[109]

Oakes implies that Ratzinger follows Przywara's more biblical (as opposed to ontological) usage by noting that in the recently published *God's Word: Scripture, Tradition, Office*, Ratzinger approvingly references Przywara's use of the term.[110] Kucer makes this more explicit claiming, "Despite Söhngen's formative influence on Ratzinger, when it comes to his definition of an analogy of faith Ratzinger leans more in the direction of Przywara who more clearly distinguishes the analogy of faith from an analogy of being."[111] Schenk, however, perceives that Ratzinger, at least in his early writings, follows Söhngen in ecumenically using Bonaventure as a classic example of a proper use of the analogy of faith.[112]

It seems to the present author that Schenk is correct about the reception of the theological programmatic of Söhngen in Ratzinger's early work. It is also clear that Ratzinger uses "analogy of faith" in a way similar to Przywara when he discusses the relation of the two Testaments. The question remains, does the more recent Ratzinger implicitly maintain the ontological claims of Söhngen's understanding of the *analogia fidei*? The answer will

---

108. Betz, "After Barth," 87n160.

109. White, "'Through Him All Things Were Made,'" 248. He defines the analogy of faith in contrast with analogy of being, by which he means "to denote the ontological resemblances between creatures and God that can be discerned and understood by powers of natural human reason."

110. Oakes, "Cross and the *Analogia Entis*," 161. Ratzinger cites Przywara, *Alter und Neuer Bund*, where he develops the notion of the analogy of faith between the two Testaments.

111. Kucer, *Truth and Politics*, 57.

112. See especially Schenk, "Bonaventura als Klassiker der analogia fidei."

determine the manner in which Ratzinger believes the church should engage the world.

In his now infamous Regensburg address, Ratzinger hoped to argue for restoring the coherence between faith and reason that once marked the experience of university life and ought to mark the relation between faith and reason in society as a whole.[113] This requires a twofold rapprochement, which he hopes will be a return to the coherence between Hellenistic *ratio* and the faith of the sacred scriptures as exhibited by the church fathers. On the one hand, the horizons of modern reason must be broadened so they are no longer closed off from asking the God question. In relativism, he sees a false humility which lacks the courage to make the distinctions necessary for recognizing the truth.[114] Ultimately, this "means that the scope of reason must be enlarged once more."[115] On the other hand, reason is necessary for faith. It is given to temper transcendence and is the antidote to violence. Accordingly, "without faith, philosophy cannot be whole, [and] faith without reason cannot be human."[116]

This means that for Ratzinger reason maintains a certain autonomy.[117] Although it can never be "self-sufficient,"[118] as Bonaventure warns, it nevertheless remains capable of rising to great heights without the aid of revelation. Ratzinger's view of the power of reason, even in fallen man, is more optimistic than Söhngen's and allows reason, and thus the *analogia entis*, a greater autonomy than Söhngen wants to give it.

According to Ratzinger, truth is manifest in faith *and* in human reason, both of which originate from and are ordered to the eternal *Logos*. Thus, the answer of faith does not obviate or excuse the free exercise of rationality. In this way for Ratzinger "*logos*" refers not only to the eternal *Logos* of the Father, but also to his reflection and projection in creation as intelligible and in the most noble dimension of humanity.

However, Ratzinger also departs from Przywara, or at least from Przywara's explicit formulations, and follows Söhngen in grounding humanity's correspondence to truth explicitly in Christ. *Logos* christology has remained a central aspect throughout his theological career. Both truth and faith are held in relation within human *logos* because of their origin and end in the

---

113. Benedict XVI, "Faith, Reason, and the University."

114. Ratzinger, *Truth and Tolerance*, 148.

115. Ratzinger, *Truth and Tolerance*, 148.

116. Ratzinger, *Truth and Tolerance*, 136.

117. See Ratzinger, *Nature and Mission*, 16.

118. For Ratzinger this means that no philosophy can ever become "a basis for faith that is independent of faith itself: for in that case, our faith would in the end be based on changing philosophical theories" (Ratzinger, *Truth and Tolerance*, 136).

divine *logos*, as noted above. This move emphasizes the givenness of life and reason and again relies upon his acceptance of the *analogia entis*. Furthermore, just as *Dei Verbum* solved the apparent opposition between scripture and tradition by finding the one source of revelation in Christ, so Ratzinger attempts to solve the apparent opposition between faith and reason by finding the one source of love and truth in Christ. Thus, while Ratzinger gives human reason a certain autonomy, he also emphasizes its givenness, often highlighting the givenness of the first gift, that of nature, more than the second, of grace. Put another way, he accepts Przywara's stronger distinction between the natural and supernatural, but also insists on the givenness and gratuity of the natural itself. In doing so, he incorporates both Przywara's conception of the *analogia fidei*—*analogia entis* relation and also hearkens back to Bonaventure's concerns of self-sufficiency.

Logos and Dialogos

In his last encyclical *Caritas in Veritate*, Pope Benedict XVI teaches that grace is the "principle driving force behind the authentic development of every person,"[119] for man receives a vocation from God to pursue love and truth. This pursuit however, must be set free by Christ from the "impoverishment" of human fallenness. While on the one hand charity-grace is the principle of the God-man relation,[120] on the other hand, it is truth which universalizes charity, freeing it from mere sentimentality and for *dia-logos*, communion in service of the common good. In the Incarnation the *Logos* opens himself up for *dia-logos* with humanity. The *Logos* is turned into *dia-logos*, because he is directed to humanity. Accordingly, the human person is a logical and dialogical being. This inclination and disposition to love and to know are elevated and amplified at the same time due to the free gift of faith.[121] Thus, as shall be seen below, Ratzinger holds that in order for the church to enter into appropriate dialogue with the modern world, Christians must first turn back to the *Logos*. Conversion must precede evangelization.

Ratzinger believes that the God of faith and the God of the philosophers should be held together, which reflects his desire to maintain the validity of the *analogia entis*. At the same time, he holds that the Christian faith revolutionized the philosophical concept of God by establishing at its very core the concepts of person, reason, and love: God is not just thought, but a Trinity of persons who love. In this way, truth and love are

119. Benedict XVI, *Caritas in veritate*, 1.
120. Benedict XVI, *Caritas in veritate*, 2.
121. See Ratzinger, *Introduction to Christianity*, 48–49, 77, 96, 126–38.

once more closely united. Here Ratzinger's own unique perspective on the *analogia entis* becomes clearer. In the analogy between God and man, because man is made "unto" God by virtue of the innate tendencies of his being and his immortal soul and because the soul is both immortal and the form of the body, the "relationship to God can be seen to express the very core of [humanity's] essence. As a created being he is made for a relationship that entails indestructability."[122] Put another way, this "being towards" or "being for God" is "part and parcel" of the "innate relationality" of the soul of the human: humanity is open to God and therefore to the relational life of the triune God. Our relationality is a kind of reflection of trinitarian life. Furthermore, while this openness to God "constitutes what is deepest in man's being" and "is nothing other than what we call 'soul,'"[123] it is not *merely* natural, or *merely* ours. The immortality that characterizes man in his innate spiritual openness to God is a gift of God, because "nature is only possible by virtue of a communication of the Creator's, yet such communication both establishes the creature in its own right and makes it a genuine participator in the being of the One communicated."[124]

He explains further, "owing to the Christological transformation, the Platonist notion of the life which flows from truth is rendered more profound, and made the vehicle of a 'dialogical' concept of humanity: man is *defined* by his intercourse with God."[125] In humanity, all of creation has the capacity for God, since the human soul is both entirely natural and made for a dialogical encounter with God. Within this context, Ratzinger describes sin as the attempt to place oneself above God, to embrace one's own autonomy and self-sufficiency, and in doing so, to attempt to cut off one's dependence on and relation with God,[126] which is precisely what he sees to be the *modus operandi* of modernity. Modern notions of freedom reject the givenness of being created. Thus, still reflecting Söhngen's concern about a naively optimistic view of human nature, Ratzinger's *logos* Christology places an emphasis on the necessity of conversion, of *metanoia*.[127]

In response to modernity's claim of autonomy and self-sufficiency, the church can only assert the reality of "original sin," which makes itself known in the brokenness of the world, and that from this reality, there is "only *one*

---

122. Ratzinger, *Eschatology*, 154; cf. Bonaventure, *Disputed Questions* 1.1.response (116).

123. Ratzinger, *Eschatology*, 155.

124. Ratzinger, *Eschatology*, 155.

125. Ratzinger, *Eschatology*, 152 (emphasis mine).

126. Ratzinger, *Eschatology*, 156.

127. Ratzinger, *Principles*, 62.

saving tradition," that of Jesus.[128] Belief in Jesus means "that there is a truth from which man proceeds and which is most signally his own, which is his true nature."[129] For Ratzinger, the formal principle of Catholicism—analogy—presumes and requires nature. Jesus himself, in his relationship to God, is the sustaining ground of authentic human *being*. His relationship to God is the "middle," connecting man with himself in order to lead man to the Father, from whom Jesus receives himself, his mission, his tradition. "The Christian sees in Jesus a point of access to the center of tradition, to that place where tradition is, in very fact, a breakthrough to what was in the beginning; where it does not range itself against reason but reveals the ground on which it rests."[130] In giving humanity access to tradition, Jesus gives access to untainted human nature. In this sense, Ratzinger's anthropology can speak with *Gaudium et Spes*: Jesus Christ reveals humanity to himself.[131]

The tradition of Jesus is the only saving tradition which gives man hope for overcoming the dehumanizing effects of sin.[132] Belief in Jesus requires the willingness to submit to the authority of the Jesus tradition. After all, "there is no Christian experience that is not the fruit of the overcoming of one's own self-will. . . . [For] God requires unselfish vessels into which to pour his own essential unselfishness."[133] Generalizing the same point, Ratzinger concludes, "religious experience in its most exalted and Christian form bears the mark of the Cross. It embraces the basic model of human existence, the transcendence of the self. The Cross redeems, it enables us to see."[134] When looking at the relation between God and the world in the context of human experience Ratzinger wishes to emphasize that grace does not merely perfect nature, but that nature requires conversion, a willingness to admit that one is sick, a willingness to go to the divine physician in search of a cure. This emphasis—which is both an echo of the similarity

128. Ratzinger, *Principles*, 93.

129. Ratzinger, *Principles*, 94.

130. Ratzinger, *Principles*, 99.

131. Cf. GS 22.

132. "In Scholastic as well as in patristic theology, Christology has two basic points: one in the past, which finds its expression in the doctrine of original sin; the other in the future, which has its critical constant in the biblical concept of Christ as the 'last man,' that is, as the revelation and the beginning of the definitive mode of human existence. If we can say with reference to the first, that Christ is necessary in order that the burden of the past—original guilt—may be overcome, we must say with reference to the second that Christ is necessary in order that the human race may come into its future, which it is not able to do unaided" (Ratzinger, *Principles*, 187–88).

133. Ratzinger, *Principles*, 350, quoting Balthasar, "Gotteserfahrung," 500, 508.

134. Ratzinger, *Principles*, 350.

within infinite difference of Przywara's *analogia entis* and also a reflection of Söhngen's more christological focus, especially as manifest in a theology of the cross—emerges as the core of Ratzinger's qualified criticism of *Gaudium et Spes*. Indeed, Ratzinger's insistence on the priority of conversion shapes his imagination and articulation of how the church can concretely function again as the dominant social dynamic force, as the universal sacrament of salvation.

2.2.3 Towards a Life in Communion and for the World

John XXIII wanted the council to enable the church to become again a culture-shaping force in the world. Ratzinger shares this desire, but he holds that that cannot be achieved via modernization. Instead, recognizing with Bonaventure the historical situation of fallen humanity, he argues the church must be a counter-cultural witness in the world. Similarly, in response to the relativism of modern society and the sequestration of God from the world, Ratzinger believes authentic reform will only come from conversion to Christ. Recall that he believes "Time and again, our world could so easily find its corrective in the Benedictine rule. . . . We need men like Benedict of Nursia, who, in an age of dissipation and decadence immersed himself in the uttermost solitude. Then, after all the purification he had to undergo, he succeeded in rising again to the light . . . where he assembled the forces from which a new world was formed."[135] For Ratzinger this *metanoia* is an act of faith that can never be individualistic but always implies that membership in the church is a communal reality ordered to worship. Conversion is conversion-into-communion with God and the church. In other words, Ratzinger believes the eucharistic liturgy is the heart of the church, which forms Christians into a spiritual and a moral communion. Christians today require conversion from the materialistic, individualistic, and hedonistic images advocated by secular society and conversion to a thoroughly biblical imagination so that they, as a people, as creative minorities, may together bear witness to the living and loving presence of Christ in the world, in their communities.

Flowing from his engagement with Przywara and Bonaventure, Ratzinger's ecclesiology calls for a renewal of ecclesial life, so that in parishes and local churches worship again leads to real, lived communion and, by offering to God what is owed him, becomes a witness to offering of God's presence. According to Ratzinger's understanding, for the church to fulfill its role as the sacrament of salvation, Christian communities must again

---

135. Ratzinger, *God and the World*, 392.

offer their lives as "a living sacrifice, holy and acceptable to God, which is spiritual worship" (Rom 12:1), λογική λατρεία. Only in doing so can they bear witness to the truth in love by providing "a pattern of common life and offer[ing] a fixed point of survival in an uncertain age."[136]

In a society in which logic often fails to gain traction, what is needed is not an adoption of secular fads or the majority's cause *du jour*, but a return to authentic Christian witness, which is always communal. In Ratzinger's latest *ressourcement*, he calls for new "creative minorities"[137] capable of showing the world the joy and peace of a life in communion with God and neighbor by becoming concrete spaces in the world where people can encounter the risen Lord.

---

136. Ratzinger, "Eschatology and Utopia," 250.
137. Ratzinger and Pera, *Without Roots*, 51–81, 107–136.

Part 2

Part 2 will feature a systematic analysis of both Ratzinger's communion ecclesiology and his theology of mission. To this end, I first explore the theological foundations of Ratzinger's communion ecclesiology by grounding it in his understanding of trinitarian communion and divine personhood. Second, I present the ecclesiology of communion, which develops from his understanding of the divine persons. Since for Ratzinger this communion of faith, which is the church, "subsists as *Liturgy* and in Liturgy,"[1] I examine the role of the Eucharist, as "source and summit" of ecclesial life in Ratzinger's ecclesiology. While the eucharistic liturgy is not oriented to mission, "it is the origin of mission."[2] Thus, the Eucharist will serve as the transition from the second step, on communion, to the third step, which examines Ratzinger's theology of mission as eucharistic offering of the ecclesial body to the Father.

---

1. Ratzinger, *God Is Near Us*, 122.
2. Ratzinger, *Pilgrim Fellowship of Faith*, 94.

3

Being as Relation: Communion in the Trinity

THE SECOND VATICAN COUNCIL defines the church theologically and sacramentally "in Christ" and as a sacrament of communion with God and the whole human race.[1] Indeed the unity of the church comes from "the unity of the Father, Son, and Holy Spirit."[2] According to the view of the council, the Father from the beginning of time wills for humanity to participate in the divine fellowship through communion with the Son.[3] The Holy Spirit realizes the communion between men and women and between humanity and the Trinity.[4] This notion of the church as "communion" has come to be seen as a primary theme of the council.[5]

Ratzinger, like the fathers of the Second Vatican Council, always intends his ecclesiological writings to be set in the "context" of talk about God and to be "theo-logical in the proper sense."[6] After all, only if the church is the people of God and the body of Christ, only if it is "from above," can it be the sacrament of salvation. Thus, for the Bavarian theologian whose theological method is often that of an interpreter of scripture and tradition, the biblical foundations of the term "communion" indicate its "theological

---

1. LG 1.

2. LG 4. With reference to St. Cyprian. Cf. UR 2: "[The Church] is a mystery that finds its highest exemplary and source in the unity of the Persons of the Trinity: the Father and the Son in the Holy Spirit, one God."

3. Cf. LG 2, 3.

4. Cf. UR 2: "It is the Holy Spirit, dwelling in those who believe and pervading and ruling over the Church as a whole, who brings about that wonderful communion of the faithful. He brings them into intimate union with Christ, so that He is the principle of the Church's unity." See also LG 4; AG 4.

5. "The ecclesiology of communion is the central and fundamental idea of the council's documents. Koinonia/communion, founded on Sacred Scripture, have been held in great honor in the early church and in the Eastern churches to this day. Thus, the Second Vatican Council did much so that the church as communion might be more clearly understood and concretely incorporated into life" (ESB, "Final Report" III.c.1).

6. Ratzinger, *Pilgrim Fellowship of Faith*, 125.

and christological character, one associated with the history of salvation and also ecclesiology."[7] From the point of view of this biblical notion of communion:

> Ecclesiology appears as dependent upon Christology, as belonging to it. Yet because no one can talk correctly about Christ, the Son, without also straightaway talking about the Father, and because no one can talk about the Father and the Son without listening to the Holy Spirit, then the Christological aspect of ecclesiology is necessarily extended into a trinitarian ecclesiology. Talking about the Church is talking about God and can be correct only in that sense.[8]

Indeed, this must be the case. After all, if the God who *is* exists precisely as the trinitarian *communio personarum*, then "'this means that the mystery of the Trinity has opened to us a totally new perspective: the ground of being is *communio*' . . . to believe in the Trinity means to become *communio*."[9] Therefore, this first section will explore the trinitarian foundation of Ratzinger's notion of *communio* by examining his trinitarian theology and his notion of person.

3.1 The Divine *Communio Personarum*

The "dynamic circle of Trinitarian love" brings about "the highest degree of unity and constancy and this in turn gives unity and constancy to everything that exists."[10] The unity of the Trinity is a perichoretic unity which is revealed to men and women by the incarnate Son who also intends to incorporate them into this unity through himself. For Ratzinger, because God chooses to reveal his triunity through the Incarnation of the Son, any inquiry into the Trinity must be focused on God as revealed by the person of Jesus.[11] Put another way, Ratzinger's Christology is the key to both his trinitarian theology and his ecclesiology, both of which can be described as christocentric.[12] In the Incarnation, the Son reveals the trinitarian face of

---

7. Ratzinger, *Pilgrim Fellowship of Faith*, 130–31.
8. Ratzinger, *Pilgrim Fellowship of Faith*, 140.
9. Ratzinger, *Principles*, 22–23, quoting de Lubac, *La foi chretienne*, 14.
10. Ratzinger, *Seeking God's Face*, 37.
11. See Ratzinger, *Introduction to Christianity*, 163.
12. See Milet, *God or Christ?*, esp. 67, 150, 216. As his title suggests, Milet, on the whole, critiques "the excesses of christocentricity" in various theologians. Nevertheless, although he identifies a degree of christocentricity in Ratzinger's theology, he ultimately concludes that Ratzinger's thought is "more markedly theocentric than christocentric."

God to humanity. Following Bonaventure, Ratzinger insists Christ is not only the center of human history but is also "the middle person of the Trinity as well as the mediator and middle between God and man."[13] In other words, he understands trinitarian unity through the person of Jesus.

Furthermore, Ratzinger's doctrine of the Trinity wanders not into esoteric abstraction, but rather bears concrete, deep, and wide-ranging implications for the church and human communion more broadly speaking. The Incarnation confirms this: "Only in the mystery of the incarnate Word does the mystery of man take on light.... Christ, the final Adam, by the revelation of the mystery of the Father and His love, fully reveals man to man himself and makes his supreme calling clear."[14] In his very person, Jesus simultaneously reveals both the triunity of God and the authentic form of humanity. Thus, the doctrine of the Trinity is eminently practical and concrete since trinitarian communion is the cypher through which authentic human communion can be perceived, and through which ecclesial communion is realized.

Ratzinger's understanding of the divine *communio personarum* takes shape in the context of his parsing of the paradox "*una essentia tres personae.*"[15] First, this formula communicates that the ground of all being is not a monadic uniformity. Rather, "it corresponds to the creative fullness of God, who himself stands above plurality and unity, encompassing both."[16] Second, only one divine principle exists; the unicity and unity of God lies on the level of substance, of essence. "Consequently the three-ness that must also be mentioned is not to be sought here. It must therefore exist on a different level, on that of relation, of the 'relative.'"[17]

3.1.1 The Son of the Father

Ratzinger unpacks the theological meaning of the "relative" by examining the relations of the divine persons. With Augustine, Ratzinger observes that "Father" is "purely a concept of relationship. Only in being-for the other is he Father: in his own being-in-himself he is simply God."[18] The unicity of

13. Ratzinger, *Theology of History in Bonaventure*, 17.
14. GS 22.
15. Ratzinger, *Introduction to Christianity*, 179.
16. Ratzinger, *Introduction to Christianity*, 179.
17. Ratzinger, *Introduction to Christianity*, 182.
18. Ratzinger, *Introduction to Christianity*, 183. Cf. Augustine in *Patrologia Latina* 36:845: "He is not called Father with reference to himself but only in relation to the Son; seen by himself he is simply God."

the Son's sonship and the Father's fatherhood becomes apparent in Jesus's so-called high priestly prayer: "I and the Father are one" (John 10:30).

> The Son as Son, and insofar as he is Son, does not proceed in any way from himself and so is completely one with the Father; since he is nothing beside him, claims no special position of his own, confronts the Father with nothing belonging only to him, makes no reservations for what is specifically his own, therefore he is completely equal to the Father. The logic is compelling: if there is nothing in which he is just he, no kind of fenced off private ground, then he coincides with the Father is "one" with him.[19]

Human sons indeed come from their fathers, but they also come to know and to be who they are through their relation to their mothers and through experiences as embodied individuals. A human father is not merely his act of begetting his son. Who he *is* is influenced by a variety of other historical persons as well as his relation to God. The same is not true of the relation between the divine Father and Son. "The first Person does not beget the Son as if the act of begetting were subsequent to the finished Person; it is the act of begetting, of giving oneself, of streaming forth. It is identical with the act of self-giving. Only as this act is it person, and therefore it is not the giver but the act of giving."[20] In short, for Ratzinger, the Father's eternal begetting of the Son is not something he does as Father or as first person. He is that eternal self-donation. The eternal act of the begetting of the Son defines who he is as a divine person.

Ratzinger's approach to the content of "Son" is similar.[21] He relies largely on the high Christology of the Johannine corpus in articulating what he calls a "spiritual Christology," which is most fully developed in *Behold the Pierced One*[22] and is an attempt to articular a Christology capable of responding to the christological tensions he perceives in modern christological treatises.[23] For Ratzinger, an adequate Christology must be sufficiently "high" or ontological—concerned with the *person* of the Son—in order to be both properly theo-logical and also capable of accounting for the

---

19. Ratzinger, *Introduction to Christianity*, 186; cf. Ratzinger, *Behold the Pierced One*, 22.

20. Ratzinger, *Introduction to Christianity*, 184.

21. In what follows, I have adapted much from Bonagura, "Logos to Son."

22. As developed in Ratzinger, *Behold the Pierced One*, 13–103. See also McGregor, "'Spiritual Christology' of Joseph Ratzinger"; McGregor, *Heart to Heart*.

23. He addresses divisions between faith and history, Christology and soteriology, theology and spirituality, the individual and the church, the Incarnation and the Cross, and faith and reason. See McGregor, "'Spiritual Christology' of Joseph Ratzinger," 82–83.

grounding of divine-human communion in the Incarnation. This is because "Trinitarian faith and faith in the Incarnation guide the idea of communion. . . . Communio must first be understood theologically. Only then can one draw implications for a sacramental notion of communio, and only after that for an ecclesiological notion."[24] Ratzinger believes the Third Council of Constantinople teaches such a Christology.

For Ratzinger, the doctrine of the Incarnation only carries its proper theological weight if the hypostatic union is understood rightly: "the affirmation of the true humanity and the true divinity in Christ can only retain its meaning if the mode of the unity of both is clarified. The Council defined this by speaking of the 'one person' in Christ."[25] The tradition maintains the *personal* mode of the union of Jesus's divine nature and human nature. Therefore, the mode of the communion between God and man is also personal.

In Ratzinger's view, the eternal relation between the Father and the Son is revealed to humanity in the incarnation of the Son's obedience to the Father.[26] In fact, "According to the testimony of Holy Scripture, the center of the life and person of Jesus is his constant communication with the Father."[27] In Jesus, this communication bears the mark of filial obedience. "When the Son is translated into creation, it means 'obedience unto death, even death on a cross' (Phil 2:8)."[28] Thus, Jesus's obedience unto crucifixion reveals the Son's unity of will with the Father. It reveals that the Son *is* eternally and completely "from" and "for." After all, "Jesus died praying. At the Last Supper he had anticipated his death by giving himself, thus transforming his death, from within, into an act of love, into a glorification of God."[29]

Furthermore, "Since the center of the person of Jesus is prayer, it is essential to participate in his prayer if we are to know and understand him."[30] From the perspective of humanity, this means that to know Jesus personally—not merely to know about him—requires truly entering into his own life of prayer.

---

24. Ratzinger, "Communio," 444, 446.

25. Ratzinger, *Behold the Pierced One*, 38.

26. "In the Son's obedience, where both wills become one in a single Yes to the will of the Father, communion takes place between human and divine being" (Ratzinger, *Behold the Pierced One*, 92).

27. Ratzinger, *Behold the Pierced One*, 15.

28. Ratzinger, *God of Jesus Christ*, 67–68.

29. Ratzinger, *Behold the Pierced One*, 22.

30. Ratzinger, *Behold the Pierced One*, 25.

> Therefore, a participation in the mind of Jesus, i.e., in his prayer, which . . . is an act of love, of self-giving and self-expropriation to men, is not some kind of pious supplement to reading the Gospels, adding nothing to knowledge of him or even being an obstacle to the rigorous purity of critical knowing. On the contrary, it is the basic precondition if real understanding, in the sense of modern hermeneutics—i.e., the entering-in to the same time and meaning—is to take place.[31]

From the divine perspective one can observe that in the resurrection Jesus is opened to incorporate humanity into his body and takes human-ness eternally into the "triune exchange of divine love."[32] Thus, he effects the exchange, having become human so that humanity might participate in his divinity. "The will of the Son embraces the one who voluntarily accepts to be in it; the will of the Son embraces the one who himself lives like a son . . . one who is not so adult, so well established in life, that it would be impossible for him to say 'Father,' to know that he owes his existence to God and to give himself back to God."[33]

Finally, this incorporation into Jesus's obedient life of prayer and love can never be isolated, never individualistic. Jesus teaches the disciples to pray to "*Our* Father," not "My Father." Ratzinger elaborates:

> Sharing in Jesus' praying involves communion with all his brethren. Fellowship with the person of Jesus, which proceeds from participation in his prayer, thus constitutes the all-embracing fellowship that Paul calls the "Body of Christ." So the Church—the "Body of Christ"—is the true subject of our knowledge of Jesus. In the Church's memory the past is present because Christ is present and lives in her.[34]

In sum, Ratzinger's "spiritual Christology" asserts the human person can only truly know Jesus by sharing in his obedient relation to the Father, by entering into his life of prayer. This entering into, this participation can never be isolated but is always communal, ecclesial, and thus always concrete. Unlike the apostles, men and women of today can only encounter the living prayer of the Lord in the church's life of love and prayer. Furthermore, this communal incorporation and sacramental participation in the life of Christ, for Ratzinger, is always an action of the Spirit,[35] to which I now turn.

31. Ratzinger, *Behold the Pierced One*, 26.
32. Ratzinger, *God of Jesus Christ*, 76; cf. 84.
33. Ratzinger, *God of Jesus Christ*, 91.
34. Ratzinger, *Behold the Pierced One*, 27.
35. Ratzinger, *God of Jesus Christ*, 110.

3.1.2 The Spirit of Love

As with the Father and the Son, Ratzinger locates the person of the Holy Spirit through the relation to the Father and the Son. Again building upon the trinitarian imagery of the Gospel of John and following Augustine's example, the Spirit is, for Ratzinger, "that which is common" to the first and second persons of the Trinity; the Spirit is "the unity of the Father and the Son, the unity in Person."[36] Just as the names of the Father and Son analogously communicate something of the respective uniqueness of the first and second persons, the name "Holy Spirit"—"being a spirit and being holy"—refers to "what is characteristic about God."[37] Ratzinger further clarifies the Augustinian implications of this: "If he is called by what is divine about God, what is shared by the Father and the Son, then *his nature* is in fact this, *being the communion of the Father and the Son*. The particular characteristic of the Holy Spirit is obviously being what is shared by the Father and the Son."[38] Thus, the Holy Spirit is the communion of the Father and the Son. What grounds the unity of the Father and the Son is not to be found in the shared divine nature but in the person of the Spirit. "The Spirit is Person as unity, unity as Person."[39]

Further, for Ratzinger, whenever pneumatology is separated from Christology the errors of Joachim of Fiore and of Montanism loom large.[40] Therefore, for Ratzinger, "the Christianity of the Spirit is in the Christianity of the lived Word. The Spirit dwells in the Word, not in a departure from the Word. The Word is the location of the Spirit; Jesus is the source of the Spirit. The more we enter into him, the more really do we enter into the Spirit, and the Spirit enters into us."[41] Indeed, the "connection between Christology

---

36. Ratzinger, *God of Jesus Christ*, 108.
37. Ratzinger, *Pilgrim Fellowship of Faith*, 41.
38. Ratzinger, *Pilgrim Fellowship of Faith*, 41; cf. *Images of Hope*, 65.
39. Ratzinger, *Pilgrim Fellowship of Faith*, 42.
40. Cf. Ratzinger, *God of Jesus Christ*, 105–6. In speaking of Möhler's move from his earlier pneumatological ecclesiology to his later Christological ecclesiology, Dennis Doyle explains: "[The later] Möhler found that his pneumatological approach ran the dual danger both of collapsing the transcendence of God into the spirit of the community and of allowing the real freedom of humans to be lost within the transcendence of God. This is because, on the one hand the Holy Spirit could become too closely identified with the community spirit," leading to a prioritization of human subjectivity and ultimately to relativism. "On the other hand, if the spirit of the community is too closely identified with the Holy Spirit, the Church can be divinized and the human elements absorbed or lost.... Möhler's solution to these problems was to shift away from a pneumatological emphasis to a distinctively Christological emphasis in his ecclesiology" (Doyle, *Communion Ecclesiology*, 35–36).
41. Ratzinger, *God of Jesus Christ*, 108. For more on this, see Heim, *Joseph Ratzinger*,

and pneumatology" is made most explicit on the cross: "the crucified Lord is the spring that makes the world fruitful. The source of the Spirit is the crucified Christ" from whose pierced side the Spirit flows as living water.[42]

For Ratzinger, this connection between Christology and pneumatology holds true for the Spirit's mission in the world and role in the church:

> A further characteristic of the Spirit is listening: he does not speak in his own name, he listens and teaches how to listen. In other words, he does not add anything, but rather acts as a guide into the hearing of the Word, which becomes light in the act of listening. . . . This already entails an additional element: the Spirit effects a space of listening and remembering, a "we," which in the Johannine writing defines the Church as the locus of knowledge. Understanding can take place only within this "we" constituted by participation in the origin.[43]

In other words, the Spirit's mission further illuminates that the person of the Spirit is to be found in the relation to the Son and to the Father who sends the Son to humanity. As the personal unity of the Father and the Son, the Spirit also brings about the personal unity in the church—both on the horizontal level with other Christians and on the vertical level with God.[44] After all, as the communion of the Father and the Son, the Spirit is love.[45] It is love that draws persons into abiding communion. "The gift of God is the Holy Spirit. The gift of God is love—*God shares himself as love in the Holy Spirit.*"[46]

In short, Ratzinger defines the Spirit as the union of the Father and the Son. This relation both constitutes the person of the Spirit and simultaneously reveals and is revealed by the Spirit's work in effecting the horizontal and vertical *communio* of the church. This communion implies both the

---

238, where he explains, "In order to demonstrate a connection between Christological and pneumatological ecclesiology, Ratzinger takes his bearings, on the one hand, from Augustine, who in opposition to the Donatists had emphasized the indivisible unity of the Spirit and the Body of Christ: 'Do you want to have the spirit of Christ? Then be in the Body of Christ! You cannot have the Spirit as something separated and free-floating, so to speak; rather, it is the Spirit of Christ's Body,' and on the other hand, from the holistic biblical and Semitic understanding of 'body.'" Heim is quoting Ratzinger, "Kirche als Tempel," 154. Heim elucidates the biblical and Semitic notion of "body" on pages 238–43.

42. Ratzinger, *Pilgrim Fellowship of Faith*, 47.
43. Ratzinger, *Nature and Mission of Theology*, 55.
44. See Ratzinger and Messori, *Ratzinger Report*, 151.
45. See 1 John 4:6–17; Augustine, *De Trinitate* XV.17, 31; Ratzinger, *Pilgrim Fellowship of Faith*, 44.
46. Ratzinger, *Pilgrim Fellowship of Faith*, 44.

divine origin of the church's being and mission and at the same time points to the existential, or concrete, implications of Ratzinger's pneumatology on his ecclesiology and missiology.

I now turn to a closer consideration of Ratzinger's understanding of divine personhood as an analog to human personhood and its import for his notion of communion, which proves to be essential for a correct understanding of his spiritual Christology and thus his ecclesiology.

3.2 Person as Relation

3.2.1 Divine Personhood

In the above overview of Ratzinger's trinitarian theology, we saw that Ratzinger identifies each of the divine persons by its relation to the other two persons. To a large degree, Ratzinger develops his notion of person via a dialogue with Augustine's trinitarian theology. Furthermore Ratzinger's method here involves an opposition to the Thomistic axiom of analogical predication, which states that one should always start with what is familiar and human, cataphatically purifying the concept in order to acceptably predicate it of God.[47] Instead, Ratzinger starts with trinitarian theology and with the divine persons as revealed in scripture in order to illuminate his understanding of human personhood.[48] On the one hand this is a response to what he perceives as the inadequacies of Boethius's definition of person where "person stands entirely on the level of substance" and is therefore unable to "clarify anything about the Trinity or about Christology."[49] On the other hand, it is a function of his assessment of Thomas and scholastic theology as having failed to incorporate the christological and theological insights of the tradition into their anthropological understanding of personhood.[50]

For Ratzinger, the trinitarian dogma of "'*una essentia tres personae*' is a function of the concept of person and is to be understood as an intrinsic implication of the concept of person."[51] Therefore, the illumination gained

47. Aquinas, *Summa Theologiae* I.1, 12, 13.
48. Ratzinger, *Introduction to Christianity*, 190.
49. Ratzinger, "Concerning the Notion of Person," 448.
50. "Scholastic theology developed categories of existence out of this contribution given by the Christian faith to the human mind. Its defect was that it limited these categories to Christology and to the doctrine of the Trinity and did not make them fruitful in the whole extent of spiritual reality" (Ratzinger, "Concerning the Notion of Person," 449).
51. Ratzinger, *Introduction to Christianity*, 179.

from a consideration of divine personhood remains relevant to the elucidation of human personhood, to any attempt at an authentic anthropology and thus to an adequate ecclesiology as well. Thus, "if the absolute is person, it is not an absolute singular. To this extent the overstepping of the singular is implicit in the concept of person."[52]

Ratzinger explains that the notion of person organically grew out of the historical questions which arose in response to the encounter with God in Christ.[53] In Jesus's relationship to the Father, the dialogical character of God is revealed.[54] Since "in God there is nothing accidental but only substance and relation,"[55] and since the substance is one, the triplicity of persons must be found elsewhere. "Relation is here recognized as a third fundamental category between substance and accident. . . . Faith gave birth to this idea of pure act, of pure relativity, which does not lie at the level of substance and does not touch or divide substance."[56] For Ratzinger, this "phenomenon of complete relativity" is apparent in Johannine theology and accurately and authentically communicates "what person must mean in terms of Scripture."[57] Additionally, since this phenomenon is fully realized in God, it signals the origin and fundamental thrust "of all personal being."[58] It is relevant not only to divine persons but also to human persons.

The second step to gaining a correct understanding of person requires a consideration of the christological notion of personhood. Ratzinger explains that the majority of the christological heresies and the debates that surrounded them flowed out of a fundamental misunderstanding of the dogma that in Christ there are two natures, divine and human—and one person, the divine *Logos*. The misunderstanding interprets the one divine person as a "subtraction from the wholeness of Jesus' humanity"[59] and has led many to perceive that while "Person is the authentic and true apex of

---

52. Ratzinger, *Introduction to Christianity*, 180. Ratzinger maintains the necessary caveat when speaking analogously of human and divine personhood: "Of course, we shall have to say at the same time that the acknowledgment that God is a person in the guise of a triple personality explodes the naive, anthropomorphic concept of person. It declares in a sort of cipher that the personality of God infinitely exceeds the human kind of personality; so that the concept of person, illuminating as it is, once again reveals itself as an inadequate metaphor."

53. Ratzinger, "Concerning the Notion of Person," 439.

54. Ratzinger, "Concerning the Notion of Person," 443

55. Ratzinger, "Concerning the Notion of Person," 444, quoting Augustine, *De Trinitate* V.4.

56. Ratzinger, "Concerning the Notion of Person," 444–45.

57. Ratzinger, "Concerning the Notion of Person," 445.

58. Ratzinger, "Concerning the Notion of Person," 445.

59. Ratzinger, "Concerning the Notion of Person," 448.

human existence. It is missing in Jesus. Therefore the entirety of human reality is not present in him."[60] However, as Ratzinger indicates, this cannot be correct; the history of the christological dogmas is the history of the church defending the fullness of Jesus's humanity. The root of the error lies in a substantialist conception of personhood.[61] Boethius's definition of "person" as "*naturae rationalis individua substantia,* as the individual substance of a rational nature" remains inadequate and stuck in fundamentally Greek philosophical categories.[62] Following the wisdom of the great creeds and the lessons of Möhler,[63] Ratzinger seeks to avoid Boethius's mistakes and those of Nestorianism in his Christology and ecclesiology. He perceives in the various quests for the historical Jesus "a one-sided separation of Christology (Nestorianism) in which, when one reflects on the humanity of Christ, his divinity largely disappears."[64] He perceives the excess focus on the humanity of Christ to ultimately divorce the man Jesus from the eternal Son which in turn renders communion between God and humanity illusory. This ultimately leaves humanity incapable of perceiving the divine *communio personarum* as the subject of theology and as relevant to the concrete historical lives of men and women.

Ratzinger turns to Richard of St. Victor as the expositor of an authentically Christian concept of personhood. Richard defines person as "*spiritualis naturae incommunicabilis existentia,* as the incommunicably proper essence of spiritual nature," a definition, which Ratzinger interprets to communicate that "person does not lie on the level of essence but of existence."[65] It is the nature of spirit to find itself in transcending itself. The hypostatic union reveals that "in [Jesus] being with the other is realized radically. Relativity toward the other is always the pre-given foundation to all consciousness as that which carries his existence."[66] In other words, in the divine person of Jesus, the *logos,* that which we associate with human personhood is not left out, cancelled out, or negated. Rather, "it comes to its highest possibility, which consists in transcending itself into the absolute and in the integration

60. Ratzinger, "Concerning the Notion of Person," 448.
61. Ratzinger, "Concerning the Notion of Person," 448.
62. Ratzinger, "Concerning the Notion of Person," 448.
63. See Doyle's exposition of Möhler's two ecclesiological phases in *Communion Ecclesiology,* 23–37. Doyle explains that Möhler "tried to avoid the extremes of ecclesiological Nestorianism and ecclesiological monophysitism." Taking the Incarnation as his guide, Möhler felt the "proper way to understand the Church is as both a human and divine reality."
64. Ratzinger, *New Song for the Lord,* 10; cf. *Introduction to Christianity,* 210.
65. Ratzinger, "Concerning the Notion of Person," 449.
66. Ratzinger, "Concerning the Notion of Person," 452.

of its own relativity into the absoluteness of divine love."⁶⁷ Thus to use the word "person" to describe the Father, the Son, and the Holy Spirit is to mean that they are their respective acts of relation:

> Person is the pure relation of being related, nothing else. Relationship is not something extra added to the person, as it is with us; it only exists at all in relatedness. . . . This means that the first Person does not beget the Son as if the act of begetting were subsequent to the finished Person; it is the act of begetting, of giving oneself, of streaming forth. It is identical with the act of self-giving. Only as this act is it person, and therefore it is not the giver but the act of giving.⁶⁸

3.2.2 Divine Persons and Human Persons

Just as Christ reveals to humanity the triune personality of God, so he also reveals the full depth, richness, and dignity of human personhood. After all, "developed Christological dogma acknowledges that the radical Christship of Jesus presupposes the Sonship and that the Sonship includes the Godship. . . . But it also acknowledges no less resolutely that in the radicalism of his service Jesus is the most human of men, the true man, and it thus subscribes to the coincidence of theology and anthropology a correspondence in which ever since then the truly exciting part of Christian faith has resided."⁶⁹ Ultimately, this requires a participationist metaphysics, which recognizes God as the ground of all being and recognizes human nature as a unique form of participating in being. Human being as personal being is ordered towards a fuller participation in God. Thus, the union of human nature and divine nature in Christ does not lead to the dissolution of human nature but to an "evolutionary leap" in human nature towards that union with God, which is its fulfillment and goal.

So the divine personhood of Jesus reveals the existential goal of all human personhood. A proper understanding of his personhood sheds light which is necessary for developing an adequate anthropology and ecclesiology.

> [Jesus's] being is pure *actualitas* of "from" and "for." But precisely because this "Being" is no longer separable from its *actualitas*, it

---

67. Ratzinger, "Concerning the Notion of Person," 452. This dynamic transcending remains "on the way" in humanity.
68. Ratzinger, *Introduction to Christianity*, 183–84.
69. Ratzinger, *Introduction to Christianity*, 211–12.

coincides with God and is at the same time the exemplary man, the man of the future, through whom it becomes evident how very much man is still the coming creature, a being still, so to speak, waiting to be realized.[70]

Put another way, just as the *Logos* receives all that he is from the Father, just as he *is* "from the Father" and simultaneously *is* "for" the world, for humanity, so human personhood is revealed to reside in the same relativity of the "from" and "for."

Since men and women are created in the image and likeness of God, the human person is created in its "essential constitution" for relation, communion, love.[71] Indeed "such a thing as the mere individual, the man-monad of the Renaissance, the pure '*Cogito ergo sum*' being does not exist."[72] In fact, the very corporeality of humanity, that which signifies the temporality and contingency of human personhood in contrast to divine personhood, nevertheless reveals the relatedness, which necessarily constitutes human personhood. After all, "existence in a corporal form necessarily also embraces history and community";[73] each human person receives her body, being, self, from her parents and indeed from all her ancestors. Therefore, the whole person "is deeply marked by his belonging to the whole of mankind—the one 'Adam.'"[74]

Thus, human being is irrevocably marked by being-from and is ordered toward being-for or being-with: "from the Trinity, the Spirit tells us what God's idea for us was: unity according to the image of God. He also tells us, however, that we men among ourselves can become one only when we find ourselves in a higher unity, as it were, in a third party. Only when we are one with God can we be united among ourselves."[75] Just as the hypostatic union does not abrogate the fullness and the freedom of Jesus in his humanity, so the communion of human persons with each other and with God does not entail the dissolution of the persons into a monadic uniformity. Rather, it is a unity analogous to that perichoretic unity of the divine persons. "God did not create the person so that he might be dissolved but so that he might open himself in his entire height and in his innermost depth—there, where

---

70. Ratzinger, *Introduction to Christianity*, 228.
71. Ratzinger, *Church, Ecumenism, and Politics*, 31.
72. Ratzinger, *Introduction to Christianity*, 247.
73. Ratzinger, *Introduction to Christianity*, 245.
74. Ratzinger, *Introduction to Christianity*, 245–46; cf. *Introduction to Christianity*, 190.
75. Ratzinger, *Images of Hope*, 66.

the Holy Spirit embraces him and is the unity of the divided persons."[76] Therefore, he continues, "the unification of men ... does not occur through the extinguishing of the person but rather through his completion, which means his infinite openness."[77] Personal being is not "closed in" upon itself, but always "opened out" to the other.[78]

Although the historical corporeality of human personhood does not allow the fullness of the "mutual indwelling," the perichoretic unity of the divine persons, it nevertheless is ordered toward participation in that perichoresis precisely because human beings are ensouled bodies, or embodied souls, if you like.

> For the unity of divinity and humanity in Christ which brings "salvation" to man is not juxtaposition but a mutual indwelling. Only in this way can there be that genuine "becoming like God," without which there is no liberation and no freedom. . . . In conjoining himself to man . . . [God] brings him for the first time to his real fullness.[79]

This fulfillment of humanity in the hypostatic union demands admitting that "when the human will is taken up into the will of God freedom is not destroyed; indeed, only then does genuine freedom come into its own."[80]

This insight allows Ratzinger to make sense of Jesus's high priestly prayer in John. Apart from communion with Christ, we can do nothing (John 15:5). We have no freedom and no hope for liberation from sin and death. Parallel to Jesus's statement of his unity with Father ("I and the Father are one" [John 17:11]) is his prayer "that they may be one, even as we are one" (John 17:22). For Ratzinger, "the significant difference" of human communion from divine perichoresis "comes to light in the fact that the unity of Christians is expressed, not in the indicative, but in the form of a prayer."[81] Human communion, in both its horizontal and vertical modes, remains communion on the way, remains marked by sin and temporality, but it remains nevertheless, really on the way.

Ratzinger's theology maintains trustworthy hope in the eschatological fulfillment of the human desire for union with God, but this hope, which theologically relies on his "spiritual Christology," is not a hope in some immediate and incorporeal communion with God. Such a communion

76. Ratzinger, *Images of Hope*, 68.
77. Ratzinger, *Images of Hope*, 70.
78. Ratzinger, "Concerning the Notion of Person," 453.
79. Ratzinger, *Behold the Pierced One*, 38.
80. Ratzinger, *Behold the Pierced One*, 38.
81. Ratzinger, *Introduction to Christianity*, 186.

would not be consistent with the bodiliness and historicity of the human person. Instead, the human person, "comes to deal with God in coming to deal with his fellowmen," or put another way, "God wishes to approach man only through man; he seeks out man in no other way but in his fellow humanity."[82] Thus, the anthropological and ecclesiological implications of Ratzinger's spiritual Christology consistently highlight the incarnational, fully human, one might even say sacramental character of the church.

In sum Ratzinger understands trinitarian communion and anthropological communion christologically, which reveals that personal being is relational being. Since the Holy Spirit is the principle of the unity of the Father and Son, and since the christological dogmas demonstrate that Jesus's humanity, as hypostatically one with the person of the *Logos*, simultaneously shares perfect communion with the Father, Ratzinger can maintain that personal being is itself being-from and being-for. The divine personhood of Christ does not diminish, negate, or subtract from his humanity but rather elevates it to the higher pitch of transcendent and perichoretic trinitarian communion. Ratzinger's spiritual Christology sheds light on the participation of humanity in the divine *communio personarum* and simultaneously recognizes the necessary corporeality and historicity of the human person. This lays the groundwork for the next chapter on Ratzinger's ecclesiology of communion which will explore the church's christological and sacramental character by examining (1) the church as locus of vertical and horizontal communion; (2) the church as sacrament of the divine *communio personarum*; and (3) the relation between Eucharist and church in Ratzinger's ecclesiology.

---

82. Ratzinger, *Introduction to Christianity*, 92–93.

4

Communio Ecclesiology

THE PREVIOUS CHAPTER EXAMINED the intrinsic link between Ratzinger's trinitarian theology and his anthropology. I argued that Christ simultaneously reveals both the meaning of person as relation in the Trinity and also the analogous thrust of the human person for communion. Human being is being ordered toward life in communion; it is made for the church. Indeed, *Lumen Gentium* makes this point in recalling the words of St. Cyprian: "The universal Church is seen to be a people brought into unity from the unity of the Father, the Son, and the Holy Spirit."[1] Other conciliar documents confirm and strengthen the theme of *Ecclesia in Trinitate*. *Gaudium et Spes* speaks of the church "proceeding from the love of the eternal Father . . . founded by Christ in time and gathered into one by the Holy Spirit."[2] The church lives from the trinitarian communion not as some merely instrumental means of bringing humanity into relationship with God, but rather in revealing the triunity of God, Jesus reveals that the entire world comes from and is made for communion. Henri de Lubac explains it well:

> God did not make us "to remain with the limits of nature" or for the fulfilling of a solitary destiny; on the contrary, he made us to be brought together into the heart of the life of the Trinity. Christ offered himself in sacrifice so that we might be one in that unity of the divine Persons. . . . There is a place where this gathering together of all things in the Trinity begins in this world; "a family of God," a mysterious extension of the Trinity in time, which not only prepares us for this life of union and gives us a sure guarantee of it, but also makes us participate in it already. The Church is the only completely "open" society, the only one that measures up to our deepest longings and in which

---

1. LG 4, quoting St. Cyprian, *De Orat Dom.* 23.
2. GS 40.

we can finally find our whole shape. "The people united by the unity of the Father and the Son and the Holy Spirit": that is the Church. She is "full of the Trinity."[3]

Therefore, this chapter will develop Ratzinger's *communio* ecclesiology by first exploring how the trinitarian and christological origins of the church are made concrete in the Eucharist, and only then analyzing how the Eucharist makes the church and what that means for the being and structure of the church. These considerations enable us to explore the eucharistic link between communion and mission in Ratzinger's ecclesiology, or better, to understand the eucharistic origins of the church's status as creative minority.

4.1 Origins of the Church

4.1.1 What the Church Is Not

For Ratzinger, like Augustine, humanity is made for communion with God, and sin is the turning in upon oneself, which negates communion. Sin is turning away from the love of God and from human community towards individualism. It is a rejection of the gift of divinization based on God's wisdom in favor of a grasping for divinization on one's own terms, a re-enactment of the original sin. Colin Starnes sums up Augustine's analysis of his theft of the pear with illuminating clarity: "Everyone knows there is a divine law which forbids theft, so if I can steal and get away with it, this will show that I am not subject to God or to any divine law. Moreover, if I am not subject to any law which defines what is good, then the good will be for me simply what I say it is. Hence, I will be free and omnipotent. I can do what I want and what I want is the good."[4] On some level, each sin is an attempt to make an idol of one's self.

God wishes to save human persons from the hell of self-divinization by bringing about a revolution of love, of self-donation, but a revolution of love can only be accomplished in freedom; it must respect the will of each person. Thus, God elects Abraham and ultimately Israel as the locus of his revolution, of his civilization of love. He must be patient with this revolution because "all must have the opportunity to come and see . . . if they want they can allow themselves to be drawn into the history of salvation that God is creating. . . . What drives them to the new thing cannot be force or moral pressure, but the fascination of a world that is changed."[5] Such change can

---

3. Lubac, *Splendor of the Church*, 237.
4. Starnes, *Augustine's Conversion*, 42.
5. Lohfink, *Does God Need the Church?*, 27.

only be wrought by an encounter with God. In Ratzinger's view, Jesus fulfills the Old Testament origins of this civilization of love by universalizing it: "Jesus' task was only to renew this People by deepening its relationship to God and by opening it up for all mankind."[6] By incarnating the truth about God and humanity, Jesus, in his person and in his gathering of the people of God, prepares a space for the horizontal and vertical communion for which humanity was created. After all, the Father does not send Jesus merely to be a moral exemplar but to offer to humanity again the possibility of *theosis*.

The Incarnation is ordered to extending to humanity a share in divinity. The church is the space in which this sharing is realized. For this reason, the church cannot merely be a club or voluntary organization, a view which Ratzinger perceives to have been creeping into theological thinking in the years following the Second Vatican Council. According to Ratzinger's reading,[7] the conciliar use of the term "People of God"[8] was co-opted and became a simply sociological term. As Heim explains, "The political and philosophical movements of the Enlightenment, as well as Marxism, pragmatism, subjectivism, skepticism, proportionalism, and, last but not least, relativism, were in [Ratzinger's] judgment influential during the post-conciliar period in contributing to the transformation of the concept of the People of God into something political and sociological."[9] When this happens, the church deteriorates into the "party of Christ."[10] In view of this perceived deterioration, Ratzinger opined, "the authentically Catholic meaning of the reality 'Church' is tacitly disappearing, without being expressly rejected."[11]

In other words, the crisis in the church is actually a crisis of faith, of Christology, of the loss of God. "The idea of God is the very thing that had been left aside [in the debates surrounding the term "People of God"] . . . and it had thereby been deprived of its entire meaning. For a church that is there only for her own sake is superfluous."[12] The church is "not a club, not a party, not even a sort of religious state within the secular state, but a body—Christ's Body. And this is why the church is not of our making but is construed by the Lord himself when he cleanses us by Word and sacrament

---

6. Ratzinger, *Behold the Pierced One*, 30.
7. See Ratzinger, *Church, Ecumenism, and Politics*, 1–28.
8. LG ch. II.
9. Heim, *Joseph Ratzinger*, 388; cf. Ratzinger, *Introduction to Christianity*, 11–26.
10. Ratzinger, *Called to Communion*, 158.
11. Ratzinger and Messori, *Ratzinger Report*, 45.
12. Ratzinger, *Pilgrim Fellowship of Faith*, 129.

and thus makes us his members."[13] The church can only really be found in its divine origin and *telos*. This properly christological and theological origin and end must be rediscovered. For this reason, he says, Vatican II intended to correlate "talk about the Church with talk about God."[14] It achieved this most clearly through its description of the church as the body of Christ, which "moved the Church out of all those mere legalities and externals and into the realm of mystery with Christ as the center."[15] Any adequate ecclesiology and truly evangelical Christian community must, therefore, worship and live in light of being from Christ and for the world.

4.1.2 Jesus and the Church

For Ratzinger, the reign of God, which must characterize God's salvific revolution, comes near in Jesus.[16] To this end, He simultaneously calls people to himself and to conversion. In doing so, Ratzinger notes, Jesus does not simply gather an amorphous mob around him; he surrounds himself with seventy-two and the twelve, with Peter, James, and John at their center. Thus, "Jesus presents himself as the patriarch of a new Israel and institutes these twelve men as its origin and foundation."[17]

Jesus institutes the Our Father as the prayer of this new community, concretely inviting the disciples to share in Jesus's place as Son of the Father. This invitation to communion with God becomes a participation in Jesus's communion with the Father in the institution of the Eucharist.

> Just as the old Israel once reverenced the temple as its center and the guarantee of its unity, and by its common celebration of the Passover enacted this unity in its own life, in like manner this new meal is now the bond uniting a new people of God. There is no longer any need for a center localized in an outward temple. . . . The Body of the Lord, which is the center of the Lord's Supper, is the one new temple that joins Christians together into a much more real unity than a temple made of stone could ever do.[18]

---

13. Ratzinger, *Called to Communion*, 161–62.
14. Ratzinger, *Pilgrim Fellowship of Faith*, 132.
15. Ratzinger, *Volk und Haus Gottes*, xi, in Heim, *Joseph Ratzinger*, 232.
16. Ratzinger, *Called to Communion*, 23.
17. Ratzinger, *Called to Communion*, 25.
18. Ratzinger, *Das neue Volk Gottes*, 79, in Ratzinger, *Called to Communion*, 27.

Thus, the Eucharist is the new covenant and therefore the making of this new universalized *communio*. "The disciples become a 'people' through communion with the Body and Blood of Jesus, which is simultaneously communion with God."[19] However, not all of Israel shares in this communion. After all, participation in this *communio* requires first believing that Jesus is who says he is and that the God of Jesus Christ is as Jesus reveals him to be, and second, entering into the historical community which Jesus gathered together:

> Belief in the Trinity is *communio*; to believe in the Trinity means to become *communio*. Historically, this means that the "I" of the credo-formulas is a collective "I," the "I" of the believing Church, to which the individual "I" belongs as long as it believes. In other words, the "I" of the credo embraces the transition from the individual "I" to the ecclesial "I."[20]

For those living after the death of the apostles, to state one's belief in the God of Jesus Christ is also to enter into communion with the believing subject, with the community in which trinitarian belief has been passed on concretely. Put another way, one can enter into the love of the triune God only through Christ, but one can encounter Christ only in the concrete place and time of one's own existence—that is to say, via the church. After all, "The Church lives from the trinitarian mystery which has opened itself to her in Christ. That there is a Church at all derives from the fact that God has opened himself."[21] For Ratzinger, this is no abstract idea. Reflecting on the origins of his own faith, he explains:

> I encountered [Jesus] initially not in literature or philosophy, but in the faith of the Church. This means that from the beginning I knew him, not as a great figure of the past . . . but as someone who is alive and at work today, someone whom people can encounter today. It means, above all, that I have come to know him within the history of the faith that has its origin in him and according to the vision of faith as given its most enduring formulation at the Council of Chalcedon."[22]

---

19. Ratzinger, *Called to Communion*, 28–29.

20. Ratzinger, *Principles*, 23.

21. Ratzinger, *Das neue Volk Gottes*, 283; cf. *Principles*, 23, 26, in Nichols, *Thought of Pope Benedict XVI*, 106.

22. Ratzinger, *Dogma and Preaching*, 122; cf. *Introduction to Christianity*, 11–29, esp. 20–29.

The church is thus the visible and tangible sign of the continued living presence of Christ in the world. "The Church is that new and greater subject in whom past and present, subject and object come together. The Church is our contemporary with Christ: there is no other. The Church is not an abstract principle but a living subject possessing a concrete content."[23] Ratzinger's ecclesiology consistently rejects a functional perspective of the church and proceeds from her sacramentality.

For Ratzinger, understanding the sign quality of the church requires entering into the mystery: "I understand it as a sign only if I enter into its referential context, if I enter upon the way that it is. But if a sign, a visible reality, points to what is invisible, what is divine, it is eminently clear that I can discover its referential context only be identifying myself with it, by allowing myself to be incorporated into the relationship that makes the sign a sign."[24] Following Augustine, Ratzinger believes the sacramental character of the church requires an adequately pneumatological and christological ecclesiology.

As the previous chapter made evident, Ratzinger observes that in Augustine the name "Holy Spirit" expresses that the particularity of the Spirit lies in his being "unity," "what the Father and Son have in common."[25] As the divine gift of unity, the Spirit manifests herself to us as the ecclesial gift of unity. This unity has both "inner" and "outer," holy and visible elements, where the inner and holy refer to what Augustine called the *ecclesia sancta*, while the outer and visible references the *ecclesia catholica*. The *ecclesiae* are not identical because the visible church remains an admixture of wheat and chaff until the end of days.[26] Following Augustine the early Ratzinger sees the Eucharist, the body of Christ, as the key to this double-unity,[27] sacramentally holding together the visible and invisible elements of the church.

This allusion to the Eucharist in conjunction with the ecclesial connection of Christology and pneumatology is no mere passing reference for Augustine or Ratzinger. As Nichols explains,

> We are united with Christ by faith whereby his Spirit dwells in us; yet the Spirit of Christ is not other than the grace of Christ, the *caritas* which is spread abroad in our hearts by the Holy Spirit; in referring to such *caritas* we overstep boundaries of the individual to enter the realm of the community, the Church

---

23. Ratzinger, *Church, Ecumenism, and Politics*, 4; cf. *Nature and Mission*, 60–61.
24. Ratzinger, *Principles*, 47–48.
25. Massa, "Communion Theme," 89.
26. Nichols, *Thought of Pope Benedict XVI*, 43.
27. Nichols, *Thought of Pope Benedict XVI*, 37–38.

which is Christ's body. And while that ecclesial *corpus Christi* is not directly accessible to us, it may be found in its "holy sign," its sacrament, the *Eucharist*.[28]

4.2 The Church as the Body of Christ

Ratzinger turns from Augustine to St. Paul in explicating the biblical understanding of the church as the body of Christ. Paul described this community in which God is encountered through Christ as the σῶμα Χριστοῦ—body of Christ. Ratzinger's Augustinian reflections on the import of these words provide him the context for elaborating on the theological nature of the church. He is careful to clarify that the original Semitic meaning of "body" in Paul's writing contains none of the dualism with which it is sometimes associated today. Thus, scripture contains

> no such opposition between body and spirit, because the talk about σῶμα Χριστοῦ, about the Body of Christ, is in no sense taken to mean a direct continuation of the earthly corporeality of Jesus as a permanent corporeality; rather, the expression σῶμα τοῦ Χριστοῦ, the Body of Christ, as applied to the Church in the New Testament, should be understood (a) with reference to the passages about the Last Supper and (b) in light of the Resurrection. And both of these, in turn, must be interpreted against the background of the Semitic biblical terminology and not according to the presuppositions of our concept of body.[29]

Therefore, when Jesus says, "This is my body," he can be understood to mean the totality of himself. "It means Jesus himself, who is present with what is his own and with the uniqueness of his 'I' and thus is fully, completely, and really present and devotes himself to man's 'I' as the one who is complete, one, and indivisible."[30] Thus to speak of the church as the body of Christ is to speak of Christ as the subject of the church.[31] Furthermore, the image of the church as the body of Christ is no mere metaphor or allegory; it does not refer to a merely moral union of Christ and Christians, because the church "is more than an organization, it is the organism of the Holy Spirit,"[32] which

---

28. Nichols, *Thought of Pope Benedict XVI*, 47, referencing Ratzinger, *Volk und haus Gottes*, 209–210.
29. Ratzinger, "Kirche als Tempel," 150, in Heim, *Joseph Ratzinger*, 239.
30. Ratzinger, "Kirche als Tempel," 151, in Heim, *Joseph Ratzinger*, 240.
31. Cf. Ratzinger, *Nature and Mission of Theology*, 54.
32. Ratzinger, *Church, Ecumenism, and Politics*, 3.

finds its source and life in Christ.[33] Ratzinger associates this pneumatological aspect with the description of the church as Mystical Body of Christ, a term which has a two-fold implication: the church grows from within, from its heart which is Christ, and Christ has formed the church as a community, a body.[34] Therefore, the external structures of the church do not define the church nor ought they to form the church, for the church is not primarily a hierarchy nor a vaguely connected group of individuals, but the body of Christ.

4.2.1 Communion in the Incarnate Son

The phrase "body of Christ" communicates that indissoluble bond between Christology and ecclesiology:

> In the Incarnation of the eternal Word there comes about that communion between God and the being of man, his creature, which had hitherto seemed impossible to reconcile with the transcendence of the one God. . . . Yet in Jesus occurs the new event, the one God entering into concrete communion with men by incarnating himself in human nature. Divine and human intermingle—"without mixing and undivided"—in the Person of Jesus Christ. . . . The Incarnation is in fact the new synthesis that has been brought about by God himself.[35]

The incarnate Christ *is* the communion between God and man, the mediator who restores to humanity the possibility of relationship with the transcendent. Here again Ratzinger relies upon the metaphysical implications of his spiritual Christology. With reference to the explanation given by the Third Council of Constantinople regarding the relationship between the human and divine wills of Christ, Ratzinger explains:

> The ontological *union* of two wills that remain independent within the unity of the person means, on the level of daily life, *communion* (κοινωνία) of the two wills. With this interpretation of the union as communion, the Council was devising an ontology of freedom. The two "wills" are united in that way in which one will and another can unite: in a common assent to a shared value. To put it another way: Both of these wills are united in the assent of the human will of Christ to the divine

---

33. Ratzinger, *Church, Ecumenism, and Politics*, 5.
34. Ratzinger, *Church, Ecumenism, and Politics*, 6.
35. Ratzinger, *Pilgrim Fellowship of Faith*, 76.

will of the Logos. Thus on the practical level—"existentially"—the two wills become one single will, and yet ontologically they remain two independent entities.... It is a unity in the mode of communion—the unity that love creates and love is. In this fashion, the Logos takes the being of the man Jesus into his own being and talks about it with his own "I": "I have come down from heaven, not to do my own will, but the will of him who sent me" (John 6:38). It is in the obedience of the Son, in the uniting of both these wills in the one assent to the will of the Father, that the communion between human and divine being is consummated.[36]

In the Incarnation of the Son, Jesus's human will and divine will are brought into communion in their common assent to a higher will, that of the Father. Another way of speaking of assent to a higher will is to speak of obedience in love for that will. The mode of union that spans the gap between humanity and divinity is personal love. Being a Christian, sharing in the communion with the Father offered by Christ means submitting one's own will in loving assent to the will of the Father. Through *imitatio Christi* men and women can participate in the communion between the God-man Jesus and the Father. Ratzinger explains that communion is the "fusion of existences," which can only occur when my "I" is opened to others in the same way that Jesus's "I" is opened to the Father and the Spirit in eternity and to man in his *kenosis*. "In this way Communion makes the Church by breaching an opening in the walls of subjectivity and gathering us into a deep communion of existence."[37] Indeed, church is communion, "not only between human beings but, as a result of the death and Resurrection of Jesus, communion with Christ, the incarnate Son, and hence communion with the eternal triune Love of God."[38]

The Second Vatican Council described the mystery of this communion with the word *sacramentum*.[39] Ratzinger explains the concept of church as sacrament according to the Tridentine definition of a sacrament as "a visible sign of invisible grace instituted for our justification."[40] Thus in speaking of the church as a sacrament, the council teaches that the church is the visible, earthly sign that points to and efficaciously mediates the saving grace of God to her members. Put another way, "sacrament" refers to the

---

36. Ratzinger, *Pilgrim Fellowship of Faith*, 81–82.
37. Ratzinger, *Called to Communion*, 37; cf. *Pilgrim Fellowship of Faith*, 130.
38. Ratzinger, *Behold the Pierced One*, 86.
39. LG 8, 48; GS 45.
40. Ratzinger, *Principles*, 47, quoting *Catechism of the Council of Trent* II.1.v.118.

"transposition from invisible to visible, from inward communion to outward community."[41]

This sacramental understanding "requires liturgical action, and liturgical action requires a community in which to exist and which embodies the fullness of power for such liturgical action."[42] Therefore, according to the definition of church as sacrament, "she is most truly Church when she celebrates the Eucharist and makes present the redemptive love of Jesus Christ."[43] This is necessary because "man cannot identify himself with God, but God has identified himself with man—that is the content of the communion that is offered in the Eucharist. A *communio* that offers less offers too little."[44] For Ratzinger, a *communio* that fails to provide hope which can span death is no *communio* at all, leaving us utterly alone in death. Hope in the face of death comes only with Christ's victory over death and communion with him in that victory. In this way, "communion between God and man that is realized in the person of Jesus Christ for its own part becomes communicable to others in the Paschal Mystery, that is, in the death and Resurrection of the Lord. The Eucharist effects our participation in the Paschal Mystery and thus constitutes the Church, the body of Christ."[45] The invisible assimilation of the Christian into Christ, her communion with him, takes visible form in the Eucharist.

4.2.2 The Eucharist Makes the Church

Ratzinger argues that for Paul and the fathers, "Church as body of Christ was indissolubly linked with the idea of the eucharist"[46] precisely because Jesus founds the church in instituting the Eucharist at the Last Supper: "Jesus gives to those who are his own this liturgy of his death and resurrection and thus gives them the feast of life. In the last supper he recapitulates the covenant of Sinai, or rather what had there been an approximation in symbol now becomes reality: the community of blood and life between God and man."[47] Thus, the church is formed "by communion through assimila-

---

41. Massa, "Communion Theme," 95.
42. Ratzinger, *Principles*, 48.
43. Ratzinger, *Principles*, 50.
44. Ratzinger, *Principles*, 53.
45. Ratzinger, *Pilgrim Fellowship of Faith*, 82–83.
46. Ratzinger, *Church, Ecumenism, and Politics*, 7.
47. Ratzinger, *Church, Ecumenism, and Politics*, 8; cf. *Called to Communion*, 75.

tion into the bread that is Christ's body."[48] Ratzinger further explains it as follows:

> The formula "the Church is the Body of Christ" thus states that the eucharist in which the Lord gives us his body and makes us one body, forever remains the place where the Church is generated, where the Lord himself never ceases to found her anew; in the eucharist the Church is most compactly herself—in all places, yet one only, just as he is one only.[49]

For this reason, Gerd Lohaus crystallizes Ratzinger's ecclesiology as follows: the "Church, as the Body of Christ, in the eucharist, is the sacrament of God's *communio*."[50]

This notion of the Eucharist as generator of the church clarifies the image of communion into which the church is formed. The Eucharist is not merely a sacrament performed by the church but is the sacrament of the risen body of Christ, which joins Christians together into one body. The eucharistic nature of ecclesial communion further illuminates the nature of said communion:

> The Church is *communio*; she is God's communing with men in Christ and hence the communing of men with one another—and, in consequence, sacrament, sign, instrument of salvation. The Church is the celebration of the Eucharist; the Eucharist is the Church; they do not simply stand side by side; they are one and the same. The Eucharist is the *sacramentum Christi* and, because the Church is *Eucharistia*, she is therefore also *sacramentum*—the sacrament to which all the other sacraments are ordered.[51]

For Ratzinger, the Eucharist is the heart of the church because through the sacramental church-forming power of the Eucharist the people of God are brought into communion with God and with each other, thus exhibiting the vertical and horizontal dimensions of ecclesial communion. "The Church is the dynamic process of horizontal and vertical unification."[52] Since man is made for more than a superficial collective unity, the sinfulness of human individuals and society makes any lasting unity extremely difficult to sustain. Indeed, "of herself, the Church is not a people but an exteriorly

---

48. Massa, "Communion Theme," 130n145.
49. Ratzinger, *Called to Communion*, 37.
50. Lohaus, "Das Verhaltnis von Ortskirche," 236, in Heim, *Joseph Ratzinger*, 271.
51. Ratzinger, *Principles*, 53.
52. Ratzinger, *Called to Communion*, 76.

very heterogeneous society."[53] Even if her members could overcome their heterogeneity and sinfulness, this apparent unity would be obliterated and exposed as fraudulence at the moment of death, because in death man is utterly alone; his earthly companions cannot accompany him beyond his final breath. Thus, Ratzinger explains, Christians "can become a people only through him who unites from above and from within: through communion with Christ."[54] Christ in the Eucharist brings Christians by the power of the Holy Spirit into the trinitarian communion.

The dynamism of this vertical and horizontal communion opens up into diachronic and synchronic communion. "For *the celebration of the eucharist* is not just *a meeting of heaven and earth*; rather, it is also *a meeting of the Church then and now* and *a meeting of the Church here and there.*"[55] Then and now, here and there. Because there is only one risen body of Christ, only one eucharistic sacrifice that one can receive, in which one can participate, and by which many may become one in Christ, christological communion bridges heaven and earth, past, present, and future.

Ratzinger's *communio*-ecclesiology recognizes that the Eucharist ever re-forms the church in the image of the Trinity and enables it to share in that communion. The Eucharist in both its visible structures and also in its invisible dimensions forms the sacramental communion that is the church.

4.2.3 Eucharist and Episcopacy

The church is the body of Christ, the sacramental communion of Christians with God and with each other. The eucharistic character of this communion points toward a) the universal nature of this communion, b) the episcopal character of the church and c) the intrinsic link between communion and mission, which I discuss in the next chapter.

First, since the Eucharist signifies and effects the reconciliation of men with God it likewise demands "reconciliation with one's brother as a prior condition (Matt 5:23)."[56] It does not allow for cliques, divisions, parties, or schisms within the communion. Just as there is only one Christ with one body so there is one church, united in Christ across all times and places, all races, genders, and socio-economic categories. At the same time, the universal character of the Eucharist does not deny the specificity of the communion of Christians gathered at this place and this time: "the eucharistic

53. Ratzinger, *Principles*, 55.
54. Ratzinger, *Principles*, 55.
55. Ratzinger, *God Is Near Us*, 53.
56. Ratzinger, *Called to Communion*, 79.

nature of the church pointed first to the local gathering."[57] However, the gathering of the congregation in the name of Christ does not thereby make the community into a church. After all, "In the Eucharist I can never demand communion with Jesus alone. He has given himself a body. Whoever receives him in Communion necessarily communicates with all his brothers and sisters who have become members of the one Body. *Communio* includes the dimension of catholicity by virtue of the range of the mystery of Christ. *Communio* is catholic, or it simply does not exist at all."[58] The episcopacy provides the guarantee of and visible form for the catholicity of eucharistic communion precisely because the episcopacy embodies the living continuity between the apostles and Christians today.[59] Since the Eucharist makes the church, a community can only become church by being sacramentally in communion with the whole church. This is accomplished in the Eucharist by means of the episcopal communion.

Ratzinger addresses this in an essay responding to the question of a given community's "right to the Eucharist."[60] He demonstrates that the notion of a community's right to the Eucharist immediately implies a right to a priest. This implies the ability to bestow orders on its own, apart from apostolic succession, which is to say, outside of a "Catholic" context. At issue is "the extent to which Catholicity is inherently essential to the Church in the deepest recesses of her life,"[61] which is to say, the extent to which catholicity is essential to a community being a church.

In exploring the roots of the modern notion of community as it relates to his stated concern, Ratzinger agrees with Afanasief that the Eucharist is present in each local church, and nothing can be added to the mystery of the Eucharist. Where the Eucharist is, there Christ and the whole church are. Since Christ only comes to us from "without," no community can bestow upon itself the presence of the eucharistic mystery. Eucharist implies orders, which implies apostolic succession. "Thus unity with all other communities is not just something that may or may not be added to the Eucharist at some later time; rather it is an inner constitutive element of the Eucharistic

---

57. Ratzinger, *Called to Communion*, 79.

58. Ratzinger, *Called to Communion*, 80.

59. Cf. Ratzinger, *Behold the Pierced One*, 74–75: "The teaching of the Apostles is the concrete way in which they continue to be present in the Church. In virtue of this teaching, even future generations, after the death of the Apostles, will remain in unity with them and thus form the same, one, apostolic Church."

60. See Ratzinger, *Principles*, 285–314.

61. Ratzinger, *Principles*, 287–88.

celebration."[62] A community becomes a "catholic" community through unity with the whole church.

After all, "no community can simply give itself its own bishop,"[63] just as no one can invent the faith on his own but must always receive it from without as a response to the handing down of the revelation of God made present in Jesus Christ. In short, "the order of unity [of the Church] is not one of purely human law but that unity is a key characteristic of the Church's essence, so that the juridical expression of unity in the office of Peter's successor and in the necessary dependence of the bishops both on one another and on him belongs to the core of her sacred order."[64] Because each bishop is a successor to the apostolic college, each bishop as the president of his eucharistic community is the representative of the episcopal college to that community even as he is the representative of his local church to the college of bishops, which is to say, to the whole church.

The Eucharist makes the church. Each community, which is gathered in reception of the celebration of the Eucharist, a celebration whose president is a member of the apostolic college, thereby shares in diachronic and synchronic communion with the Catholic Church, which is the communion of all similarly gathered eucharistic communities. The bishop guarantees that the communion which is signified and effected in the Eucharist is the same communion instituted by Christ and effected the Holy Spirit and made real in the church of all times and places. Therefore, authentically ecclesial creative minorities, of the sort Ratzinger has in mind, must live from and for the Eucharist both liturgically and in the concrete contexts of their lives. In addition, this eucharistic living demands that the local community and the universal church mutually recognize their shared faith and ecclesial life.

In the next chapter, I explore the liturgical aspects and missionary implications of Ratzinger's eucharistic ecclesiology. Specifically, I examine his understanding of the church which eucharistically becomes both a participation in Jesus's own λογική λατρεία offered to the Father even as it sacramentally brings his offer of salvation to the nations.

---

62. Ratzinger, *Principles*, 293.
63. Ratzinger, *Called to Communion*, 88.
64. Ratzinger, *Called to Communion*, 94.

5

Eucharist and Mission

IN COMING TO SAVE humanity via this offering of communion, Jesus also and always reveals the proper way to relate to the Father, which is to say he reveals the proper form of worship. One could say that Jesus comes to offer right worship to the Father on behalf of humanity and to invite humanity to participate in his liturgical offering. In a sense the mission of the church, the mission of the body of Christ, is to worship God rightly. This chapter first explores the relation between communion and mission more generally before examining Ratzinger's understanding of the liturgical mission of the church from its origins in the Old Testament through its fulfillment in Christ and the "new worship," which he institutes, to the eucharistic participation of the church in Jesus's "new worship." After this background in the christological and ecclesial nature of worship, I then argue that the Eucharist, as the source and summit of the Christian life, serves as the middle term connecting Ratzinger's notion of *communio* with his idea of mission. Lastly, I unpack what this means for his understanding of missiology and evangelization.

5.1 Communion and Mission

5.1.1 Abrahamic Origins

In his book *Does God Need the Church?*, Gerhard Lohfink explains the ecclesiological and missiological implications of the first few chapters of Genesis. "From the beginning" God is not merely concerned with calling a person and founding a people all his own; his concerns are universal, for "humanity as a whole."[1] God desires the salvation of the whole world, Jews and Gentiles. He calls Abram and chooses a people for the purpose of establishing a concrete place, a particular people, in whom his attempt to "reconcile the

---

1. Lohfink, *Does God Need the Church?*, 21.

world to Himself" might be performed and made present as an invitation to the Gentiles. Only in this way can the authentic freedom of sinful humanity be respected. From the moment of his call to Abram, God makes clear his intention to bless all of humanity. To Abram God says, "by you all the families of the earth shall bless themselves."[2] Lohfink explains, "Abraham and the new thing that God is bringing into the world with him will be salvation for those who come into contact with him and share in this new thing."[3] This call to Abram, which is in the first place a gratuitous gift, also contains within itself significant responsibility, a mandate. Abram and his descendants who will become Israel, the chosen people of God, are chosen for the sake of the nations. "Israel's being chosen is not a privilege or a preference *over others*, but existence *for others*, and hence the heaviest burden in history."[4] Through the prophets, God consistently reminds the Jews of their responsibility, calling them back to him so that they may continue to be a *lumen gentium*.

In short, the Jews are gathered so that they might bear witness to the presence of God in the world. They are called to communion for the purpose of fulfilling a universal mission.

5.1.2 Gathered around Jesus and Sent by Jesus

Jesus's public ministry, the words and deeds which enflesh his mission, starts with his gathering of the twelve. Jesus calls and gathers the apostles in order to send them into the world—"that they might be with him and he might send them forth to preach and to have authority to drive out demons" (Mark 3:13–15).[5] This preaching is always done in Jesus's name. It is a participation in his mission. As the Father has sent him, so Jesus sends them to share in his mission of "drawing all people to himself" (John 12:32). The eloquence of their preaching and witness depends upon the reality of their communion in Christ: "I in them and you in me [Father], that they may be brought to perfection as one, that the world may know that you sent me, and that you loved them even as you loved me" (John 17:23).

After Jesus's resurrection and ascension, this gathering around Jesus and being sent by Jesus takes place in the context of the Lord's Supper, the Eucharist, and is characterized as *"koinonia"*:

2. Gen 12:3c, in Lohfink, *Does God Need the Church?*, 28.
3. Lohfink, *Does God Need the Church?*, 30.
4. Lohfink, *Does God Need the Church?*, 37; cf. Ratzinger, *Introduction to Christianity*, 233; *Meaning of Christian Brotherhood*, 75–92.
5. Bracketed text present in the original.

> They devoted themselves to the teaching of the apostles and to the communal life, to the breaking of the bread and to the prayers. Awe came upon everyone, and many wonders and signs were done through the apostles. All who believed were together and had all things in common; they would sell their property and possessions and divide them among all according to each one's need. Every day they devoted themselves to meeting together in the temple area and to breaking bread in their homes. They ate their meals with exultation and sincerity of heart, praising God and enjoying favor with all the people. And every day the Lord added to their number those who were being saved. (Acts 2:42–47)

But this communal life devoted to "the teaching of the apostles" and the "breaking of the bread" was itself preceded by Pentecost. Here, "The Church was publicly displayed to the multitude, the Gospel began to spread among the nations by means of preaching, and there was presaged that union of all peoples in the catholicity of the faith by means of the Church of the New Covenant, a Church which . . . supersedes the divisiveness of Babel."[6] The community is formed as a communion ordered toward mission.

5.1.3 Communion Is Missionary

The Gospels hand on two very clear missionary mandates. The Matthean mandate emphasizes proclamation: "Go therefore and make disciples of all nations, baptizing in the name of the Father and of the Son and of the Holy Spirit, teaching them to observe all that I have commanded you" (Matt 28:19–20). On the other hand, the Johannine missionary mandate highlights the importance of Christian unity: "May they become perfectly one, so that the world may know that you have sent me" (John 17:23).[7] This latter mandate has become more prominent in recent decades as the ecumenical movement has gained momentum, but they ought not to be read in opposition to each other. Proclamation that does not emanate from concretely lived communion is empty and unpersuasive. A community, which is not "ready to give an explanation to anyone who asks" (1 Pet 3:15), cannot effectively bear witness to Christ. Communion and mission are deeply intertwined. The liturgy attests to this: the faithful are gathered in order to be sent. Or, in the words of Pope John Paul II:

---

6. AG 4.

7. For more detailed accounts of the missionary mandates and the emphases of each, see John Paul II, *Redemptoris missio*, 23.

> Communion with Jesus, which gives rise to the communion of Christians among themselves, is an indispensable condition for bearing fruit: "Apart from me you can do nothing" (John 15:5). And communion with others is the most magnificent fruit that the branches can give: in fact, it is the gift of Christ and His Spirit.
>
> At this point *communion begets communion:* essentially it is likened to a *mission on behalf of communion.* . . . Communion and mission are profoundly connected with each other, they interpenetrate and mutually imply each other, to the point that *communion represents both the source and the fruit of mission: communion gives rise to mission and mission is accomplished in communion.* It is always the one and the same Spirit who calls together and unifies the Church and sends her to preach the Gospel "to the ends of the earth" (Acts 1:8). On her part, the Church knows that the communion received by her as a gift is destined for all people. . . . The mission of the Church flows from her own nature. Christ has willed it to be so: that of "sign and instrument . . . of unity of all the human race." Such a mission has the purpose of making everyone know and live the "new" communion that the Son of God made man introduced into the history of the world.[8]

However, where there is disunity in the church, where there is no communion, the reign of God is not evident. If God does not reign in a given community, how can they proclaim Him? Paul VI explains it well in *Evangelii nuntiandi*:

> The power of evangelization will find itself considerably diminished if those who proclaim the Gospel are divided among themselves in all sorts of ways. Is this not perhaps one of the great sicknesses of evangelization today? Indeed, if the Gospel that we proclaim is seen to be rent . . . how can those to whom we address our preaching fail to be disturbed, disoriented, even scandalized?
>
> The Lord's spiritual testament tells us that unity among His followers is not only the proof that we are His but also the proof that He is sent by the Father. It is the test of the credibility of Christians and of Christ Himself. As evangelizers, we must offer Christ's faithful not the image of people divided and separated by unedifying quarrels, but the image of people who are mature in faith and capable of finding a meeting-point beyond the real tensions, thanks to a shared, sincere and disinterested search for

---

8. John Paul II, *Christifidelis laici*, 32.

truth. Yes, the destiny of evangelization is certainly bound up with the witness of unity given by the Church.[9]

John Paul II echoed the above words of his predecessor when in *Redemptoris missio* he observed, "People today put more trust in witnesses than in teachers, in experience than in teaching, and in life and action than in theories. The witness of a Christian life is the first and irreplaceable form of mission. . . . The first form of witness is *the very life of the missionary, of the Christian family, and of the ecclesial community*, which reveal a new way of living."[10] Contemporary men and women, often hear the proclamation of the Gospel not as good news but as hypocrisy and pharisaism. Many people seem to have been inoculated against the traditional forms of evangelization. Yet, disillusioned by Christian disunity and scandal they remain all the more in need of truly good news. The current situation calls for concrete communion, for communities in whom others can experience the reign of God. Only as members of such communities can persons credibly bear witness to the profound reality of the love of Christ, who comes "to enable people to share in the communion which exists between the Father and the Son."[11] In short, communion is necessary for mission and is ordered towards mission, but authentic communion cannot be fabricated; it can only be received. For Ratzinger this takes place in the Eucharist. I now turn to Ratzinger's own understanding of the relation between liturgy and mission.

5.2 Liturgy and Mission in Ratzinger

For Ratzinger ecclesial communion is essentially a participation in the triune love of God, a participation that is entirely gift and which takes the form of foretaste. It remains a pilgrim participation. This participation in the divine communion of persons is mediated to humanity through the Incarnation of the Son who offers humanity a share in his sonship by opening up his body on the cross and in the Eucharist. Thus, the Eucharist ever re-forms ecclesial communities into the body of Christ. However, the gathering of the people of God, even before the Incarnation of the Lord, has always been about liturgy, about worship. Thus, before exploring the relation between liturgy and mission in Ratzinger's ecclesiology it is necessary to pay attention to what he means by "liturgy."

---

9. Paul VI, *Evangelii nuntiandi*, 77.
10. John Paul II, *Redemptoris missio* 42.
11. John Paul II, *Redemptoris missio*, 23.

5.2.1 Worship in the Old Covenant

In *The Spirit of the Liturgy* Ratzinger begins his exploration of the essence of the liturgy in Egypt. He explains that while the goal of the Exodus at first glance seems to have been the inheritance of the promised land, a closer look reveals that Pharaoh was asked to let Israel go into the wilderness "that they may serve" the Lord (Exod 7:16). "Israel is my first-born son.... Let my son go that he may worship me" (Exod 4:22–23). Pharaoh offers to compromise, allowing only the men to go, and later allowing all the people to go but without their livestock. Moses rejects these offers as inadequate, for, "we do not know with what we must serve the Lord until we arrive there" (Exod 10:26). These exchanges reveal that "the only goal of the Exodus is ... worship, which can only take place according to God's measure."[12] The land is not the goal of the Exodus, nor was it primarily about liberating the people from slavery. Rather, the promised land is to be the "place for the worship of the true God"[13] and for establishing the covenant. The land is a means to the *telos* of the gathering of the people of God and "only becomes a true good, a real gift, a promise fulfilled, when it is the place where God reigns."[14] Indeed when God no longer reigns in Israel, the land ceases to be the land of the promise. The people cease to be a people with a place. They become exiles.

Ratzinger then points out the concrete character of Israelite worship. In the Sinaitic covenant, "a covenant concretized in a minutely regulated form of worship,"[15] God reveals the manner in which he wills to be worshiped. By connecting this worship with the covenant, with the commandments, God communicates the degree to which right worship is liturgical, but liturgical in a way that always demands right living.[16] Thus the Sinaitic covenant reveals the inseparability of worship and ethos because without a common ethos the Israelites cannot truly become (and remain) a people. "Israel is constituted as a people through the covenant and the divine law it contains. ... Whenever Israel falls away from the right worship of God, when she turns away from God to the false gods (the powers and values of this world), her freedom, too, collapses."[17] In this way, true worship, "goes beyond the action of the liturgy," beyond the altar, and "embraces the ordering of the

---

12. Ratzinger, *Spirit of the Liturgy*, 16.
13. Ratzinger, *Spirit of the Liturgy*, 17.
14. Ratzinger, *Spirit of the Liturgy*, 17.
15. Ratzinger, *Spirit of the Liturgy*, 17.
16. See Ratzinger, *Spirit of the Liturgy*, 17–18. Here, Ratzinger quotes St. Irenaeus: "The glory of God is the living man, but the life of man is the vision of God" (Irenaeus, *Adversus Haeraeses* 4.20.7).
17. Ratzinger, *Spirit of the Liturgy*, 18–19.

whole of human life."[18] Put another way, "it is the very life of man, man himself as living righteously, that is the true worship of God, but life only becomes real life when it receives its form from looking toward God. Cult exists in order to communicate this vision and to give life in such a way that glory is given to God."[19]

Ultimately, this clarifies what worship is about: relating to God rightly. After all, right relationship with God is "essential for the right kind of human existence in the world.... Worship gives us a share in heaven's mode of existence, in the world of God, and allows light to fall from that divine world into ours," imbuing right worship with an eschatological character and with authentic hope.[20]

Approaching from the perspective of the covenant as the establishment of God's relationship to his people and vice versa,[21] brings to light the connection between covenant, worship, and the *Shema Israel*. The various covenants of the Old Testament are ordered towards concretizing the relationship between God and his people so that they may worship him rightly, live uprightly, and bear witness to his presence in the world forthrightly. "The goal of creation is the covenant, the love story of God and man."[22] In this view, God creates the cosmos as the space for his encounter, his marriage, with humanity. Indeed, the Holy Land ceases to be the land of the promise when Israel is no longer living out its covenant with God. The exile bears witness to the connection between creation and covenant, and also between covenant, worship, and ethics. After all, the exile is preceded both by acts of idolatry and acts of injustice. Thus, the covenant, communion with God, is the *telos* of creation and worship is "the soul of the covenant."[23]

Across time and space, religion has nearly universally centered on sacrifice offered to the deity, which usually entails handing over to God something important to humanity, and/or to the community, by destroying it. Thus, shortly after receiving the Ten Commandments (Exod 19–20), Moses "built an altar at the foot of the mountain" (Exod 24:4). Then they proceed to worship God sacrificially:

> Then, having sent young men of the Israelites to offer burnt offerings and sacrifice young bulls as communion offerings to the

---

18. Ratzinger, *Spirit of the Liturgy*, 19.
19. Ratzinger, *Spirit of the Liturgy*, 18.
20. Ratzinger, *Spirit of the Liturgy*, 21.
21. "Then I will take you for My people, and I will be your God; and you shall know that I am the LORD your God" (Exod 6:7).
22. Ratzinger, *Spirit of the Liturgy*, 26.
23. Ratzinger, *Spirit of the Liturgy*, 27.

LORD, Moses took half of the blood and put it in large bowls; the other half he splashed on the altar. Taking the book of the covenant, he read it aloud to the people. . . . Then he took the blood and splashed it on the people, saying, "This is the blood of the covenant which the LORD has made with you according to all these words." Moses then went up with Aaron, Nadab, Abihu, and seventy elders of Israel, and they beheld the God of Israel. . . . They saw God, and they ate and drank. (Exod 24:5-11)

This clarifies the connection between a life well lived (the Ten Commandments), covenant, and sacrificial worship. The blood of the sacrifice is the sign of covenant. It is sealed in blood. Moses's pouring of the "blood of the covenant" on the people and on the altar—which represents God—is the sacramental, as it were, the sign that effects the covenantal bond between God and Israel.

But does such "sacrifice" actually please God? Does it actually hand anything over to God? Does it serve him? The author of Psalm 50 expresses the point clearly, writing on behalf of God to Israel: "If I am hungry, I will not tell you, because the world is mine and all it contains. Am I going to eat the flesh of bulls, shall I drink the blood of goats? Offer to God a sacrifice of thanksgiving, fulfill your vows to the Most High" (Ps 50:12-14). Further, when sacrifice becomes divorced from ethos, from the Law, then it ceases to be meaningful: "For it is loyalty that I desire, not sacrifice, and knowledge of God rather than burnt offerings" (Hos 6:6). This is oft repeated throughout the prophets.[24]

Of what then does sacrifice consist? Ratzinger explains: "True surrender to God looks very different. It consists . . . in the union of man and creation with God. Belonging to God has nothing to do with destruction or non-being: it is rather a way of being."[25] This elucidates the prophetic rejection of Israel's sacrifice and indicates the radical connection between worship and ethics. True worship is not found in destruction but in the transformation of man into conformity with God's will. God's will is love. Thus Augustine can say, "All the commands that we read were given by God in relation to the many modes of sacrifice offered in the ministry of the tabernacle or the Temple refer back, therefore, as signs, to the love of God

---

24. To quote two further instances: "I hate, I despise your feasts, I take no pleasure in your solemnities. Even though you bring me your burnt offerings and grain offerings I will not accept them; your stall-fed communion offerings, I will not look upon them" (Amos 5:21-22); "What do I care for the multitude of your sacrifices? Says the LORD. I have had enough of whole-burnt rams and fat of fatlings; In the blood of calves, lambs, and goats I find no pleasure" (Isa 1:11).

25. Ratzinger, *Spirit of the Liturgy*, 28.

and neighbor."²⁶ But the Christian way, the achievement of God's reign in the world, of God's revolution, can never be reduced to mere moralistic norms. The connection between ethos and worship prevents this. This sacrifice of love that God desires demands first that he take the initiative. For Ratzinger, "The initiative of God has a name: Jesus Christ, the God Who Himself became man and gives Himself to us."²⁷ As the self-revelation of the Father, the Word-made-flesh reveals to humanity true worship by instantiating what Ratzinger calls a "new worship." Next, I explore Ratzinger's understanding of Jesus's cultic actions.²⁸

5.2.2 Jesus and the New Worship

In Ratzinger's mind the connection that Jesus draws between the Last Supper and his death and resurrection, inaugurates the new worship which is true worship. The "for you" of Jesus's institution of the Eucharist at the Last Supper preemptively transforms Jesus's death from an instance of capital punishment into a self-offering, a sacrifice:

> The Cross and Resurrection give him authority as the one who ushers in true worship. Jesus justifies himself through his Passion—the sign of Jonah that he gives to Israel and to the world. ... The era of the Temple is over. A new worship (*ein neuer Kult*) is being introduced, in a Temple not built by human hands. This Temple is his body, the Risen One, who gathers the peoples and unites them in the sacrament of his body and blood. He himself is the new Temple of humanity. The crucifixion of Jesus is at the same time the destruction of the old Temple. With his Resurrection, a new way of worshipping God begins (*beginnt eine neue Weise, Gott zu verehren*), no longer on this or that mountain, but "in spirit and truth" (John 4:23).²⁹

What is the content of this new worship? What are the implications of true worship for communion and mission? These questions I explore in what follows.

In his discussion of Jesus's entry into Jerusalem, Pope Benedict XVI, writing not under the authority of his office but "solely as an expression of

---

26. Augustine, *City of God* X.5 (310).
27. Ratzinger, "Theology of the Liturgy," 20.
28. Here I rely heavily on Wainwright, "'New Worship.'" Wainwright relies primarily on the English translation of Ratzinger's *Jesus of Nazareth: Part Two*.
29. Ratzinger, *Jesus of Nazareth: Part Two*, 21–22, in Wainwright, "'New Worship,'" 993.

[his] 'personal search for the face of the Lord,'"[30] first highlights the early church's identification of this event with the coming of the Lord in the Eucharist in the *Didache*: "Let his grace draw near, and let this present world pass away. Hosanna to the God of David. Whoever is holy, let him approach; whoever is not, let him repent. *Maranatha*. Amen."[31] Here the pope emeritus sees evidence for the early church's eucharistic participation in Jesus's new worship. Wainwright explains that although the early church still gathered in the Temple in Jerusalem, the "breaking of bread," which took place in house-churches, became "the new 'cultic' center (*die neue 'kultische' Mitte*) of the lives of the faithful."[32] Of course, to identify something other than the Temple as the cultic center of a Jewish sect is to speak of a radical reorientation of their worship. Thus, in Jesus

> the entire Old Testament theology of worship (and with it all the theologies of worship in the history of religions) is "preserved and surpassed" [*aufgehoben*] and raised to a completely new level. Jesus himself is the presence of the living God. God and man, God and the world, touch one another in him. The meaning of the ritual of the Day of Atonement is accomplished in him. In his self-offering on the Cross, Jesus, as it were, brings all the sin of the world deep within the love of God and wipes it away. Accepting the Cross, entering into fellowship with Christ, means entering the realm of transformation and expiation.[33]

In his hour, which encapsulates the intrinsic unity between the Paschal Mystery and the Eucharist, Jesus becomes the new high priest, whose self-offering accomplishes the atonement to which the old feast pointed. He becomes the new and true Passover lamb, whose blood spares God's people not from death wrought by God's angel, but from the second death wrought from sin. Jesus himself, his body, is now the temple where this truly efficacious sacrifice is offered. Only in placing him at the cultic center of life can a community praise God rightly. Ratzinger expands upon the meaning and depth of this new center of worship by reflecting upon the Last Supper and Jesus's Paschal Mystery. Ratzinger reads Jesus's high priestly prayer (John 17) in light of the Day of Atonement of the Old Covenant:

---

30. Ratzinger, *Jesus of Nazareth: Part One*, xxiii.

31. Ratzinger, *Jesus of Nazareth: Part Two*, 10, in Wainwright, "'New Worship,'" 997. Ratzinger is quoting from the *Didache* 10:6.

32. Wainwright, "'New Worship,'" 998, quoting Ratzinger, *Jesus of Nazareth: Part Two*, 35–36.

33. Ratzinger, *Jesus of Nazareth: Part Two*, 38, in Wainwright, "'New Worship,'" 998.

> Just as the high priest makes atonement for himself, for the priestly clan, and for the whole community of Israel, so Jesus prays for himself, for the Apostles, and finally for all who will come to believe in him through their word—for the Church of all times (cf. John 17:20). . . . His Cross and his exaltation is the Day of Atonement for the world, in which the whole of world history—in the face of all human sin and its destructive consequences—finds its meaning and is aligned with its true purpose and destiny.[34]

In this way, Jesus replaces the sacrificial animals with "the Word" whom he is and for whom "a body has been prepared" (Heb 10:5). In his high priestly prayer, Jesus illuminates the Eucharist in its true depth. Here—in this prayer, at the institution of the Eucharist, on the cross—"Jesus transforms his cruel death into 'word,' into the radical expression of his love, his self-giving to the point of death. Thereby he himself becomes the 'Temple.' Insofar as the high-priestly prayer forms the consummation of Jesus' self-gift, it represents the new worship and has a deep inner connection with the Eucharist."[35] The prayer elevates his death from an act of capital punishment to a gift of life and liturgical sacrifice offered for the many. The celebration of the Eucharist fulfills and transcends *Yom Kippur* and becomes "the new atonement liturgy of Jesus Christ, the liturgy of the New Covenant, in its entire grandeur and purity."[36]

Furthermore, the Last Supper not only fulfills the Day of Atonement but also reveals the full meaning of the Passover. For Ratzinger, the evangelists clearly understood Jesus's actions as "echoes of both Exodus 24:8 [the Mosaic covenant] and Jeremiah 31:31 [the promise of a new covenant] in Jesus' words."[37] Therefore, "very early on, Jesus' Last Supper—which includes not only a prophecy, but a real anticipation of the Cross and Resurrection in the eucharistic gifts—was regarded as a Passover: as his Passover. And so it was."[38] In this way Jesus's words and actions imbue the Eucharist with a liturgical character, which encompasses the two major feasts of the Old

---

34. Ratzinger, *Jesus of Nazareth: Part Two*, 78–79, in Wainwright, "'New Worship,'" 999–1000.

35. Ratzinger, *Jesus of Nazareth: Part Two*, 80, in Wainwright, "'New Worship,'" 1000.

36. Ratzinger, *Jesus of Nazareth: Part Two*, 88, in Wainwright, "'New Worship,'" 1000.

37. Ratzinger, *Jesus of Nazareth: Part Two*, 126, in Wainwright, "'New Worship,'" 1001.

38. Ratzinger, *Jesus of Nazareth: Part Two*, 114–15, in Wainwright, "'New Worship,'" 1001.

Covenant and also fulfills those feasts. It is the reality to which they point. Put another way, in the "dual action of praise/thanksgiving and breaking/distributing that is recounted at the beginning of the institution narrative, the essence of the new worship established by Christ through the Last Supper, Cross, and Resurrection is made manifest: here the old Temple worship is abolished and at the same time brought to its fulfillment."[39] Jesus thus makes the celebration of the Eucharist truly the source and summit of the Christian life. Further, Ratzinger's "spiritual Christology" enables him to perceive the celebration of this new worship performed by disciples—then and now—in terms of participation and vicarity.[40] This vicarious participation is in itself transformative because it is a participation in Jesus's obedience unto death and thus also in his victory over death.

However, it is not only the anticipatory words of the Last Supper and those of the high priestly prayer which give the crucifixion its liturgical character. The event itself as depicted in the Gospel communicates its central place in the new worship:

> The new cosmic liturgy is accomplished. The Cross of Jesus replaces all other acts of worship as the one true glorification of God, in which God glorifies himself through him in whom he grants us his love, thereby drawing us to himself. The Synoptic Gospels explicitly portray Jesus' death on the Cross as a cosmic and liturgical event: the sun is darkened, the veil of the Temple is torn in two, the dead rise again. Even more important than the cosmic sign is an act of faith: the Roman centurion—the commander of the execution squad—in his consternation over all that he sees taking place, acknowledges Jesus as God's Son: "Truly this man was the Son of God" (Mark 15:39). At the foot of the Cross, the Church of the Gentiles comes into being. Through the Cross, the Lord gathers people together to form the new community of the worldwide Church. Through the suffering Son, they recognize the true God.[41]

---

39. Ratzinger, *Jesus of Nazareth: Part Two*, 130, in Wainwright, "'New Worship,'" 1001; cf. Ratzinger, *Jesus of Nazareth: Part Two*, 141.

40. See Ratzinger, *Jesus of Nazareth: Part Two*, 134.

41. Ratzinger, *Jesus of Nazareth: Part Two*, 223, in Wainwright, "'New Worship,'" 1006; cf. pages 230–31. "Ratzinger places the death of Jesus—with John's Gospel—at the time of the slaying of the Jewish Passover lambs. Now 'the Temple sacrifices, the cultic heart of the Torah, were a thing of the past. Christ had taken their place. In the New Testament literature there are various attempts to explain Christ's Cross as the new worship, the true atonement, the true purification of this corrupted world,'" (Wainwright, "'New Worship,'" 1006–7).

Nevertheless, Jesus's crucifixion remains only a statistic, only another Jew put to death by the Romans, without the event of the resurrection. Here, on the third day, something truly remarkable happens, something with enough gravity to affect the radical re-centering of life and worship that occurred in the early Christian community. This event as experienced by the apostles is the impetus for making Jesus the center of the new worship.

> If we bear in mind the immense importance attached to the Sabbath in the Old Testament tradition on the basis of the Creation account and the Decalogue, then it is clear that only an event of extraordinary impact could have led to the abandonment of the Sabbath and its replacement by the first day of the week. Only an event that marked souls indelibly could bring about such a profound realignment in the religious culture of the week. Mere theological speculations could not have achieved this.[42]

For this reason, Sunday becomes the new day of worship when the new people come before the new temple to participate in the true priest's true offering, an offering in "spirit and truth." As Ratzinger explains, "The Day of Resurrection is the exterior and interior locus of Christian worship, and the thanksgiving prayer as Jesus' creative anticipation of the Resurrection is the Lord's way of uniting us with his thanksgiving, blessing us in the gift and drawing us into the process of transformation that starts with the gifts, moves on to include us, and then spreads out to the world 'until he comes' (1 Cor 11:26)."[43]

In this way, the Resurrection also indicates the eschatological character of the new worship, which is clarified further in Jesus's ascension to the right hand of the Father.[44] With Jesus's bodily departure comes the apostles' awareness of his presence in a new form; they become "convinced of a new presence of Jesus. They are certain (as the risen Lord said in St. Matthew's account [cf. Matt 28:18–20]) that he is now present to them in a new and powerful way. They know that 'the right hand of God' to which he 'has been exalted' includes a new manner of his presence; they know that he is now permanently among them, in the way that only God can be close to us."[45] This new presence is necessary for the new worship. Jesus's presence must become a presence mediated by the Spirit so that in the Eucharist and in

---

42. Ratzinger, *Jesus of Nazareth: Part Two*, 223.

43. Ratzinger, *Jesus of Nazareth: Part Two*, 144, in Wainwright, "'New Worship,'" 1002.

44. See Ratzinger, *Jesus of Nazareth: Part Two*, 283.

45. Ratzinger, *Jesus of Nazareth: Part Two*, 281, in Wainwright, "'New Worship,'" 1010.

the church his body, his being, can be present in all legitimately formed eucharistic communities.[46]

Thus, the liturgical celebration of the Lord's coming is an anamnesis of his Incarnation, a participation in his sacramental presence, and an anticipation of his parousia. In reflecting on the *Didache*'s exclamation and plea "Maranatha!"[47] Ratzinger explains:

> Christian prayer for the Lord's return always includes the experience of his presence. It is never purely focused on the future. The words of the risen Lord make the point "I am with you always, to the close of the age" (Matt 28:20). He is with us now, and especially close in the Eucharistic presence. Yet, conversely, the Christian experience of the Lord's presence does include a certain tension toward the future, toward the moment when that presence will be definitively fulfilled: the presence is not yet complete. It pushes beyond itself. It sets us in motion toward the definitive.[48]

Earlier in his career Ratzinger reflected on the liturgical character of the parousia and on the eschatological character of the Christian liturgy. First, he makes note of the "language of cosmic symbolism in the New Testament," which he argues is an attempt on the one hand to usurp the cosmic and liturgical claims of the Roman polity and on the other hand to incorporate and fulfill the cosmic character of liturgical language in the Old Testament. For this reason, "The cosmic imagery of the New Testament cannot be used as a source for the description of a future chain of cosmic events."[49] Since they are not merely attempts to predict future events, the parousia cannot be deduced by reading the "signs of the times."

> Instead, these texts form part of a description of the mystery of the Parousia in the language of liturgical tradition. The New Testament conceals and reveals the unspeakable coming of Christ, using language borrowed from that sphere which is graciously enabled to express in this world the point of contact with God. The Parousia is the highest intensification and fulfillment of the

---

46. LG 26. Cf. Ratzinger, *Church, Ecumenism, and Politics*, 18–20; *Principles*, 285–98.

47. Cf. Ratzinger, *Jesus of Nazareth: Part Two*, 289, where he explains that the Greek can be legitimately interpreted as either *marana tha*, which would be translated as "Lord, come!" or as *maran atha*, which is rendered "the Lord has come!"

48. Ratzinger, *Jesus of Nazareth: Part Two*, 289–90, in Wainwright, "'New Worship,'" 1011.

49. Ratzinger, *Eschatology*, 202.

> Liturgy. And the Liturgy is Parousia, a "parousial" event taking place in our midst.[50]

Ratzinger finds scriptural evidence for the eschatological character of the eucharistic liturgy in the Letter to the Hebrews and the Book of Revelation. Since each Eucharist is a participation in the heavenly liturgy, "every Eucharist is Parousia, the Lord's coming, and yet the Eucharist is even more truly the tensed yearning that he would reveal his hidden glory."[51] In this way, the Christian liturgy reflects the "already but not yet" character of the reign of God made present in Jesus and operative in the church. "In touching the risen Jesus, the Church makes contact with the Parousia of the Lord. She prays and lives, so to speak, into that Parousia whose disclosure will be the definitive revelation and fulfillment of the mystery of Easter."[52]

This straining towards the eschatological fulfillment of the reign of God means the church must embrace that reign. The new worship is not merely the gift of participation offered to the baptized. Participation in the glory of the resurrection requires participation in the Lord's obedience, in God's reign in him.

> The motif of the Parousia becomes the obligation to live the Liturgy as a feast of hope-filled presence directed towards Christ, the universal ruler. In this way, it must become the origin and focus of the love in which the Lord can take up his dwelling. In his Cross, the Lord has preceded us so as to prepare for us a place in the house of the Father. In the Liturgy the Church should, as it were, in following him, prepare for him a dwelling in the world. The theme of watchfulness thus penetrates to the point where it takes on the character of a mission: to let the Liturgy be real, until that time when the Lord himself gives to it that final reality which meanwhile can be sought only in image.[53]

In other words, participation in Jesus's new worship has "existential" implications. True worship obliges the Christian to "live the Liturgy," to embody Jesus in the concrete actions of her life so that the Lord "also comes in ways that change the world."[54] The liturgy has a missionary character, and the

---

50. Ratzinger, *Eschatology*, 202–3. Ratzinger continues: "This helps us to realize that whereas in the Liturgy the Church appears to be engaged in self-contemplation, in reality she enters into the heart of the world, and works actively for the latter's liberating transformation."

51. Ratzinger, *Eschatology*, 203.

52. Ratzinger, *Eschatology*, 204.

53. Ratzinger, *Eschatology*, 204.

54. Ratzinger, *Jesus of Nazareth: Part Two*, 291–92.

mission of the church has a liturgical character. In the next section, I unpack Ratzinger's reading of Romans 12 and the Letter to the Hebrews in order to clarify what Ratzinger means in alluding to the missionary character of the liturgy. The Eucharist as it is related to Ratzinger's notion of true worship is, I argue, the key to understanding the relation between communion and mission in his ecclesiology, between the fellowship of the church *ad intra* and the church's proclamation of the Gospel *ad extra*.

5.3 Becoming Eucharist

Ratzinger's theology is always an exercise in recognizing the *prius* of God, the importance of hearing his word and allowing it to give meaning and direction to our lives. The same is true of his understanding of worship. In order for worship to be true worship, the people of God must receive the form of their worship from God. Ratzinger argues that the church's listening to the word and participation in the liturgical work of the Lord together "afford a transparent view of the salvific work of Jesus Christ and thus allow the eternal to shine through into the temporal."[55] Elsewhere, he describes a legend purporting to explain how Russia became Christian: the prince found the Byzantine liturgy more persuasively to bear witness to transcendent reality than the arguments made by adherents of other religious traditions. "What impressed onlookers about the liturgy was precisely . . . the fact that it was celebrated for God and not for spectators, that its sole intent was to be . . . pleasing and acceptable to God. Precisely this 'disinterest' of standing before God . . . was what caused a divine light to descend on what was happening and caused that divine light to be perceptible even to onlookers."[56] Thus, for Ratzinger, when adoration reflects one's confident faith and hope that the ground of all being is present here, when it is done for no other reason than to glorify the Lord, the act of worship, in and of itself, becomes transparent to the Lord. It becomes a credible word, enabling and ennobling the worshiping community to bear witness to the presence of God. So, while liturgy is not explicitly oriented to mission and should not be reduced to a missionary event, "its aim is to please God and to lead men to see this as being the measure of their lives. . . . As such, in this profound sense, it is the origin of mission."[57]

After all, faith is handed on successfully when children see in their parents that God is more important to them than anything else in the world.

---

55. Ratzinger, *Theologie der Liturgie*, 16, in Heim, *Joseph Ratzinger*, 517–18.
56. Ratzinger, "We Experienced," 43.
57. Ratzinger, *Pilgrim Fellowship of Faith*, 94.

However, considering the church's relative inability to keep young people present and active in the community after their confirmation, one may ask whether Catholic worship today adequately reflects the belief that the Lord is in *this* place. Why is Christian witness often not convincing, not moving, even to Catholic children, much less to the rest of the world?

Only a people that has allowed itself to be gathered into communion by God in Christ, can convince the world of God's presence therein. The political, socio-economic, and denominational divisions in the church today are among the greatest arguments against the credibility of the faith. After all, faith is aroused only when God's "closeness is felt." It is only "where human intentions take second place to reverence before him, that the credibility comes that creates belief."[58] For Ratzinger, Christian communities have lost their credibility because the lives of Christians are not transparent to God often enough. This transparency and the credibility that comes with it can only come from God: "Only a power and a love that are stronger than our own initiatives can build up a fruitful and reliable community and impart to it the impetus of a fruitful mission. . . . The love of Christ, which is present for all ages in the Sacrament of his Body, awakens our love and heals our love: the Eucharist is the foundation of community as it is of mission."[59] Thus, Eucharist not only makes the church but also sends the church into the world.

Ratzinger understands the Second Vatican Council to confirm this. The first constitution promulgated by the council was *Sacrosanctum Concilium*. For Ratzinger, this makes sense because "Worship, adoration, comes first. And thus God does. This beginning is in accordance with the Rule of St. Benedict (XLIII): 'Operi Dei nihil praeponatur.'"[60] *Lumen Gentium* followed as the next major document, and "should be seen as inwardly bracketed together with [*Sacrosanctum Concilium*]."[61] This bracketing communicates that the "Church derives from adoration, from the task of glorifying God. Ecclesiology, of its nature, has to do with liturgy."[62] But the other two constitutions add to and further fill out this liturgical ecclesiology. Thus, "the third Constitution talks about the Word of God, which calls the Church together and is at all times renewing her. The fourth Constitution shows how the glory of God presents itself in an ethos, how the light we have received from God is carried out into the world, how only thus can

---

58. Ratzinger, *Pilgrim Fellowship of Faith*, 93.
59. Ratzinger, *Pilgrim Fellowship of Faith*, 89.
60. Ratzinger, *Pilgrim Fellowship of Faith*, 126.
61. Ratzinger, *Pilgrim Fellowship of Faith*, 126.
62. Ratzinger, *Pilgrim Fellowship of Faith*, 126.

God be fully glorified."⁶³ Not only is the church derived from adoration, but adoration only truly glorifies God when it is embodied in an ethos which evangelizes the world, an ethos by which Christian lives become transparent to God.

This follows from Ratzinger's understanding of the nature of worship. What happens on the altar, in the Mass properly speaking, is part of true worship, "but so too is life according to the will of God; such a life is an indispensable part of true worship."⁶⁴ For Ratzinger, this new and true worship is summed up in the concept of λογική λατρεία, "which we encounter in the epistle to the Romans (12:1),"⁶⁵ and in which the "sacrifice is the 'word,' the word of prayer, which goes up from man to God, embodying the whole of man's existence and enabling him to become 'word' (*logos*) in himself."⁶⁶ In this way, "It is man, conforming himself to *logos* and becoming *logos* through faith, who is the true sacrifice, the true glory of God in the world."⁶⁷ For Paul λογική λατρεία results from the implicit and inherent link between his theology of the cross and his understanding of the Eucharist. "Without the Cross, the Eucharist would remain mere ritual; without the Eucharist the Cross would be merely a horrible, profane event. Thus something else becomes clear: *the close connection between life as it is lived and experienced and sacral actions in worship.*"⁶⁸

Therefore, to recognize that the Gospel is no longer credible because Christian communities and Christian lives are no longer credible is to admit that in many Christian communities, liturgy and life have ceased to be λογική λατρεία, worship in accord with the *logos*, and have become, often enough, something else entirely. But when worship is in accord with the *logos*, then

> The Logos . . . makes us sons in the sacramental fellowship in which we are living. And if we become sacrifices, if we ourselves become conformed to the Logos, then this is not a process confined to the spirit, which leaves the body behind it as something distanced from God. That is why we are . . . urged [by St. Paul] to present our bodies as a form of worship consistent with the

---

63. Ratzinger, *Pilgrim Fellowship of Faith*, 126.
64. Ratzinger, *Spirit of the Liturgy*, 17–18.
65. Ratzinger, *Spirit of the Liturgy*, 44.
66. Ratzinger, *Spirit of the Liturgy*, 45–46.
67. Ratzinger, *Spirit of the Liturgy*, 46.
68. Ratzinger, *Pilgrim Fellowship of Faith*, 98.

Logos, that is to say, to be drawn into fellowship of love with God in our entire bodily existence.[69]

As Ratzinger's analysis of the Exodus revealed the link between worship, covenant, and life in the Old Testament, so too here he communicates that in Christian liturgy worship and ethics remain inseparably interwoven. "Cult seen in its true breadth and depth goes beyond the action of the liturgy. Ultimately, it embraces the ordering of the whole of human life."[70] The credibility of the gospel today depends in part on the degree to which the deep truth of Christian worship is attested to in the lives of the faithful and leads to the *vita apostolica*.

It is this fact of the public nature of liturgy, of true adoration, which allows communion to be missional. Although the situation of the early church cannot be reconstructed today, the need remains for local churches to develop appropriate forms of community life, which overflow from the liturgy in order to make fellowship possible.[71] After all, if faith without works is dead, then worship that does not also become the concrete experience of communion fails to be λογική λατρεία. Put another way, it is true that "the word 'Eucharist' points to the universal form of worship that took place in the Incarnation, Cross, and Resurrection of Christ, and so it can happily serve as a summary of the idea of λογική λατρεία and may legitimately serve as an appropriate designation for Christian worship."[72] Nevertheless, the above does not imply that true worship can be limited to what happens at the altar and in the church building. After all, "Christian liturgy [remains] liturgy on the way, a liturgy of pilgrimage toward the transfiguration of the world."[73] Since humanity is made for worship of God and communion with God, the Mass remains a gathering in order to be sent, and the liturgy retains its missionary mandate until that time when God is "all in all."

This also implies that the ethos of the reign of God, of Christian fellowship, is no mere moralism. It is the concrete form, the existential reality, of his eucharistic ecclesiology. Following Paul in his letter to the Philippians, Ratzinger examines the liturgical character of martyrdom. "Paul views his expected martyrdom as liturgy and as sacrificial event. . . . In martyrdom he is fully drawn into the obedience of Christ, into the liturgy of the Cross, and hence into true worship."[74] He continues by reflecting on the martyrdoms

---

69. Ratzinger, *Pilgrim Fellowship of Faith*, 117.
70. Ratzinger, *Spirit of the Liturgy*, 20.
71. Ratzinger, *Meaning of Christian Brotherhood*, 69.
72. Ratzinger, *Spirit of the Liturgy*, 50.
73. Ratzinger, *Spirit of the Liturgy*, 50.
74. Ratzinger, *Jesus of Nazareth: Part Two*, 239.

of Ignatius of Antioch: "Christ's grain of wheat, ground through martyrdom in order to become the bread of Christ (cf. *Ad Rom.* 4:1)," and of Saint Polycarp, in which the fire "formed a wall around the martyr's figure, and there was he in the center of it, not like burning flesh, but like a loaf baking in the oven," and it spread "a delicious fragrance, like the odor of incense."[75] Since martyrdom is the act of offering one's life as a sacrifice to God, through her death the martyr enters into the eucharistic mystery and bears witness to the depth of her faith in God. "We can, as it were, become bread, to the extent that the mystery of Christ is communicated through our life and our suffering, and to the extent that his love makes us an offering to God and to our fellow men."[76]

But liturgy as *res publica* does not stop with martyrdom strictly speaking. Each Christian ought to present herself, her life, as a living sacrifice to God; each Christian ought to become Eucharist. This and this alone is spiritual worship, worship characterized by *logos*. The Eucharist makes the church and demands *caritas*. It is the sacramental means by which Christ gathers his ecclesial body. It builds Christians into a people, a communion, a body. "A Christian life that did not involve being drawn into the pascha of the Lord, that was not itself becoming a Eucharist, would remain locked in the moralism of our activity and would thus again fail to live up to the new liturgy that has been founded by the cross."[77] This means that a Christian community that truly worships, which lives λογική λατρεία will bear witness to the presence of God in the world, will be an efficacious sign of grace active in the lives of the Christians therein.

Accordingly, for Ratzinger, "a principal need is for a reconstruction of the existential context of the Catechumenate . . . the common experience of the Spirit that can thus become also a foundation of realistic reflection."[78] In other words, those being evangelized ought to be able to experience the *communio* of the church, and by being inserted into this horizontal *communio*, they ought to be able to perceive the church's communion with the Father through the Son and in the Spirit.

Creative minorities,[79] communities in which this communion can be experienced, are existential prerequisites for the church's ability to answer the challenges of evangelizing the modern world. For Ratzinger though, true reform is not the result of making but of wonder; true reform requires

---

75. Ratzinger, *Jesus of Nazareth: Part Two*, 239.
76. Ratzinger, *Jesus of Nazareth: Part Two*, 240.
77. Ratzinger, *Pilgrim Fellowship of Faith*, 120.
78. Ratzinger, *Principles*, 26.
79. Ratzinger and Pera, *Without Roots*, 51–81, 107–136.

personal conversion and grows out of faith, which is always ecclesial. This does not mean that Ratzinger's vision of "creative minorities" reflects some perfected Donatist church. Rather, it reflects his conviction that true penitence bears witness. In light of the recent abuse scandals and loss of Christian credibility, it is vital to remember that the communion of the church is precisely the communion of those in need of the divine physician. Thus, while the eucharistic communities necessary for evangelization do require an ethos of love, for Ratzinger, they also will be always threatened by sin. The church can bear credible witness only by being a communion of penitents. Ratzinger explains, "Forgiveness, together with its realization in me by way of penance and discipleship, is first of all the wholly personal center of all renewal. But because forgiveness touches the very core of the person, it gathers people together and is also the center of the renewal of the community."[80] Thus, liturgical communities that bear witness to the presence of God will do so not only through their holiness, but also by embodying the theology of the cross. The more the church is rooted as a community forgiven in the Lord, the more will Christian lives become worship according to the *logos*, capable of bearing witness to the hope, love, and joy, that comes with faith and forgiveness.

This bearing witness and being a space where the presence of Christ can be experienced is essential to the success of the New Evangelization. Because today,

> only with great difficulty can the faith touch the hearts of people by means of simple or moral speeches, and even less by a general appeal to Christian values. The courageous and integral appeal to principles is essential and indispensable; yet simply proclaiming the message does not penetrate to the depths of people's hearts, it does not touch their freedom, it does not change their lives. What attracts is, above all, the encounter with believing persons who, through their faith, draw others to the grace of Christ by bearing witness to him.[81]

Thus, the classic means of evangelizing remain necessary, he says, but insufficient in themselves. People need to encounter the Lord. Being a Christian is not "the result of an ethical choice or a lofty idea, but the encounter with an event, a person, which gives life a new horizon and a decisive direction."[82] To be truly creative minorities, Christian communities must become places where Christianity takes on its nature as encounter, where λογική λατρεία

---

80. Ratzinger, *Called to Communion*, 153.
81. Benedict XVI, "Address to Bishops of Portugal."
82. Benedict XVI, *Deus caritas est*, 1.

overflows into our lives, such that our communion becomes the sacrament of an encounter with the Lord.

It is the sacramental character of Ratzinger's eucharistic ecclesiology that communicates and preserves the church's properly christological and theological character, while simultaneously pointing toward her mission. Just as Ratzinger's ecclesiology is built up from his trinitarian theology, so his understanding of the mission of the church depends on his Christology. Put another way, for Ratzinger, the church is missionary because of the sacramental relation to Christ, which gives the church the responsibility of participating in Jesus's mission of drawing all people to himself. The church derives her mission entirely from that of Christ:

> The Church has no nature and no significance of her own besides Christ; instead, she must find her meaning in being the instrument of Christ's movement. If this is so, then on this basis her course and her mission are charted clearly enough. The Church has no option of becoming self-enclosed in her contentment about what she has already achieved. She is herself the gesture of self-opening and hence must continually place herself at the service of this gesture and must carry it out historically. But this gesture is by no means an end in itself; its real goal is to introduce [souls] into that *sacrum commercium*, into that holy exchange which began when God became man.[83]

The church sacramentally becomes the body of Christ so that she can be an efficacious sign of Jesus's mission to the world. She exists to adore the Father and "to hand on the message about divine love."[84]

Thus, for Ratzinger the mission of the church is essentially the call to evangelize, to spread the good news of the reign of God and the salvation that comes with it as offered by Jesus. This evangelization is not merely a passing on of a message, of information. Only love can communicate love. Thus, Jesus's high priestly prayer in John:

> I pray not only for them, but also *for those who will believe in me through their word*, so that they may all be one, as you, Father, are in me and I in you, that they also may be in us, *that the world may believe that you sent me*. And I have given them the glory you gave me, so that they may be one, as we are one, I in them and you in me, that they may be brought to perfection as one, *that the world may know that you sent me, and that you loved them even as you loved me*. (John 17:20–23, emphasis mine)

83. Ratzinger, *Das neue Volk Gottes*, 110, in Heim, *Joseph Ratzinger*, 297.
84. Ratzinger, *Das neue Volk Gottes*, 111, in Heim, *Joseph Ratzinger*, 298.

The lived communion of believers is a prerequisite for the successful handing on of God's love to the world. In this way, Ratzinger can remark, "the Christian liturgy . . . in a certain sense is more realistically celebrated in everyday life than in the ritual execution of it."[85] He explains that this was a common understanding of the church fathers, for whom "the everyday practice of charity is an essential part of the eucharistic event, and furthermore only in this way is the status of Christians as the Body of Christ fully achieved—a status that has in the eucharistic celebration its definitive and therefore also its demanding center."[86] If a community truly believes it has found the pearl of great price, they will worship and live accordingly. Thus, their lives will be lived in a manner that is convincing to others. In a society flooded with relativism, materialism, and individualism, the church cannot settle for good ad campaigns and popular tweets but must be a concrete place and a communal, indeed eucharistic, people whose very lives are transparent to God.

Thus, an evangelical and credible common experience of the Spirit can result only from an ethos of love and a missionary "openness to the world." Ratzinger explains this conciliar phrase by highlighting its missionary rootedness:

> One could say that the Council marks the transition from a conservationist to a missionary attitude, and the conciliar alternative to "conservative" is not "progressive," but rather "missionary." In this antithesis is found basically the precise meaning of what the conciliar "opening-up to the world" means and what it does not mean. It does not provide the Christian with greater comfort by setting him free to conform to the world in a fashionable mass culture—the Council could never do that, because as a Christian event it was bound to the nonconformism of the Bible: "Do not be conformed to this world" (Rom 12:2).[87]

A loving openness to the world that is simultaneously an act of nonconformism is necessarily an act of making oneself vulnerable. The mission of the church to share God's message of love to the world thus also bears within itself the theology of the cross intertwined with the theology of the Eucharist. Living out of true worship calls the church to be the true body of the Lord opening herself up and laying herself down on the altar of the world. True worship, λογική λατρεία, is found in the Eucharist where the High Priest offers his body "unblemished to God" (Heb 9:14). Further, it is

---

85. Ratzinger, *Das neue Volk Gottes*, 22, in Heim, *Joseph Ratzinger*, 246.
86. Ratzinger, *Das neue Volk Gottes*, 22, in Heim, *Joseph Ratzinger*, 246.
87. Ratzinger, *Das neue Volk Gottes*, 128, in Heim, *Joseph Ratzinger*, 196.

accomplished where the Eucharist makes the church, and the church allows herself to become His "flesh for the life of the world," when her members "offer [their] bodies as a living sacrifice, holy and pleasing to God, [their] spiritual worship," λογική λατρεία (Rom 12:1).

To recap and conclude part 2, recall that for Ratzinger the mission of the church is grounded in his communion ecclesiology and is a sacramental participation in the mission of the Son. By means of the Eucharist, the Lord aims to heal the individualistic and egoistic wounds of sin by restoring communion among men and communion between man and God. This restoration of communion occurs in part through a participation in the new worship instituted by Christ, through his own eucharistic offering. In that the Eucharist makes the church it also calls upon members of the church to "be what they see," to concretely embody a eucharistic ethos in their lives. In doing so, the existential context of ecclesial communion becomes transparent to God and to the joy that comes with his reign. This life of concrete communion once again can become credible. Where this communion is rejected by a sinful world, indeed in the midst of whatever persecutions may come, the grace of the Eucharist and the habit of a eucharistic ethos will strengthen Christians to maintain their credible witness to love that is stronger than death. In this way, just as Christ offered his body for the church, so the church, as the body of Christ, offers herself for the life of the world.

Part 3

In Part 3 I outline three critiques of Ratzinger's ecclesiology from the trinitarian perspective, the ecclesiological perspective, and the missiological perspective respectively. Chapter 7 offers a qualified response to those critiques, recognizing the manner and degree to which they contain truth, but also correcting their misperceptions and further filling out the picture of Ratzinger's ecclesiology of communion and communion missiology. Chapter 8 summarizes what has been said and attempts to articulate a concrete example of Ratzinger's ideas by means of an examination of the Focolare movement and the thoughts of its founder Chiara Lubich. The Focolare will serve as an example of Ratzinger's notion of creative minorities and offer evidence of the manner in which such communities might advance a fitting model for successfully evangelizing men and women in our time.

6

Questions and Critiques

HAVING SET FORTH THE foundations and logic of Ratzinger's theology of the church and mission, I must address whether his theology and its ecclesiological answers to the problems of the modern age are consistent and adequate to the task at hand.

Over the course of his career, scholars have critiqued Ratzinger's ecclesiology for its "abstract" nature and its "latent idealism," with a corresponding view that his theology fails to address the contextual nature of the church. Of course, it is precisely the situation of the church in its predicament vis-à-vis the world that Ratzinger's theology must address. If he does not adequately ground his understanding of the church in sound theology, then his ecclesiology may ultimately lead the church astray. At the same time, if his ecclesiology is too abstracted, failing to address the problems the church actually faces, then his solutions will prove unhelpful at best. Since it has been argued that his ecclesiology is insufficiently incarnational and lacks a properly sociological character, these questions cannot be ignored.

This chapter seeks to listen with an attentive ear to some of this criticism and thereby to better elucidate the strengths and weaknesses of Ratzinger's work. Recall that in Ratzinger's view the church is "at the same time a mystery of faith and a sign of faith, mysterious life and the visible phenomenal form of this life,"[1] which is one way of pointing toward the sacramentality of the church. Ratzinger's identification of Christ with the church is a vital part of his response to the contemporary theological attempts perceived to reduce the church to functional concerns, to reduce ecclesiology to sociology.[2]

Ratzinger's arguments against sociological reductionism—by means of emphasizing the church's sacramental and thus pneumatological character—and his insistence that the church can only be received from above

---

1. Ratzinger, *Das neue Volk Gottes*, 11, in Heim, *Joseph Ratzinger*, 236.
2. See Ratzinger and Messori, *Ratzinger Report*, 46.

have exposed him to sharp criticisms from various theologians. Miroslav Volf[3] and Gerard Mannion classify his ecclesiology as "top-down," "hierarchical," and universalist. They claim he fails to account for the empirical reality of the church as experienced at the community level.[4] Joseph Komonchak argues that Ratzinger's sacramental view of the church prioritizes the universal church and thereby reduces the human dimensions of the church to passivity. Mary Ehle maintains that Ratzinger's "spiritual mission" fails to convey concrete good news to contemporary men and women in the midst of their profound trials and tribulations.[5] I briefly consider the arguments of Volf, Komonchak, and Ehle in order to explore the subtleties of Ratzinger's thought with greater clarity and precision. The following chapter will respond to these critiques by emphasizing Ratzinger's existential ecclesiality, the habit of life in the church that is prior to ecclesiological reflection.

6.1 Volf's Critique: The Ecclesiological Implications of Person as Relation

6.1.1 Volf's Trinitarian Approach

Miroslav Volf, the well-known Free Church theologian, advances his arguments on the theological level in his impressive book, *After Our Likeness*, in which he engages with Ratzinger and Orthodox theologian John Zizioulas in order to contemplate the church in light of trinitarian theology. Volf's misgivings about Ratzinger's ecclesiology start with the latter's allegedly monistic ecclesiology.[6]

As an adherent to the Free Church tradition, Volf is predisposed to push back against the "universalistic Catholic ecclesiology" and the hierarchical structure of the church.[7] However he bases his ecclesiological argument on properly theological grounds with reference to trinitarian theology. He believes that "the thesis that ecclesial communion should correspond to trinitarian communion enjoys the status of an almost self-evident proposition."[8] What is at issue is the manner in which trinitarian communion is made visible in the life of the church. However, he perceives the correspondences and limits of the analogy between the Trinity and

---

3. Volf, *After Our Likeness*, 38.
4. Mannion, *Ecclesiology and Postmodernity*, 58–59.
5. Ehle, "Trinitarian Ecclesiology of Communion."
6. Volf, *After Our Likeness*, 71.
7. Volf, *After Our Likeness*, 47.
8. Volf, *After Our Likeness*, 191.

the church have not been accorded sufficient attention. Mistakes are often made: "The result is that reconstructions of these correspondences often say nothing more than the platitude that unity cannot exist without multiplicity nor multiplicity without unity, or they demand of human beings in the church the (allegedly) completely selfless love of God."[9] Volf references Ratzinger in describing the latter mistake as depicting an image of ecclesial communion "so divine that no one can live it."[10]

Volf rightly recognizes that "*all* the crucial elements in [Ratzinger's] ecclesiology and entire theology are rooted in the doctrine of the Trinity."[11] Therefore, he seeks the foundations of Ratzinger's alleged ecclesial monism in his trinitarian theology. For his own part, Volf explains that the analogy between the triune God and the church requires escaping the "dichotomy between universalization and pluralization," and so "unity and multiplicity must enjoy a complementary relationship" in the drama of the church in history.[12] All the same, he cautions:

> Trinitarian models, however, are not simply projections of ideal social models. Insofar as trinitarian models do in fact speak of the triune God who is to be distinguished from human beings, models of the triune God and of the church must also be distinguished. "Person" and "communion" in ecclesiology cannot be identical with "person" and "communion" in the doctrine of the Trinity; they can only be understood as *analogous* to them.[13]

The end of the above refers to the point at which Volf identifies the origin of Ratzinger's trinitarian and ecclesiological error. Volf perceives that in Ratzinger's theology Christ is no mere "ontological anomaly"[14] but "is the model for how the human personality is to be understood."[15] Thus, the human person, like the divine person, *is* pure relation.[16] Volf identifies two problems with this approach—he argues it leads to the dominance of the one divine substance[17] and thus to hierarchical monism in the church and

---

9. Volf, *After Our Likeness*, 191.
10. Volf, *After Our Likeness*, 191.
11. Volf, *After Our Likeness*, 67.
12. Volf, *After Our Likeness*, 193.
13. Volf, *After Our Likeness*, 199.
14. Volf, *After Our Likeness*, 68.
15. Volf, *After Our Likeness*, 68. Volf explains that for Ratzinger, with regard to method and substance, "the trinitarian concept of person is the key to the anthropological and ecclesial concept of person" (Volf, *After Our Likeness*, 68n210).
16. Volf, *After Our Likeness*, 68.
17. Volf, *After Our Likeness*, 204–5. Note that for Volf, contra the dominant strands

also thinks it leaves Jesus's humanity and the humanity of persons in the church short-changed, demanding divine love of them.

6.1.2 Volf's Personal Problem

Volf explains that the concept of person as pure relation demands that trinitarian unity be located not in "a differentiated unity of persons standing in these relations, but rather [in] a unity in which the Father, Son, and Holy Spirit 'coincide' and in this way are '*pure* unity.'"[18] For this reason and in agreement with the dominant approach of Western trinitarian thought, Volf claims that "Ratzinger locates the unity of the triune God not at the level of persons, but . . . at the level of substance."[19] Therefore, the divine substance has a priority over the persons. Ecclesiologically speaking, this raises problems for Volf who argues that Ratzinger's "sketchy" trinitarian theology moves him "*to conceive ecclesial structures by way of the one substance of God. The one, externally acting divine substance corresponds to the one church that, together with Christ, constitutes one subject and in that way becomes capable of action. A monistic structure* for the church emerges from this."[20] For Volf this fails to do justice to the rootedness of multiplicity within the triune God by making the relations ultimately "so transparent that it is difficult to distinguish them from the one, sustaining, divine substance."[21] Therefore, put another way:

> Because the persons are "pure relations," God can act externally only as the one undifferentiated divine being, that is, as *one* "person." This one divine nature acting externally corresponds to the one church that together with Christ constitutes one subject and thus itself becomes capable of action. Hence for both the Trinity and for the church, the "one" is structurally decisive: the one divine nature, the one Christ, the one Pope, and the one Bishop.[22]

---

of the trinitarian theology in the tradition, the perichoresis and co-equality of the divine persons implies and demands no hierarchy within the Godhead, no monarchy of the Father. As one might expect, this corresponds to his free-church ecclesiology.

18. Volf, *After Our Likeness*, 70, referencing Ratzinger, *Introduction to Christianity*, 135.

19. Volf, *After Our Likeness*, 70.

20. Volf, *After Our Likeness*, 71.

21. Volf, *After Our Likeness*, 204.

22. Volf, *After Our Likeness*, 214.

Not only does this view offend Volf's trinitarian and ecclesial sensibilities as a Free Church theologian, but he argues that since human persons are not in fact divine persons, nor even perfected eschatological persons, Ratzinger's ecclesiology "is unable to do justice structurally to the abuse of power because persons understood in this way are also embedded in a monistic hierarchical structure of the relations, the understanding of person as pure relation can easily degenerate into repressive ideology."[23] In light of the sex abuse crisis and the failure of bishops to address it adequately, this critique must be taken seriously.

6.1.3 Volf on Ratzinger's Christological Anthropology

The second major problem Volf identifies with Ratzinger's theology involves Ratzinger's "thesis that Christ does not represent an ontological exception,"[24] which means the divine definition of person as relation can be applied to human persons. This ultimately places divine demands on the pilgrim wayfarers who make up the church because it implies that just as the Son *is* his relation to the Father, so also human persons. But, unlike divine persons who simply *are* pure relationality, the concept of relation in human persons, precisely in their pilgrim existence, cannot be applied "purely" or "totally." Ratzinger's goal "is to integrate human beings into the trinitarian life of God."[25] While Volf admits that it is true that ecclesial persons are made for communion with God, he maintains that although there is a correspondence between ecclesial persons and divine persons, "a distinction does remain between the two,"[26] a distinction that he claims Ratzinger fails to clarify sufficiently. In Volf's reading of Ratzinger, historical human persons can only be described as more or less "standing in relation" to God, until they eschatologically receive and achieve the fullness of human existence in "pure relation" to God. However, this either requires that the difference between protological human personhood and divine personhood is merely quantitative—in essence denying the transcendence of God—or results in an untenable and "radical discontinuity . . . between protological and eschatological anthropology."[27] Put another way, the method by which Ratzinger hopes "to integrate human beings into the trinitarian life of God,"[28] does

23. Volf, *After Our Likeness*, 214.
24. Volf, *After Our Likeness*, 70.
25. Volf, *After Our Likeness*, 70.
26. Volf, *After Our Likeness*, 206.
27. Volf, *After Our Likeness*, 68, where he develops the above argument in detail.
28. Volf, *After Our Likeness*, 70.

violence to either an authentically human anthropology or an adequately transcendent theology. Indeed, for Volf, Ratzinger's notion of personhood even fails to sufficiently account for the humanity of Christ: "Given the inner logic of Ratzinger's thinking, one must say that if anything comes up short, it is not the divinity of Christ . . . but rather his humanity and the humanity of human beings themselves."[29] Here Volf anticipates something akin to Komonchak's critique, which I will explore below: in Ratzinger's theology the emphasis on protecting the divine and sacramental character of Christ and the church respectively ultimately diminishes the humanity of both Christ and the church.

Thus, Volf argues that Ratzinger's articulation of the correspondence between his trinitarian theology and his ecclesiology leads to a hierarchical and monistic view of the church. Volf perceives that this view could devolve easily into a repressive ideology, and he understands Ratzinger's theology to demand that men and women can only be fully themselves by receiving their divinization from above in such a way that they are abstracted from their own historical, cultural, and sociological *Sitz im Leben*.

6.2 Komonchak's Critique

6.2.1 Komonchak's Ecclesiological Method

Joseph Komonchak, a well-respected specialist in the history and theology of Vatican II, was heavily influenced by Bernard Lonergan,[30] among others.[31] His *Foundations in Ecclesiology*[32] bears witness to this influence, attending to methodological issues in ecclesiology with reference to sociology and concrete human communities. Komonchak's critique of Ratzinger flows from his methodological considerations.[33] Thus, I briefly examine some of

---

29. Volf, *After Our Likeness*, 70.

30. Komonchak studied under Bernard Lonergan at the Gregorian University in Rome.

31. Komonchak wrote his dissertation on John Henry Newman's discovery of the visible church, received much of his theological formation via engagement with neo-scholastic manuals, and was heavily influenced by the ecclesiology of the Second Vatican Council, to name just a few of his influences.

32. Komonchak, *Foundations*.

33. For Komonchak, method in ecclesiology seems to be always present in the background of his thought. Many of his essays attend to methodological issues. The following are some of his most important engagements with method in ecclesiology: *Foundations*; *Who Are the Church?*; "Ministry and the Local Church"; "Towards a Theology of the Local Church"; "The Church: God's Gift and Our Task"; and "The Epistemology of Reception."

Komonchak's thoughts on method in ecclesiology in order to set his criticism of Ratzinger's ecclesiology into context.

Method in theology refers to the means by which a theologian gathers information in arriving at an interpretation. Roger Haight puts it this way:

> Method involves the premises and presuppositions of a theologian's position. Method concerns the starting point and the elementary data the theologian appeals to in taking a position. Method includes the logic, the kind of argument and its coherence, through which the theologian understands experience. In other words, a theologian's method generates the position he or she takes, so that beneath every position taken lies the method that generated the position.[34]

One's theological method does not predetermine one's position on a given subject, but it is the means by which one arrives at that position.

For Komonchak method in ecclesiology is in part a means of laying the groundwork for his theology of the local church which calls for theological considerations of the church to start methodologically at the local level with concrete human communities rather than with the idea of the universal church. For Komonchak this interest in the local church is not merely academic or theoretical but reflects the priority of experience in local churches. He explains: "Over several years I became convinced that one of the chief challenges was to bridge the gap between the lofty theological language which the Council restored to the center of ecclesiology and the concrete reality of the Church as realized in communities of believers."[35] One might say that for Komonchak, method in ecclesiology is an attempt to articulate the manner in which the church bears "no weak analogy"[36] to the hypostatic union. Komonchak wants to explore "how the quite human could be the locus of the quite transcendent."[37] He perceives this to be a particularly important task because he understands more recent ecclesiologies to have failed sufficiently to account for the human and sociological aspects of the church as "classical ecclesiology" once did: "At its origins, classical ecclesiology was not hesitant in applying what passed for social theory

---

34. Haight, "Critical Witness," 187, in Madar, "Contribution of Joseph A. Komonchak," 106.

35. Komonchak, *Foundations*, vii.

36. "For this reason, by no weak analogy, it is compared to the mystery of the incarnate Word. As the assumed nature inseparably united to Him, serves the divine Word as a living organ of salvation, so, in a similar way, does the visible social structure of the Church serve the Spirit of Christ, who vivifies it, in the building up of the body" (LG 8).

37. Komonchak, *Foundations*, viii.

to the Church, whether in the borrowing from Aristotle's political theory in the Middle Ages or in the imitation of modern juridic thought in the last two centuries."[38] Komonchak does not recognize similar methodologies in the ecclesiology of many post-Vatican II scholars, including Joseph Ratzinger. As far as Komonchak is concerned, Ratzinger and others like him emphasize the divine or transcendent dimensions of the church and fail to address sufficiently the existential realities of concrete communities precisely because they do not address the sociological aspects of ecclesiology.

Komonchak thinks that anyone attempting to understand how the church is a human community and the people of God must first address in what sense the church is a community. Following Lonergan's analysis of religious conversion Komonchak focuses on the communal aspects thereof.

> Conversion is existential, intensely personal, utterly intimate. But it is not so private as to be solitary. It can happen to many, and they can form a community to sustain one another in their self-transformation and to help one another in working out the implications for filling the promise of their new life.[39]

With this in mind, Komonchak explains, "the Church is an achievement in the world mediated and constituted by meaning and value. Its substance is the inner gift of God's love, embodied and interpreted by Christ's message."[40] The church and conversion in it is concrete, personal, and communal. It is not ideal or esoteric. Thus, the substance of the church for Komonchak is the common experience of God's love and the meaning given it by the community.[41] This demands the active reception and appropriation of that experience, which, in Komonchak's method, does not simply allow a given community of believers to make themselves "church." In his view, the church is a community constituted by meaning. Thus, he maintains the centrality of doctrines for the church: "doctrines are not just doctrines. They are constitutive both of the individual Christian and of the Christian community."[42] So in a sense, the church constitutes itself by communicating the Christian message by means of catechesis and evangelization, by passing on doctrines geographically and historically, across space and time, which is to say socially. In today's global and complex, ideological and technocratic society, characterized in part by personal alienation, the church has

---

38. Komonchak, "Local Church," 4–5, in Madar, "Contribution of Joseph A. Komonchak," 218.
39. Lonergan, *Method*, 130–31, in Komonchak, *Foundations*, 38.
40. Komonchak, *Foundations*, 39.
41. Komonchak, *Foundations*, 39.
42. Lonergan, *Method*, 319, in Komonchak, *Foundations*, 41.

the responsibility to be a redemptive community in human society.[43] Again quoting Lonergan, Komonchak explains:

> The church is a redemptive process. The Christian message . . . tells not only of God's love but also of man's sin. Sin is alienation from man's authentic being . . . and sin justifies itself by ideology. As alienation and ideology are destructive of community, so the self-sacrificing love that is Christian charity reconciles alienated man to his true being, and undoes the mischief initiated by alienation and consolidated by ideology.[44]

For the church to fulfill its mission, its redemptive purpose, the church must "recognize that theology is not the full science of man, that theology illuminates only certain aspects of human reality, that the church can become a fully conscious process of self-constitution only when theology unites itself with all other relevant branches of human studies."[45] In other words for the church to fulfill its mission it must be a community that attends to sociology and other relevant disciplines.

6.2.2 Komonchak: Local Church and Church Catholic

Since Komonchak's methodological concerns emphasize the local church, which is precisely the context in which he thinks the sociology of concrete communities should be studied, I now examine an important essay of his, "The Local Church and the Church Catholic: The Contemporary Theological Problematic," which is relevant to his critique of Ratzinger.

Komonchak explores the manner in which the New Testament and Christians thereafter use the term "church" both to refer particularly to local Christian communities and more generally to the universal church, which is the one body of Christ. Frequently the methodology of such studies exhibits a bias, which tends to emphasize the universal and neglect the local.[46]

There is some general agreement that "Word, Sprit, Eucharist, apostolic ministry" can be considered "generative principles" of the church.

> Where all of these principles generate a community, there is the Church, not simply a "part" of the Church but the full reality of the People of God, the Body of Christ, and the Temple of the Spirit. For this very reason, the whole Church cannot be said

---

43. Komonchak, *Foundations*, 41–42.
44. Lonergan, *Method*, 364, in Komonchak, *Foundations*, 42.
45. Lonergan, *Method*, 364, in Komonchak, *Foundations*, 42.
46. Komonchak, "Local Church," 419.

to result from the addition or sum of all the local churches. The generative principles . . . generate a local church as the catholic Church, the communion constitutive of any local church generating also the other local Churches and the communion among them that is the one catholic Church.[47]

Of course, any further examination requires determining in which communities the church is realized.[48] A straightforward reading of the generative principles might lead one to conclude that the church is realized in each parish, although the diocese is normally considered the smallest community which exhibits all of the principles. Can ecclesial communities smaller than a diocese be called a church? If not, why not? What of ecclesial communities larger than a diocese? Komonchak explains: "This issue is settled in advance if the presence of the fullness of apostolic ministry is considered the necessary and sufficient defining characteristic of the Church; it is addressed differently, however, if the values of locality or particularity may be included among the constitutive elements of a Church."[49] Therefore, how one defines "church" or where one recognizes it to be realized is in part informed by the methodological decision one makes with regard to the constitutive principles.

Some theologians have posited the priority of the universal church over local churches,[50] fewer have asserted the priority of the local church over the universal church,[51] and still others prefer to speak of them as si-

---

47. Komonchak, "Local Church," 420–21.
48. Komonchak, "Local Church," 422.
49. Komonchak, "Local Church," 426.

50. As one might expect different authors mean different things by "priority" and offer various reasons to support their argument. Komonchak lists the following variations of prioritizing the universal over the local: "It means . . . that the local church depends on the universal Church, and that the universal Church has pre-eminence and absolute ontological priority (Mondin); that is the Church-from-above, the mystery of salvation, it exists in all the local churches (Boff); that Christ founded only the universal Church and not the particular churches (Bertrams, C. Colombo, Bandera, d'Ors); that the universal Church is the exemplary, efficient, and final cause of the local church (Bertrams); that only the universal Church can be the universal sacrament of salvation (Bertrams, Bandera) and is assured of being indefectible and infallible (C. Columbo, Bandera), and holy (C. Colombo); that the universal Church precedes the local church's temporally (Ratzinger)" (Komonchak, "Local Church," 428–29).

51. Komonchak references only Bruno Forte and Severino Dianich. Forte argues that every true ecclesial act has its origin in a local church, and Dianich claims that "the necessarily particular event of the communication and reception of the faith is the 'first principle' of the Church from which, methodologically, all other elements are derived as the developments of its universal virtualities" (Komonchak, "Local Church," 429).

multaneous.[52] After all, is not the universal church present and active both in the missionary activities of the church in Bangkok and in the church in Bogota? While some may argue that this only supports the priority of the universal church, since no individual local church can be claimed to be "holy, catholic, indefectible," etc., is it not also the case that the universal church, which is holy, catholic, and indefectible, can only concretely exist and be located in and out of the local churches? For Komonchak, "that is why a discussion of the relation between the local church and the universal Church . . . has to include a treatment of the ecclesiological significance of locality or particularity."[53]

The fundamental issue is "whether the local, socially, culturally, and historically specific elements can be constitutive characteristics of the local churches."[54] Giuseppe Colombo argues that geographical and cultural designations, those that pertain to the category of locality, are external and therefore theologically insignificant.[55] He explains, "No culture can make the Church; only the Word of God, the Eucharist, and the charisms can make the Church."[56] Ecclesial diversity arises from the varying interplay of these constitutive elements. The different cultures "have only the value of an introduction or of a pre-understanding."[57] The local, sociological, or human characteristics do not make a particular community of Christians a church in the proper sense. "It is somewhat like matter in relation to form, but in a conception of matter as continually predetermined and modified by the form."[58]

This conception of the sociological and human aspects of Christian communities as mere matter predetermined by the more properly theological constitutive elements certainly seems to negate the positive contributions of human freedom and creativity. The International Theological Commission offered a more nuanced version:

52. Komonchak himself probably falls into this camp, which argues that "the Church which first emerges at Pentecost is at once local and catholic" (Komonchak, "Local Church," 431–32). Others referenced in support of this view include Bouyer, de Lubac, Legrand, and Tillard.

53. Komonchak, "Local Church," 434.

54. Komonchak, "Local Church," 436.

55. Colombo, "La teologia della chiesa locale," 17–38, esp. 32–38. Referenced and quoted here and in the following paragraph in Komonchak, "Local Church," 436–37.

56. Komochak, "Local Church," 437, quoting Colombo, "La teologica della chiesa locale," 32–38.

57. Komonchak, "Local Church," 437, quoting Colombo, "La teologica della chiesa locale," 32–38.

58. Komonchak, "Local Church," 437, quoting Colombo, "La teologica della chiesa locale," 32–38.

The new people of God is not, then, characterized by a way of existence or a mission which substitute for an existence and for human projects already present. The memory and hope of Jesus Christ must rather convert or transform from within the way of existence and the human projects already being lived in a group of people. One might say that the memory and hope of Jesus Christ by which the new people of God lives are like the "formal" element (in the scholastic sense of the term) which must structure the concrete existence of the people. The latter, which is like the "matter" (again in the scholastic sense), free and responsible, of course, receives one or another of a variety of determinations in order to constitute a way of life "according to the Spirit." These ways of life do not exist *a priori* and cannot be determined in advance; they display a great diversity and are thus always unforeseeable even if they can be related to the constant action of the one Holy Spirit. On the other hand, what these different ways of life have in common and as a constant is that they express the demands and joys of the Gospel of Christ "in the ordinary conditions of family and social life in which human existence is interwoven."[59]

Here Komonchak sees an improvement, perceiving a recognition of "the freedom and responsibility of the 'material element'" as evidence of a perspective that allows a particular church to be generated by a "co-mediation of culture and gospel."[60] Komonchak is not trying to argue that a given community of Christians in a particular place can make itself a church. He admits, "It is the gospel and not the cultural particularities which primarily generate a Church."[61] However, in order to clarify the freedom and charisms of the local human culture, he continues, "A local church arises out of the encounter between the gospel and a particular culture, a set of specific social and historical experiences, and this encounter, as it differs from other encounters of gospel and culture, must also generate a constitutively different local church."[62]

Komonchak builds on this by following the arguments of Severino Dianich,[63] who claims that the constitutive principles of a particular church can be located with reference to its mission. Each particular church must attempt to instantiate or embody the one mission of the one church in its

59. ITC, "Select Themes of Ecclesiology" III.4, in Komonchak, "Local Church," 438.
60. Komonchak, "Local Church," 438.
61. Komonchak, "Local Church," 439.
62. Komonchak, "Local Church," 439.
63. See Dianich, *Chiesa in missione*, 65, 172–73; *De caritate ecclesiae*, 27–107.

historical, geographical, political, and cultural circumstances. Thus, "A Church confronting the challenge of the world religions will have a different self-awareness from one facing the challenges of post-colonialism, or poverty, or of post-Christian secularization."[64] These subjectively human and sociological differences are precisely the principles that constitute a given local church as this church and not that one. Further, they evince the indispensable role of human freedom, creativity, and subjectivity in receiving the Gospel in a given community and subsequently living it in these particular circumstances. In Komonchak's own words:

> The objective principles of the Church's realization do not constitute the Church except insofar as they are received and appropriated in the acts of faith, hope, and love of the human members of the Church. Under the Word and by the power of the Spirit men and women are also the subjects of the Church's self-realization. Thus the formal principle of the Church's genesis includes not only the gifts of God but also the freedom of men and women with which they receive them.[65]

Komonchak reiterates that this is not an option in favor of the priority of the local churches over the universal church, but it demands that an adequate ecclesiology consider "the co-constituting freedom of the human subjects of the Church's realization."[66] Moreover, it is from this perspective that Komonchak criticizes Ratzinger's ecclesiology.

6.2.3 Ratzinger's Neglect of the Humanity of the Church

In a contribution to the *Festschrift* in honor of Hervé Legrand, Komonchak traces Ratzinger's persistent arguments in favor of the priority of the universal church over local churches, arguments which began, according to Komonchak in 1983,[67] when Ratzinger's concerns were primarily ecumenical.[68] Just two years later, prior to the extraordinary Synod of 1985, Ratzinger emphasized the historical priority of the universal church:

---

64. Komonchak, "Local Church," 444.
65. Komonchak, "Local Church," 447.
66. Komonchak, "Local Church," 447.
67. Komonchak, "A propos," 245–68. I will be quoting from the author's unpublished translation: "On the Priority of the Universal Church: Analysis and Questions."
68. Komonchak, "On the Priority," 1. Ratzinger argues, "There is a priority of scriptures as witness and a priority of the Church as the vital environment for such witness, but both are linked together in constantly alternating relationships, so that neither can be imagined without the other. This relative priority of the Church to Scripture

> If on the one hand it must be said that the Church is not a papal monarchy, on the other hand neither can it be considered a confederation of particular Churches whose unity results only as something secondary from the addition of individual Churches, so that the ministry of unity would consist only in moderating the agreement of the Churches. As in a body the unity of the organism precedes and sustains the individual organs, since the organs would not exist if the body did not, so also the unity of the catholic Church precedes the plurality of particular Churches which are born from this unity and receive their ecclesial character from it.[69]

In multiple places, Ratzinger refers to the Lukan Pentecost narrative as evidence of the historical and ontological priority of the universal church.[70]

Komonchak recognizes Ratzingerian arguments being made in official documents of the Congregation for the Doctrine of the Faith, including most prominently *Communionis Notio*,[71] the 1994 paperback edition of which features an introduction by Ratzinger. Here Ratzinger claims that the document intended to counter "an anti-hierarchical idea of a Church that would be rather a federation of local churches that in every sense precede the universal Church."[72] Thus, Ratzinger's theological position seems in part to be a response to perceived threats against the unity of the church in the form of arguments in favor of the priority of the local churches. In his concluding remarks Komonchak questions whether such threats even exist.[73]

Overall, Komonchak argues, "Ratzinger's writings display a disconcerting tendency to downplay the significance of or even to pass over completely the actions of the local Church,"[74] and therefore of the human persons in the local churches. He asks whether Ratzinger's ecclesiology "comes close

---

obviously presupposes also the existence of the Universal Church as a concrete and active reality, for only the whole Church can be the locus of Scripture in this sense. So the question of defining the relation between a particular Church and the universal Church has obviously already claimed amongst the fundamental problems" (Ratzinger, *Church, Ecumenism, and Politics*, 71). I have used the English translation Komonchak offers from the original German.

69. Ratzinger in Komonchak, "On the Priority," 2. Komonchak cites Ratzinger, "De Romano Pontifice deque Collegio Episcoporum," 3. Typescript in my possession.

70. See, for example, Ratzinger, *Called to Communion*, 44.

71. CDF, *Communionis notio*. Hereafter, CN.

72. Ratzinger in Komonchak, "On the Priority," 5. Komonchak translates from the Italian, Ratzinger, "Introduzione," 9.

73. Komonchak, "On the Priority," 11–12.

74. Komonchak, "On the Priority," 12.

to denying the theological consistency of the local Church, which seems to be reduced to a place where the universal Church alone is considered to be at work? Does not the question have to be asked: *where*, that is, *in whom*, is the universal Church at work? Who are the agents of this sacrament?"[75] For his part, Komonchak concludes that "in Ratzinger's efforts to explain 'what the universal Church is practically and how it works,' the local or particular Church nearly disappears from view, mentioned only to warn people not to make too much of it."[76]

According to Komonchak, ecclesiological conceptions like that of Ratzinger might be grouped with those of Giuseppe Colombo discussed above. In other words, they present the risk of oversimplifying "the nature of Christian experience" by presenting the local, human, and cultural elements of the church as unformed matter "that receives its determination by the 'form' of the distinctive elements generative of the Church."[77] For Komonchak and Donato Valentini, "this runs the danger of regarding the human element in the construction of the Church as merely passive and receptive and thus of 'interpreting the Word of God, the Eucharist, and the Spirit's charisms as realities which somehow pass over man's head.'"[78] Thus, for Komonchak the ecclesiological problem of Ratzinger's argument for the priority of the universal church can be traced to a problem in Ratzinger's anthropology, to a problem in his understanding of the relation between grace, sin, and human freedom.

If Komonchak is right, if Ratzinger's ecclesiology fails to account for the freedom and responsibility of human subjectivity in the church, how can it be an appropriate and effective answer to the crises of today? How can it point the way forward for the mission of the church and the practice of the New Evangelization?

Before exploring these questions in detail, let us turn to Mary Ehle's critique of Ratzinger's missiology.

---

75. Komonchak, "On the Priority," 12.
76. Komonchak, "On the Priority," 12.
77. Komochak, "Local Church," 437.
78. Komochak, "Local Church," 437, quoting Valentini, *Il nuovo popoli di Dio*, 56. Komonchak adds in the footnote: "This seems to me to be a crucial point: the freedom of the human subjects of the Church's self-realization, which cannot be separated from their concrete historical situation, is not related to the divine freedom as matter to form; in fact, it is an intrinsic element of the formal principle itself."

6.3 Ehle's Missiological Critique

6.3.1 Ehle's Perspective

In her dissertation, "A Trinitarian Ecclesiology of Communion and the Mission of the Church: Beyond the Debate between Joseph Cardinal Ratzinger and Leonardo Boff; the Contribution of Bernd Jochen Hilberath," Mary Ehle articulates an argument similar to that of Volf and Komonchak but does so also on the missiological level.

Ehle recognizes that just as Ratzinger's ecclesiology finds its ground in his trinitarian theology, so does his missiology. Just as he conceives of God as relational, so he also conceives of the church:

> Since, for him, the nature of the Church as a communion proceeds both christologically from the "masculine" act of ordering the ecclesial institution, which occurs in relation to the person of the Son, and "pneumatologically" from the feminine act of listening and receiving the Word, made possible through relation to the persons of the Holy Spirit, these relations form the nature of the Church.[79]

And so Ehle's treatment of Ratzinger's ecclesiology focuses on how Ratzinger understands the correspondence of "relation" as it applies to the Trinity and to the church and on how this understanding influences his "mission of communion."[80] Ehle identifies two aspects of Ratzinger's trinitarian starting point: first, Ratzinger associates the sending of the church with the sending of the Son into the world by the Father, and second, relying on the Johannine understanding of mission, Ratzinger holds together the mission of the Son with the mission of the church by means of the concept of relation. For Ehle, "In Ratzinger's missiology, this relation to Christ is not only the ground of the Church's mission, but also the end of the Church's mission. The Church is missionary because of its relation to Christ, and this relation to Christ brings with it a specific task for the Church in the world: to draw all men and women into relation with Christ . . . who leads to communion with the triune God."[81] This also means that for Ratzinger the church's mission is not primarily about social concerns or about transforming political systems, rather "the Church's missionary proclamation 'is the historical execution of divine salvation.'"[82] Ehle admits that the church

---

79. Ehle, "Trinitarian Ecclesiology of Communion," 98.
80. Ehle, "Trinitarian Ecclesiology of Communion," 98.
81. Ehle, "Trinitarian Ecclesiology of Communion," 99.
82. Ehle, "Trinitarian Ecclesiology of Communion," 101. Ehle quotes from Ratzinger, *Das neue Volk Gottes*, 387.

cannot serve as the sacrament of salvation and cannot realize its mission of communion if love of God and love of neighbor are not united. Indeed, she explains, "grounding the unity of the Church communion in the unity of the trinitarian communion centered in the Son, allows Ratzinger to articulate love of the neighbor as a constitutive element of the Church's mission such that one could not justifiably argue that he dismisses the importance of the Church's social mission."[83] However, she hastens to add that for Ratzinger reference to love of neighbor as constitutive of the church's mission is understood "primarily as a spiritual mission."[84] Thus, she quotes Ratzinger: "Real love of neighbor desires to give the deepest things human persons need: knowledge, truth, and love."[85] The church lives her mission of communion by being the communion of people who bear witness to the truth of the word in love.

Due to the focus of her work in comparing Ratzinger and Boff, Ehle spends some time on Ratzinger's understanding of the relation of the mission of the church to political involvement. Since for Ratzinger the unity and mission of the church come from and through communion with Christ, the church's sacramental reality takes precedence over ethical actions. Consequently, the Christian impulse to address suffering and injustice in the world ought first to be directed to the "spiritual mission, bringing men and women to love their neighbor through love of the triune God in the Church."[86] For Ratzinger, "to imagine that one can inaugurate a sorrow-free world through social reform and the abolition of government and the rule of law, and the demand that this be accomplished here and now represents an erroneous doctrine, a serious error concerning the nature of man."[87] This is because what man ultimately needs he can only receive from God through the church.

For Ehle, Ratzinger understands the church to be accomplishing her mission, "first, insofar as it remains in relation to its center—the Son—in the celebration of the Eucharist so as to be a sign of communion with God (love of God); and second, as it proclaims to others their need for relation

---

83. Ehle, "Trinitarian Ecclesiology of Communion," 105.

84. Ehle, "Trinitarian Ecclesiology of Communion," 105.

85. Ratzinger, *Nature and Mission*, 27, in Ehle, "Trinitarian Ecclesiology of Communion," 105.

86. Ehle, "Trinitarian Ecclesiology of Communion," 110.

87. Balthasar and Ratzinger, *Two Say Why*, 85, in Ehle, "Trinitarian Ecclesiology of Communion," 110. In the footnote to this reference Ehle explains, "The underlying fear of Ratzinger's criticism of Christians who believe that they can completely change the world is rooted in Marxism, specifically as appropriated in liberation movements."

with Christ (love of neighbor)."[88] Further, she recognizes the eucharistic origin of Ratzinger's missiology, which I have explored above, and which she describes as "the origin of the mission in the sense that this sacramental celebration enables and fosters belief in God and the relation of God that is the basis of ethics lived out in mission. In the eucharist the Church recognizes its mission to bring others into its communion with the objective of making all things one in Christ."[89] And this remains a pilgrim mission, on the way to the wedding feast of the lamb and awaiting the communion of all things in God and in the church.

6.3.2 Ehle on Ratzinger's Mission of Communion

Following her exposition of Ratzinger's ecclesiology and missiology Ehle critiques Ratzinger's "mission of communion" on three levels: first she examines the problems that the notion of person as relation creates for his understanding of mission; second, she explores the submission to Christ and passivity of the disciples which flows from the christocentric focus of his missiology; third, she criticizes the priority which he gives to the church's spiritual mission, desiring a more sociological and political missiology.[90]

First, for Ehle, if the human person like the divine person is pure relation, then "the mission of the human person is participation in the person of Christ—in his mission, which is his person. . . . The human person's relation with Christ and participation in the Trinitarian communion *is* the goal of mission."[91] Ehle interprets this to mean that Christians are both to imitate Christ and to bring others into that relation of imitation. In Ehle's view, Ratzinger reduces the Christian life to *imitatio Christi* in such a way that "the true freedom and diversity of human persons, Christians and those to whom they reach out in mission, are relegated to the background, if not dissolved into the relations that, in Ratzinger's communion missiology, are themselves the goal of mission."[92] A person's concerns, troubles, joys, and ideas do not *ultimately* matter in comparison with whether she has been brought into communion with God through Christ. In view of such communion, troubles, joys, and sufferings take on a new light.

---

88. Ehle, "Trinitarian Ecclesiology of Communion," 112–13.

89. Ehle, "Trinitarian Ecclesiology of Communion," 113. Admittedly, Ehle's description seems to miss part of the sacramental and martyrial thrust of Ratzinger's argument.

90. Ehle, "Trinitarian Ecclesiology of Communion," 128–35.

91. Ehle, "Trinitarian Ecclesiology of Communion," 129.

92. Ehle, "Trinitarian Ecclesiology of Communion," 129.

Second, like Komonchak and Volf, Ehle locates in Ratzinger a tendency to overlook the human element of the church. She argues that this is confirmed by Ratzinger's articulation of the relation between Christ and mission, which "accentuates the theme of obedience—the Son's submission to the Father and the Christian's imitation of this submission to Christ in the Church."[93] While she admits that Ratzinger's emphasis on "the primacy of receptivity" in the Son's relation to the Father "is not intended to condemn man to passivity,"[94] she insists that his christomonism and insistence on the priority of the universal church over the local churches fails to balance unity with multiplicity. Missiologically speaking, it implies something like passivity on the part of the local churches, since the particular aspects of their missions are subsumed into the one mission of the one church.[95]

Third, the universality of this "spiritual mission" is problematic for two reasons: "the consequence of Ratzinger's accentuation of the spiritual nature of the Church's mission, while probably not intended, may well be to render Christians passive in the face of sinful and oppressive persons and structures in the world."[96] For Ehle, the pervasive presence of suffering in the current historical situation demands a response which aims not merely at pointing people to heaven, but also works to resolve economic, political and social injustices.[97] In addition, the spiritual mission of the Christian is essentially to participate in the salvific mission of the Son to bring men and women into communion with God by bringing them into the communion of the church, but in the present pluralistic age of ecumenical and interreligious dialogue, does not such a view of mission amount to ecclesial triumphalism? "For if the focus of mission is on the Church itself, then how can the Church truly be for others in the world? Or said differently, to some extent it could be the case the [sic] Ratzinger's trinitarian theology and communion ecclesiology have led him to develop a missiology—however explicitly or not—that proceeds as if salvation is found in the Catholic Church alone."[98]

93. Ehle, "Trinitarian Ecclesiology of Communion," 130.
94. Ehle, "Trinitarian Ecclesiology of Communion," 130.
95. Ehle, "Trinitarian Ecclesiology of Communion," 130–31.
96. Ehle, "Trinitarian Ecclesiology of Communion," 133.
97. Ehle explains her position in detail: "Congar's criticism of the charismatic renewal movement addresses this point directly: 'The Renewal may be so situated at the level of *res* that the *sacramentum* may be underestimated. It may be so oriented towards the vertical dimension of religion, that is, the relation with the absolute, that the horizontal aspect is neglected, if not in regard to relationships with one's immediate neighbor, at least in the more extended, and in this sense more strictly social.'" (Ehle, "Trinitarian Ecclesiology of Communion," 133n218, quoting Congar, *I Believe in the Holy Spirit*, 2:168).
98. Ehle, "Trinitarian Ecclesiology of Communion," 134.

Such triumphalism is, at least according to Ehle, contrary to the demands of the current ecumenical situation.

6.4 Summary of the Critiques

All three of the critics I have surveyed have ultimately accused Ratzinger's ecclesiology of passing over the freedom and creativity of the human contributions to the communion and mission of the church. Volf contributes to the conversation his unease with the monistic and hierarchical tenor of Ratzinger's trinitarian theology and ecclesiology. Komonchak emphasizes the degree to which the local churches are left passive and in danger of disappearing from view. Ehle expresses concern about the failure of Ratzinger's missiology to engage in the redeeming of structures of sin. She sums up their collective concerns well when she concludes:

> The wholeness and unity evident in Ratzinger's trinitarian theology informs his communion ecclesiology and his missiology such that in the eschaton this unity will include all men and women who have been drawn to the Word in the Church. As Ratzinger's trinitarian theology takes on a monistic structure through his definition of divine person as relation, so too, does his ecclesiology, and missiology. In the end, however, the harshest critic may well argue that the ultimate consequence of Ratzinger's emphases on person as pure relation—divine persons as their innertrinitarian relations and human persons as their relation to Christ in the Church—removes the breadth of human nature and the reality of human existence from human persons while depriving divine persons of their personal properties. . . . The fact that in his description of relations he prioritizes the immanent trinity over the economic trinity, and the spiritual communion and mission of the church over its sociological nature and mission leaves one yearning for a socio-politically committed Church *qua* Church that is faithful to its nature as sacrament, a sign *and* instrument of the trinitarian communion.[99]

The critiques leveled at the correspondence between communion and mission in Ratzinger's ecclesiology run to the core of his theology. They cannot simply be ignored or set aside. If Ratzinger's trinitarian theology is as flawed as Volf claims, then his whole theological project is likely to have serious, perhaps insurmountable, problems. If his ecclesiology passes over the heads of persons in the pews and ignores their freedom and responsibility as

---

99. Ehle, "Trinitarian Ecclesiology of Communion," 134–35.

Komonchak insists it does, then how can the church be the communion she is called to be in the world today? Does it effectively address the church and people the world over in the current crises? If Ehle is right that Ratzinger's communion of mission both smacks of triumphalism and simultaneously fails to address the suffering of the lost whom Christ came to seek and save, then how can his missiology encourage the church to live and offer the λογική λατρεία, which can again credibly communicate the Gospel to the world?

We will see that the link between the incarnational nature of Ratzinger's "spiritual Christology" and his eucharistic ecclesiology suggests an image of the church as a contextual form of community, which might provide the right trajectory for answering the questions even if he does not explicitly articulate those answers. Such a contextual form of living and loving comports well with his call for creative minorities which function in a manner analogous to St. Benedict's monasteries.

7

Response and Analysis

IN THE PREVIOUS CHAPTER, I summarized the arguments with which Miroslav Volf, Joseph Komonchak, and Mary Ehle critique Joseph Ratzinger. Here I offer Ratzingerian responses to those critiques and indicate areas where they illuminate gaps or weaknesses in Ratzinger's elucidation of the relation between communion and mission.

7.1 Del Colle's Trinitarian Response

7.1.1 The Dominance of the One or the Agency of the Three?

Recall that Volf's critique relies on drawing ecclesiological and anthropological conclusions from trinitarian and christological assertions. For Volf, Ratzinger's definition of person as relation yields a problematic view of trinitarian unity: because all persons are total relationality, their unity cannot come about by way of their specific personal selfhood, but must be located "at the level of substance."[1] Thus, he finds in Ratzinger a trinitarian monism, "the pyramidal dominance of the one"[2] substance, from which follows Ratzinger's "monistic structure of the church."[3]

However, Del Colle convincingly argues that Volf misreads Ratzinger on these fundamental points. For Del Colle, Volf interprets Ratzinger's thought to be consistent with the dominant lines of trinitarian predication in the West, which Volf perceives to leave no "density" to the personal distinctions in the Trinity and to result in the dominance of the divine substance.[4] Del Colle indicates this is not the case with Ratzinger:

---

1. Volf, *After Our Likeness*, 70.
2. Volf, *After Our Likeness*, 216.
3. Volf, *After Our Likeness*, 71.
4. Del Colle, "Communion and the Trinity," 314.

Ratzinger is aware of this tendency [to the dominance of the one] and consistently counters it: "To him who believes in God as tri-une, the highest unity is not the unity of inflexible monotony." In fact, the absolute in God cannot be "an absolute singular" but that of a person, mindful that any statement that the God of Jesus Christ is a person must be rendered "in the guise of a triple personality [which] explodes the naive, anthropomorphic concept of person."[5]

Indeed, in the very section from which Volf detects the "all-embracing dominance of oneness of substance," Ratzinger advances the thesis of *"the absoluteness of the relative, of that which is in relation."*[6] All the same, Del Colle pauses to ask whether Ratzinger's notion of person as pure relation nonetheless mutes his attempts to emphasize the plurality of the persons and ultimately results in trinitarian monism. How one answers this "depends on what we mean by relation. The identification of person with relation is either the explication of personhood or the reduction of personhood to something ontologically less than personhood."[7] Put another way, "we may legitimately ask whether Ratzinger in his utilization of this language and conceptuality fails to affirm what Thomas Aquinas identifies as the defining truth of persons, namely, that they are subsisting relations (*Summa theologiae* Ia.29.4)."[8] Volf attempts to articulate just this point: "if all persons are total relationality with regard to one another, then the agent in the deity can only be the one substance, both internally and externally."[9] Does Ratzinger's notion of person as relation empty the divine persons of their agency?

If it does, it contradicts the consistent Western tradition in which, "the unity of the divine operation *ad extra* is not inconsistent with the unity of divine life *ad intra* since in neither case is the substance an agent! . . . It is the three divine persons who act as one by virtue of the unity of the divine nature."[10] Indeed Ratzinger seems to take this for granted, as one might expect, and focuses on a different issue:

> In God, person means relation. Relation, being related, is not something superadded to the person, but it *is* the person itself.

---

5. Del Colle, "Communion and the Trinity," 314. The quotes are from the 1979 edition of Ratzinger, *Introduction to Christianity*, 128, 129, respectively.
6. Ratzinger, *Introduction to Christianity*, 180-81.
7. Del Colle, "Communion and the Trinity," 317.
8. Del Colle, "Communion and the Trinity," 319.
9. Volf, *After Our Likeness*, 71.
10. Del Colle, "Communion and the Trinity," 319.

In its nature, the person only exists *as* a relation. Put more concretely, the first person does not generate in the sense that the act of generating a Son is added to the already complete person, but the person *is* the deed of generating, of giving itself, of streaming itself forth. The person is identical with this act of self-donation.[11]

Ratzinger is not referring here to the one substance at all but is attending to the dialogical character of personhood. In short, Volf's argument—that Ratzinger's theology ultimately asserts the dominance of the one substance as the one acting agent of the triune God—does not hold.

7.1.2 The Role of the Spirit in Ratzinger's Christology

However, Volf's critique cannot yet be dismissed *in toto*. He further argues that Ratzinger's insistence on Christ as "no mere ontological anomaly" inevitably means that the latter's theological and anthropological definition of person as relation ultimately fails to do justice to the humanity of Christ and of Christians. The key to properly understanding Ratzinger here lies in his spiritual Christology[12] and his notion of sacrament. Recall that Ratzinger refers to the Third Council of Constantinople to show that the human and divine wills of Christ "are united in the assent of the human will of Christ to the divine will of the Logos. Thus on the practical level—'existentially'—the two wills become one single will, and yet ontologically they remain two independent entities. . . . It is a unity in the mode of communion—the unity that love creates and love is."[13]

The eternal relation between the Father and the Son is revealed to humanity in the incarnation of the Son's obedience to the Father. In the resurrection, he is opened up to incorporate humanity into his body and to take human-ness eternally into the "triune exchange of divine love."[14] In so doing, He effects the exchange, having become human so that humanity might participate in his divinity. This incorporation and participation, for Ratzinger, is always an action of the Spirit.[15] The effect of the "Spirit" in Ratzinger's spiritual Christology (and thus his ecclesiology) is not to negate humanity nor does it imply some unreal or ideal abstraction. Rather, it uses trinitarian language to talk about human freedom in a participationist

11. Ratzinger, "Concerning the Notion of Person," 444.
12. See chapter 5, section 3.1.1 of the current work for my exposition of this idea.
13. Ratzinger, *Pilgrim Fellowship of Faith*, 81–82.
14. Ratzinger, *God of Jesus Christ*, 76.
15. Ratzinger, *God of Jesus Christ*, 110.

metaphysic. In its content and its implications for human freedom, it is not much different from Servais Pinckaers's freedom for excellence.[16]

Thus, the Spirit becomes the ground upon which Ratzinger's theology builds up trustworthy hope in the eschatological fulfillment of the human desire for union with God, but this hope is not a hope in some immediate and incorporeal communion with God. It is not a mere idea. Such a communion would not be consistent with the bodiliness of the human person. After all, "God has become man so that men might become like God,"[17] and so, "God wishes to approach man only through man; he seeks out man in no other way but in his fellow humanity."[18] Thus the anthropological implications of Ratzinger's spiritual Christology remain incarnational, fully human, indeed, sacramental.

In this way the divine personhood of Christ does not diminish, negate, or subtract from his humanity, contra Volf, but rather elevates it to the transcendent and perichoretic trinitarian communion. Because of this participationism, Ratzinger's trinitarian theology, his spiritual Christology, and his ecclesiology allow the participation of humanity in the divine *communio personarum* and simultaneously recognize the necessary corporeality and historicity of the human person without denying the transcendence of God or demanding divinity of humanity.

Ratzinger articulates a similar point from a pastoral perspective in *Dogma and Preaching*, where he argues that Christian education and preaching is not about a "metaphysical system" or speculative thinking about Christ, church, or Trinity. Rather, it is *"the exposition of the way of Christian existence through Christ in the Spirit to the Father."*[19] In other words, the way of Christian existence is the concrete experience of trinitarian life. Indeed, at its core Christianity can be viewed as a "reality" in which catechumens "are to be trained."[20] There is no negating of humanity here. In fact, where Volf claims Ratzinger's explication of the uniqueness of Christ diminishes his humanity and the freedom of human persons in the church, Ratzinger explains:

> The uniqueness of the Christ-event does not devalue the life of mankind; rather it gives to that life a share in the strength of its own presence. The great figures of the faith from Polycarp to Maximilian Kolbe, really demonstrate what a life of following

16. See Pinckaers, *Morality*, esp. "Freedom and Happiness."
17. Ratzinger, *Dogma and Preaching*, 129.
18. Ratzinger, *Introduction to Christianity*, 92–93.
19. Ratzinger, *Dogma and Preaching*, 46–47.
20. Ratzinger, *Dogma and Preaching*, 47.

Christ means; in them we can see the demands made by this life and the hope that it offers. They are all interpretations of Jesus Christ; in them he becomes concrete.... Only when we rediscover the Saints will we also find the Church again.[21]

The implications of Ratzinger's trinitarian theology and Christology for men and women are expressed in the very real, human, and concrete lives of the saints. After all, "In the last analysis, following Christ is nothing other than man's becoming man by integration into the humanity of God."[22]

Nevertheless, any adequate appreciation of, and response to, Ratzinger's critics must bear in mind the concrete and contextual implications thereof. Having demonstrated that Miroslav Volf's trinitarian critique of Ratzinger cannot be sustained under close inspection, I admit that Volf's caution of the dangers of ecclesiological monism ought to be heard and considered well, especially in light of the clerical abuse scandals and episcopal malfeasance. Volf's concern—that Ratzinger's ecclesiology "is unable to do justice structurally to the abuse of power because persons understood in this way are also embedded in a monistic hierarchical structure of the relations, the understanding of person as pure relation can easily degenerate into repressive ideology"[23]—demands a response. Ratzinger himself provides some preliminary answers to the questions of the structure of the church, monism, and the abuse of power.

For Ratzinger, as Del Colle explains, "the inseparability of sacramental *ordo* and sacramental mediation of grace is essential for any Catholic ecclesiology."[24] In other words, in a Catholic conception, normative manifestations of grace will occur in and through the sacraments, which, by the fact of their constitution, demand an *ordo*, a hierarchy. However, this does not necessitate ecclesiological monism. For Ratzinger, the papal primacy is always tied up with collegiality. Furthermore, he argues that primacy, like all Christian life, is first ordered toward service, and second, in a more particular way, it possesses a martyrological structure, which serves church unity.[25] Thus, "the primacy is to be understood first of all as witness to the confession of Christ on the basis of witness given personal warranty in martyrdom as verification of testimony for him who was crucified and victorious on the cross."[26] Ratzinger, the student of Augustine and Bonaventure, maintains

---

21. Ratzinger, *Dogma and Preaching*, 55.
22. Ratzinger, *Dogma and Preaching*, 129.
23. Volf, *After Our Likeness*, 214.
24. Del Colle, "Communion and the Trinity," 324.
25. Ratzinger, *Church, Ecumenism, and Politics*, 36–40.
26. Ratzinger, *Church, Ecumenism, and Politics*, 38.

that just such a martyrological structure is called for by the responsibility of bearing witness to Christ in the world, which "has hated me before it hated you" (John 15:18). Thus, Ratzinger explains, "on the basis of this kind of theology of martyrdom the primacy represents the guarantee of the opposition of the Church in its catholic unity to all particular secular power."[27] In more practical terms, the exercise of the papacy is not a monarchical or tyrannical operation of power but is rather "a vicariate of obedience and of the cross."[28] Furthermore, Ratzinger does not place his hope in the pope or the hierarchy for ecclesial reform or evangelization of the modern world. Rather he calls for local creative minorities, acting and worshipping in communion with the universal Church, martyrologically to offer their corner of the world a witness to the love, joy, and forgiveness inherent in life with Christ.

7.2 Ratzinger's Intercultural Ecclesiality

Recall Komonchak's convincing argument that throughout Ratzinger's theological career he consistently argued for the ontological and temporal priority of the universal church.[29] Komonchak interprets these arguments both to minimize the activity of local churches and to lean in the direction "of regarding the human element in the construction of the Church as merely passive and receptive and thus of 'interpreting the Word of God, the Eucharist, and the Spirit's charisms as realities which somehow pass over man's head.'"[30] Komonchak is basically correct in his overview of Ratzinger's ecclesiological arguments. To cite one example, Ratzinger explains, "The place, the geographical element, is less constitutive of the local church than is communion with the bishop—that is, the theological element."[31] This follows from Ratzinger's belief that a community can only be received as church by the universal church. Being a member of a certain community in a certain place does not make one a member of a church unless that community has communion via episcopal collegiality and apostolic succession with the whole church. Yet, such a view does not necessarily imply a

---

27. Ratzinger, *Church, Ecumenism, and Politics*, 38.
28. Ratzinger, *Church, Ecumenism, and Politics*, 40.
29. Komonchak, "On the Priority."
30. Komochak, "Local Church," 437, quoting Valentini, *Il nuovo Popoli di Dio*, 56. Komonchak adds in the footnote: "This seems to me to be a crucial point: the freedom of the human subjects of the Church's self-realization, which cannot be separated from their concrete historical situation, is not related to the divine freedom as matter to form; in fact, it is an intrinsic element of the formal principle itself."
31. Ratzinger, *Principles*, 290; cf. 297, 308.

denial of the local element or reduce the human element to passivity. Does Komonchak's interpretation necessarily follow?

Answering this requires an examination of the degree to which Ratzinger's ecclesiology might in other ways account for the concrete and contextual character of the experience of "local Church." Since locality is necessarily tied up with culture, I first explore the interaction of faith and culture in Ratzinger's thought. Second, I consider whether his notion of sacramentality safeguards the contextual and embodied character of human experience in the church, rather than diminishing it.

7.2.1 Coming to Terms with "Culture"

Ratzinger most clearly addresses the relationship between faith and culture in *Truth and Tolerance*,[32] where he is concerned with issues of evangelization and inculturation through the lens of the church's right and responsibility to mission and her ability to encounter human culture—to heal and elevate it without destroying it.

Ratzinger defines "culture" as a "social form of expression as it has grown up in history of those experiences and evaluations that have left their mark on a community and have shaped it."[33] He argues that history has shown religion to be the "determinative center" of every culture,[34] with the possible exception of modern Europe in which the *ratio* of this technical culture closes itself off to transcendence.[35] However, just as human nature tends to seek the true, the good, and the beautiful, so cultures exhibit an openness to the transcendent and a capacity for the universal.[36] The degree to which a community is open to God and to universality depends upon the correctness of that culture's perception of reality and the proper ordering of its values. The Greece of Plato and Aristotle was more open to receiving the Gospel than would have been the culture of the ancient Aztecs, with their propensity for human sacrifice. Because cultures have a potential for universality, when cultures meet they will inevitably influence each other. Ideally, each culture would purify the other's perceptions of reality and ordering of values. This can occur organically without any violation of one culture by the other,[37] but it could only occur via the medium of "their shared truth

---

32. Ratzinger, *Truth and Tolerance*, 148.
33. Ratzinger, *Truth and Tolerance*, 60.
34. Ratzinger, *Truth and Tolerance*, 59.
35. Ratzinger, *Truth and Tolerance*, 58.
36. Ratzinger, *Truth and Tolerance*, 61.
37. Ratzinger, *Truth and Tolerance*, 62–64.

concerning man," which necessarily also touches upon the questions of God and reality.[38] However, this purification does not often take place in its fullness, because the effects of original sin upon a culture cause a degree of closedness to other cultures, to universality, and to transcendence. This closeness leads to alienation and erects a wall between cultures,[39] a wall that Christ came to abolish by reconciling all men to himself.[40]

With this in mind, how might one articulate the "cultural" nature of a global community, one that transcends the normal geographical limits of a people? When a culture encounters the church, the people of God, what is it encountering?

7.2.2 Church: Not a Naked Faith and Not a Classical Cultural Agent

When speaking of the encounter of faith and culture, Ratzinger prefers to speak of "interculturality" rather than inculturation. This is because "inculturation presupposes a naked faith transferred into a culture that is indifferent from a religious point of view."[41] Just as grace presupposes nature, so faith presupposes culture. No man or society has ever encountered a culture-free faith, and faith is no mere abstraction of ideas. Rather, faith itself is cultural. Tracing its roots back to the Old Testament, the Christian faith bears within it the purified aspects of the nomadic peoples of Abraham's time and place, the Exodus generation and borrowed pieces of Egyptian culture, the monarchy and aspects of the various kingdoms with which it came into contact, the culture of the Jews in exile, etc. To the degree that Christianity claims to speak the truth about humanity, who we are and how we should live, faith is always "creating culture and is culture."[42]

However, Ratzinger is quick to point out that the people of God, "differ from classical cultural agents" in that it "subsists within various different cultural entities"[43] without destroying them. An implication of this is that there is not merely one "Christian culture." The people of God can, do, and have lived out their whole faith in its integrity in a variety of places, times, and cultures. This does not mean that it merely "lives through borrowed

---

38. Ratzinger, *Truth and Tolerance*, 66.
39. Ratzinger, *Truth and Tolerance*, 65.
40. 2 Cor 5:18.
41. Ratzinger, *Truth and Tolerance*, 64.
42. Ratzinger, *Truth and Tolerance*, 67.
43. Ratzinger, *Truth and Tolerance*, 68.

cultures,"[44] for this would make universality a fiction. The culture of Christians in New Orleans would mean nothing to Christians in Bangkok, and the faith itself would be "dematerialized into a mere spirit, ultimately lacking in reality."[45] The church would lose its sacramental character.

Upon applying these reflections to the local church, one might reasonably surmise that Ratzinger believes that all Christians exist to a certain extent within two cultures. Upon becoming Christian, a person does not cease being American, French, or African.[46] Nevertheless, her life in a Christian community bears a form that is common to all Christians regardless of locality. She ever remains in the secular culture but is no longer of it. This "tension between 'secular' culture and church culture must be upheld to constantly renew the faith and heal culture."[47] However, because Christianity is not intended to be esoteric or merely private, for Ratzinger, becoming Christian requires conversion from a secular culture to the church. This is consistent with Ratzinger's view of nature and grace, influenced as it is by St. Bonaventure, which insists upon accounting for the sin-wounded situation of historical man. For this reason, no culture can simply be adopted by the church *in toto*. Ratzinger explains, "Without a certain exodus, a breaking off with one's life in all its aspects, one cannot become a Christian."[48] However, while Christianity always implies the cross, Ratzinger does not intend this breaking off absolutely. In baptism, one becomes Christian and a new creation without ceasing to share the food, music, and other tastes and habits of one's "natural" culture, just as Saul becomes Paul without ceasing to maintain and incorporate many Jewish ideas and habits into his new life in Christ.

In the Incarnation, the Son binds divinity to history and links himself with a particular culture: "Christ remains man to eternity."[49] He remains a Jewish man to eternity. The Christ event, the Incarnation and Paschal Mystery, is a once for all event. It cannot simply be repeated in a different culture. "That means that because the people of God is not just a single cultural entity, but is gathered together from all peoples, therefore the first cultural identity [Jesus'], rising again from the break that was made, has its place therein."[50] In other words, although the "culture" of the church spans

---

44. Ratzinger, *Truth and Tolerance*, 69.
45. Ratzinger, *Truth and Tolerance*, 69.
46. Ratzinger, *Truth and Tolerance*, 68.
47. Ratzinger, *Truth and Tolerance*, 70.
48. Ratzinger, *Truth and Tolerance*, 71.
49. Ratzinger, *Truth and Tolerance*, 71.
50. Ratzinger, *Truth and Tolerance*, 71.

across many cultures of many times and places, certain cultural forms remain normative. In *Truth and Tolerance* Ratzinger means this in reference to that cultural milieu within which Jesus and the apostles lived. However, in his Regensburg address, Pope Benedict XVI describes as providential the process by which Judaism and Christianity encountered Greek culture, and more specifically its philosophy, and he implies that the culture of European Christendom also should be, to some extent, normative for all of Christianity because in it the pinnacle of the faith-reason synthesis was reached.[51]

Nevertheless, Ratzinger maintains that local churches possess a responsibility to share with the whole church their particular gifts and insights. Supra-local ecclesial institutions must be sensitive to movements of the Spirit in local communities in order to identify and distinguish genuinely "catholic" expressions of the church from that which needs purifying. The role of the universal here is not to issue mandates; rather, it has "the task of inspiring, of distinguishing, of purifying, of mediating."[52] On the other hand and contra Komonchak's understanding, Ratzinger attributes active responsibility to the local communities who should not wait for mandates but, rather, must always be open to the responsibility of rendering "mediation to the whole."[53] Thus, "[the local church] must fructify the universal Church by its experience of faith, its patience and its creative imagination. The universal Church, for her part, must be open to this enrichment, must disseminate it to the whole Church through the communion of bishops with the pope and, where necessary, must purify and deepen it in terms of the whole."[54]

Upon looking more closely at the local-universal relation, Ratzinger notes that the Second Vatican Council rediscovered the authentic relation between plurality and unity that had been de-emphasized in the Middle Ages. In this context, he explains that the council "defined 'local church' as the Fathers had defined it, in terms of the bishop, not in terms of a geographical oneness of 'place.'"[55] Thus, just after attributing an active responsibility to the whole on the part of the local, Ratzinger adds that the "local," the "geographical" has no theological or constitutive role for the particular church. He finds the word "local" itself to be misleading, because "no one thinks of the local church in terms of geographical criterion."[56] However, he

51. Benedict XVI, "Faith, Reason, and the University."
52. Ratzinger, *Principles*, 304.
53. Ratzinger, *Principles*, 304.
54. Ratzinger, *Principles*, 309.
55. Ratzinger, *Principles*, 307.
56. Ratzinger, *Principles*, 308.

does not intend either of the above statements to reject or deny all import to the local culture; rather, he means to affirm that these elements are *not* what make a local community a church. After all, "the separation of the non-theological factors from that which actually forms the Church (the office of bishop) destroys the *ecclesia localis* and rends the *ecclesia universalis*."[57] Because a community cannot bestow upon itself sacramental powers, its "catholicity" and its being as "church" must come from without, from the universal church; just as no man can save himself but can only receive the sacraments of salvation through the ecclesial sacrament of Christ. So while Ratzinger insists that no community can become a local church without a bishop to unite it with the whole church, he also highlights the existential import of lived *communio* on the local level in order for people to experience powerfully the communion of the church in a technocratic society increasingly distant and anonymous.[58] The very call for the church to exist as creative minorities in the world implies the activity of particular Christian communities in the one mission to the world.

In sum, Ratzinger has a nuanced and complex view of culture and of the active contribution of Christians in a local church as members of *that* church. The church does not have its own culture, but it is a cultural agent of sorts which "subsists" in a plurality of localities and cultures and yet maintains a certain, as yet undefined, normative cultural form. It does so without destroying and alienating the "natural" culture, without denying human freedom. Rather, those in that culture who convert ought to see their participation in the structures of sin inherent in their culture purified and ought to observe the best aspects of their culture—the aspects that had most fully opened up to God and most accurately reflected reality—taken up and fulfilled by the culture of faith. Thus, converts can and should contribute unique insights and particular contributions to the whole church. This contribution occurs precisely through the type of sacramental participation in the divine communion described above and at the same time begins to clarify, contra Komonchak, the manner in which Ratzinger's spiritual Christology and ecclesiology recognize the corporeality and historicity of the human person.

Komonchak claims that Ratzinger's ecclesiology condemns Christians in local churches to passivity by failing to do justice to human freedom in the church. However, while in the ecclesiological writings surveyed by Komonchak Ratzinger fails to bring human responsibility to the fore; he clearly

---

57. Ratzinger, *Principles*, 308. Ratzinger here does not intend to reject the notion that the Eucharist makes the church but wishes to emphasize the sacramental character of the Eucharist in order to exhibit its being bestowed upon the local by the universal.

58. Ratzinger, *Principles*, 309.

does take human responsibility seriously. Indeed, he places upon Christians in local churches the responsibility both to bear witness to a graced and thus healed and elevated form of the "natural" culture inhabited by their neighbors and also to offer their particular embodiment of Christian life for the enrichment of the universal church.

In fact, Ratzinger offers a concrete example of just this point in an essay entitled "The Anthropological Basis of Brotherly Love,"[59] which lauds the work of local Catholic groups who ministered to young job-seeking women who were leaving rural life for the city in order to shelter them from the two-fold dangers of the mobility (or instability) and anonymity of the modern age. Their work was "an attempt to set up, in the midst of mobility, a context that would support and shelter" the young women "from the modern highwaymen who waylaid and misused people in many ways as the objects of their own business dealings."[60] It was simultaneously "an attempt, in the midst of anonymity, to offer personal communication."[61] Ratzinger explains that the dawning of the "age of the technopolis" presented the world and the church with a new situation, and the work done by the Catholic *Mädchenschutzvereine* corresponds to the human needs of that time and place but also to the "nature of the Church and signifies the application of her commission to the given historical situation."[62]

In other words, the nature of church demands and calls for local Catholic communities to fulfill the mandate of bringing the Gospel to all peoples by offering hospitality to any "strangers and sojourners" who may be passing by.[63] After all, "Church, correctly understood and living correctly, does not look to herself; rather, she goes out from herself and works for others."[64] But, this can only happen if "the layman demonstrates his freedom and his indispensability by doing what the Church *must* do."[65] Thus, Ratzinger concludes the first part of his lecture by summarizing as follows: "we can say that the work of the Mädchenschutzverein applies the universality and

---

59. Published in Ratzinger, *Dogma and Preaching*, 210–21. According to the footnote on 210, this was a "Lecture presented at the celebration of the seventy-five years of service by the Catholic *Mädchenschutzvereine* [associations for the protection of young women] in Bavaria . . . on April 25, 1970, in Munich."

60. Ratzinger, *Dogma and Preaching*, 213.

61. Ratzinger, *Dogma and Preaching*, 213.

62. Ratzinger, *Dogma and Preaching*, 213.

63. See Ratzinger, *Dogma and Preaching*, 213–14.

64. Ratzinger, *Dogma and Preaching*, 216.

65. Ratzinger, *Dogma and Preaching*, 216.

identity of the one Church to a concrete place in human history and human life in a practical way and tries to translate it into the reality of daily life."[66]

This is precisely the role of the local church as creative minority in Ratzinger's ecclesiology. Komonchak can rightly claim that a majority of Ratzinger's ecclesiological essays and arguments fail to give the local church and the men and women therein sufficient attention. Ratzinger's insistence on the normativity of Judaic and European Christianity could lead one to dismiss forms of ecclesial life that do not reflect the cultural norms of Western Christian life. Nevertheless, Ratzinger's thought as a whole, rather than passing over the freedom and responsibility of men and women in local churches, calls upon them to embody the one church, the one body of Christ, in the context of their daily lives. Furthermore, Ratzinger trusts the ecclesial movements and their work in various cultures and places to bear fruit for the future of the church.

7.3 An Embodied Communion and a Performance of Caritas

Mary Ehle's arguments against Ratzinger's missiology can be summarized in two points: First, she believes the emphasis which Ratzinger places on the "spiritual mission" of the church fails to respond adequately to the suffering and injustice so prevalent in the here and now. Second, she thinks the identification of the mission of the church with the mission of Christ amounts to Catholic triumphalism. Like Volf she locates the origin of these missiological problems in his alleged christomonism and in his notion of person as relation. As a result, "the true freedom and diversity of human persons, Christians and those to whom they reach out in mission, are relegated to the background, if not dissolved into the relations that, in Ratzinger's communion missiology, are themselves the goal of mission."[67]

We have already determined that Ratzinger's notion of person and his spiritual Christology do not in fact "condemn man to passivity" but rather offer men and women participation in the freedom and love of God. This participation takes place through and in the church, which remains a concrete communion and does not pass over humanity's head. Rather, it is the work of the Spirit manifested at a contextual level in the life of the church. This is an essential aspect of the council's definition of the church as sacrament. After all, the notion of sacramentality highlights both the gratuitousness of God's initiative and the specifically visible, incarnate character of God's actions. The sign-value of the sacrament requires living the mystery,

---

66. Ratzinger, *Dogma and Preaching*, 217.
67. Ehle, "Trinitarian Ecclesiology of Communion," 129.

entering its referential context: "if a sign, a visible reality, points to what is invisible, what is divine, it is eminently clear that I can discover its referential context only by identifying myself with it, by allowing myself to be incorporated into the relationship that makes the sign a sign."[68] Thus, Ratzinger's eucharistic ecclesiology demands concrete communion. To paraphrase William Cavanaugh, it requires a performance of the Eucharist.[69]

Komonchak is correct to recognize that much of Ratzinger's ecclesiological writings focus on the priority of the universal church over the local churches and does so through an ecclesiology from above which emphasizes the priority of God's action over those of men and women. Ehle is right that Ratzinger's view of mission as a "spiritual mission" is nearly equivalent to evangelization and is not directly concerned with missionary work understood as social action. Yet, his notion of Eucharist as the origin of mission simply does not conform to the critiques offered by Komonchak and Ehle. A study of the sources of his work and of the concrete and pastoral character of much of his writing clarifies that his ecclesiology is not merely pie in the sky but demands to be embodied and practiced.

7.3.1 Ratzinger's Augustinianism and Embodied Ecclesiology

For his doctoral thesis, Ratzinger studied the ecclesiology of Augustine by exploring the latter's use of "People of God" and "House of God." Ratzinger argues that Augustine, influenced as he is by John Chrysostom, Tertullian, and Cyprian, takes the Incarnation as the ground of his ecclesiology, which ultimately gives it a thoroughly concrete and embodied character[70]—concrete in that it takes the physicality of humanity seriously and embodied in that it takes the communal nature of ecclesial life seriously. For Augustine, as for Ratzinger, the Eucharist effects the incarnational and embodied character of ecclesial life. In the Eucharist, the Christians become what they see and receive what they are. Thus, men and women are eucharistically brought into communion with Christ by the power of the Spirit in the ecclesial body.[71] As is the case with Ratzinger's spiritual Christology so here, the reference to the "spiritual" character of ecclesial communion does not mean this communion is somehow only symbolic, ideal, or even unreal. Rather,

---

68. Ratzinger, *Principles*, 47–48; cf. *Principles*, 53–54.

69. See Cavanaugh, *Torture and Eucharist*, 253–82; Cavanaugh, *Migrations of the Holy*, 63–68.

70. Ratzinger, *Volk und haus Gottes*, 295–96. Hereafter VHG.

71. Ratzinger, VHG, 287.

the Spirit animates the ecclesial body, makes it something new. Ratzinger explains:

> What does it mean that the Church is Christ's spiritual body? There is no reason why a different meaning should be given that which is usually spoken of as the Church of the body of Christ. We have to consider that "spiritual" is not spiritual in the modern sense, which is to say, only spiritual but not real, but rather wants to testify to the nature of the new Christian reality, of *pneuma*.[72]

In the Eucharist, the Spirit effects the communion between Christ and his members so that they may also live according to the Spirit, which is to say in obedience to the Father. This obedience, which is embodied in the praxis of love, is the way in which the church, as a body, testifies to the new Christian reality. By living in accord with the Spirit, the church testifies to the presence of the Spirit, to the presence of God in the world. This loving obedience takes on the character of a participation in the new worship offered by Christ to the Father.[73] After all, the city of God is set apart by the performance of love of God rather than self-love.

From another perspective one might say that since "faith by itself, if it has no works, is dead" (Jas 2:17), a church whose members embody life according to the Spirit is therefore "spiritual" and really alive.

Following Augustine, Ratzinger's ecclesiology demands communion concretely embodied—communion performed. The Eucharist makes the church and demands caritas. After all, "caritas is not a mystical inner reality which says nothing to human realisation; rather, it is Church unity, more: it is the real, sober, acting love of the Christian heart."[74] The communion at the heart of the church is about a concrete love of others in the Spirit. Just as Ratzinger's spiritual Christology relies upon the close connection between pneumatology and freedom, so the implications of his ecclesiology stand on the ground of the Spirit whose role it is to liberate human freedom for participation in the life of Christ, for the concrete loving of neighbor. For Ratzinger the Spirit effects the connection of the eucharistic offering at the altar with the moral life of Christians as self-sacrifice. In Ratzinger's adoption of the Pauline notion of the Christian becoming Eucharist by offering his body as λογική λατρεία to God in Christ, he also perceives that the Eucharist is not merely the sacrament of Jesus's worship. It is also the efficacious sign of λογική λατρεία offered by Christians united in caritas. This means both

---

72. Ratzinger, VHG, 149.
73. Ratzinger, VHG, 283; cf. *Pilgrim Fellowship of Faith*, 82.
74. Ratzinger, VHG, 290–91.

true worship and real, concrete love. The moral life of Christians is then the embodied *sacramentum*, the cultic offering of the Eucharist.

> This means every act of genuine Christian love, every work of mercy, is in a true and proper sense a sacrifice, a setting of the one unique Christian sacrifice. There is not on the one hand an inauthentic moral or personal offering and beside it an authentic cultic one. Rather the first is the res of the latter, in which the latter has its authentic reality.[75]

The Spirit transubstantiates Christian love into eucharistic offering, enabling and ennobling the Christian community that concretely loves—and thus lives the Eucharist—to bear witness thereby to the presence of God in the world, precisely because Christ is truly present there. The Spirit inspires the local church to be a creative minority.

Rather than condemning the local church and the Christians therein to passivity, Ratzinger's eucharistic ecclesiology demands of local churches both concrete communion and embodied caritas. Since he envisions Eucharist as the origin of mission, any merely ideal communion and passive charity on the part of the church would lead to entirely ineffective mission and evangelization, precisely because it would lack the animation of the Spirit and true Christian praxis. Only a people that has allowed itself to be gathered into communion by God in Christ, can convince the world of God's presence therein. Faith is only aroused when God's "closeness is felt."[76]

For this reason, Ehle's claim, that "the consequence of Ratzinger's accentuation of the spiritual nature of the Church's mission, while probably not intended, may well be to render Christians passive in the face of sinful and oppressive persons and structures in the world,"[77] completely misses the thoroughly sacramental and incarnational nature of his ecclesiology and missiology, which explicitly call for concrete love. Further, Ratzinger anticipates and rejects Ehle's call for "a socio-politically committed Church qua Church."[78]

---

75. Ratzinger, VHG, 292.

76. Ratzinger, *Pilgrim Fellowship of Faith*, 93.

77. Ehle, "Trinitarian Ecclesiology of Communion," 133. "The importance [Ratzinger places] on the receptivity of the Word in imitation of Mary's *fiat* implies a passive stance of the Christian toward suffering. While vertical and spiritual communion with God and the Church can, and indeed does, provide some consolation in the midst of suffering, for human persons living in the world and facing day-to-day economic struggles and the reality of violence and discrimination, the Church's mission has to address more adequately the failures of liberal society" (Ehle, "Trinitarian Ecclesiology of Communion," 132n215).

78. Ehle, "Trinitarian Ecclesiology of Communion," 134–35.

7.3.2 Concrete Love in Ratzinger's Mission of Communion

Here I first discuss Ratzinger's recognition of the depths and seriousness of the problems in today's world both on a human level—as problems of suffering—and on an evangelical level—as arguments against the validity of Jesus's claims. Second, I explain Ratzinger's reasons for rejecting Ehle's proposed solution and articulate his alternative. With regard to the former, Ratzinger admits that the fact of the near ubiquitous suffering and evil in the world, of abuse and neglect in the church, highlights the unfulfilled nature of scripture's claims about the messianic age and Jesus's claims about the nearness of the reign of God. Referencing the eschatological peace prophesied by Isaiah 11:6–9, he explains, "It is talking about the peace that will be characteristic of redeemed mankind . . . how they no longer act in an evil or malicious way, because the land is filled with the knowledge of God, which covers the earth as water does. Redeemed people . . . live on the basis of their closeness to God and on his reality, so that quite of their own accord they become people of peace."[79] Yet, despite the proliferation of Christianity nigh to the ends of the earth, Christians, it seems, can only respond to such passages with shame and embarrassment. Some two millennia after the dawn of redeemed humanity, we must admit, the world remains "a place of strife where there is no peace . . . in which the knowledge of God does not cover the land like water but which lives in a state of being far from God, having God blacked out."[80] And so, the quite real and concrete men and women who are the church remain embarrassed, not only by Old Testament prophecies but also by the unfulfilled promises of the Lord who proclaimed the presence of the kingdom of God and proclaimed it as good news. The temptation to doubt the efficacy of the Gospel, of Jesus, and of its and his relevance for the concrete world arises from this embarrassment.[81] Often, in an attempt to shed the embarrassment, preachers and theologians have responded by postponing the coming of the kingdom to the end of time or by abstracting it from any concrete impact into a merely "spiritual" reality, as Ehle might describe it. Contra this tendency and as evidence of his concern with the Gospel's existential impact on the lives of people, Ratzinger explains,

---

79. Ratzinger, *What It Means*, 22–23.

80. Ratzinger, *What It Means*, 23.

81. "What really confronts us today, what bothers us much more is the inefficacy of Christianity: after 2,000 years of Christian history, we can see nothing that might be a new reality in the world; rather, we find it sunk in the same old horrors, the same despair, and the same hopes as ever. And in our own lives, too, we inevitably experience time and again how Christian reality is powerless against all the other forces that influence us and make demands on us" (Ratzinger, *What It Means*, 25–26).

> Christian theology ... in the course of time turned the kingdom of God into the kingdom of heaven that is beyond this mortal life; the well-being of man became a salvation of souls, which again comes to pass this life. But the analogy does not thereby provide an answer. For what is sublime in this message is precisely that the Lord was talking not just about another life, not just about men's souls, but was addressing the body, the whole man, in his embodied form, with his involvement in history and society; that he promised the kingdom of God to the man who is bodily with other men in this history.[82]

In other words, for Ratzinger, the mission of the church—the preaching of good news to the ends of the earth—must concern itself with the embodied and historical lives of real men and women. It must be proclaimed precisely as concrete good news to people in the midst of their trials and tribulations. This is the meaning of salvation history: "The history of Israel and the mystery of the Church are both intended to teach us one and the same thing: that God wants to come to man only through other men. . . . Thus, being a Christian, means constantly and in the first instance, letting ourselves be torn away from the selfishness of someone living only for oneself and entering into the great basic orientation of existing for the sake of another."[83] In short, to be Christian is to love, and in attempting and failing to love as freely and fully as Christ loves, we learn we need to receive love and forgiveness from he who is love so that our love may better bear witness to the Lord. For Ratzinger, this is what it means to be a Christian. This is the essence of the new and true worship. This is the heart of the church's mission.

Second, despite sharing Ehle's concern for the present situation of the world and to her apparent dismay, Ratzinger's demand for concrete caritas on the part of the church does not coincide with her desire for a socio-politically involved church. "Nowadays people object to the service of Christian brotherly love by questioning whether it bypasses necessary changes to the situation, whether it helps the individual, but overlooks the collective problem."[84] But, while he admits the need to bring to the city of man, to the new technopolis, resources and virtuous planning,[85] like Augustine, he believes it will remain the city of man, ultimately defined by love of self. Rather, an authentic Christian anthropology recognizes, contra Marx and his social concern for the whole, which ultimately devalues the individual, that "man

---

82. Ratzinger, *What It Means*, 28.
83. Ratzinger, *What It Means*, 56.
84. Ratzinger, *Dogma and Preaching*, 219.
85. Ratzinger, *Dogma and Preaching*, 219.

is not just raw material for the future; he himself is the ultimate purpose. . . . That is why there will never be circumstances that make personal, caring, and loving action on man's behalf superfluous."[86] Whenever society forgets this fundamental anthropological truth, "Planning for the future . . . is love of those who are most distant. It does not replace love of neighbor, of those who are closest."[87] Rather it often forgets to care for those who are closest.

To be fair to Ehle, Ratzinger does reject the kind of political theology she appreciates in someone like Boff. In addition, although Ratzinger is reasonably skeptical of such claims, there may be legitimate ways of engaging the polis that nevertheless keep the brother near at hand ever in view. Persons like Dorothy Day and Oscar Romero bear witness to this possibility. In their own ways each of them gave their lives for the poor, the disenfranchised, the powerless, and they did so in such a way so as to speak truth to power and to challenge the "rotten, decadent, putrid . . . system"[88] in which they were living. A non-violent, evangelical political theology based on the Gospel, which acts for the future precisely by loving the brother in the present, is possible. Nevertheless, for Ratzinger such political engagement is not at the core of the Gospel or the mission of the church.

In the end, Ehle's claim that Ratzinger's missiology of communion is "spiritual," not sufficiently concrete, and unconcerned with a big picture view of society's problems overlooks the existential implications of his theology and misses the *telos* of his missiology. Ratzinger's sacramental view of reality recognizes that humanity can only experience the divine through concrete love and that it is precisely the societal reforms for which Ehle calls, Dorothy Day and Oscar Romero excepted, which often fail to care for the concrete individuals in our midst. After all,

> Man does not live on bread alone. . . . Someone who is as well-fed as can be and can afford everything he wants starts to notice that that is still much too little. If someday everybody has everything he wants, he will still be far from happy. On the contrary, the Western world of today proves that when he is just beginning to be completely unhappy, that that is where his problems start. In this respect, man cannot be redeemed by bread. He hungers for more. . . . It is quite obvious how foolish it is to describe [Christian faith and love] as "the opiate of the people," now that people

---

86. Ratzinger, *Dogma and Preaching*, 219.
87. Ratzinger, *Dogma and Preaching*, 220.
88. Day, "On Pilgrimage," 6–7.

do in fact take opium precisely because they have the prosperity that is supposed to make the opiate superfluous.[89]

Christian love and authentic Christian mission, on the other hand, recognize that "if a person has been able to give meaning to an individual, to just one person, through his love, then his life has been infinitely worthwhile."[90] But of course it is not enough to have lived a worthwhile life. The mission of the church is the mission of the redeemer. Moreover, "in all circumstances it has been redemptive when, in the midst of a world of hostility and alienation, someone has appeared who emerged from the collectivity and has been a brother. These redemptive encounters . . . are the true, the inner church history. For only by helping to redeem others are we ourselves redeemed."[91] Only by concretely loving our neighbor do we offer λογική λατρεία to the Lord. Only by thus receiving and living his sacramental bread do we thus become his "flesh for the life of the world." Only thus does the church become creative minority.

---

89. Ratzinger, *Dogma and Preaching*, 225.
90. Ratzinger, *Dogma and Preaching*, 220.
91. Ratzinger, *Dogma and Preaching*, 220.

8

Communion and Mission Made Concrete in the Movements

WE HAVE SEEN THAT Ratzinger's ecclesiology does not reduce his notion of creative minorities to some divine ideal that passes over the heads of those in the pews, but one might yet ask, what concrete form his ideas could take. Ratzinger's theology is broad and flexible enough to allow for a variety of charisms and particular forms to put flesh on his notion of creative minorities. Here I offer a concrete example of a Christian community's embodiment of Ratzinger's ecclesiology and argue that such embodiments might exemplify how the church can once again efficaciously be a culture-shaping force of goodness in the world today. To this end, I first clarify the need for concrete communion of the sort demanded by creative minorities. Second, I explore how Ratzinger places his hope in the new ecclesial movements as fruits of the Spirit, which can express in their communal life and in their charisms the existential link between communion and mission. Third, I examine one such movement, the Focolare, and the thought of its founder, Chiara Lubich, as an example of what Ratzinger's ecclesiology might look like if made concrete and lived out in Christian communities.

8.1 The Need for Concrete Communion

Before exemplifying how Ratzinger's understanding of communion can be and has been made incarnate in some of the ecclesial movements and how they invigorate and strengthen the church for mission let us clarify precisely why this modern age greatly needs what Ratzinger calls "communion."

The great errors of the modern age rest "on the fact that it noticeably misjudged the roots and the living foundation of the idea of freedom and pushed towards an emancipation of reason that fundamentally contradicted the essential nature of human reason as a non-divine reason and for that reason must itself become irrational."[1] The now *de facto* autonomous and irrational use of reason ultimately means that it has "become blind and so becomes inhumane and hostile to creation in the destruction of its rational basis."[2] Hostility to creation leads to hostility towards creatures, toward humans and humanity. Ethics loses its foundation and in fact becomes superfluous. Mammon replaces Manna as that which sustains men and women; technology replaces Torah as that which guides and directs human society.

Furthermore, the secular hegemony is incessantly reinforced not only by the constant consumption of media, of which nearly all men and women and many children now partake, but also by the secular liturgies enacted whenever people go shopping, attend a football game, browse the internet, or drive to work.[3] Such relentless exposure to powerful formative practices subtly shapes desires. As a result, the so-called First World is full of societies that were traditionally Christian but are now thoroughly "secular." The world has been flattened, eliminating the transcendent. In Ratzinger's view this seismic shift philosophically takes truth out of the ethical equation and leads to individualism and a "tyranny of relativism," while in the order of *techne* it works toward building a society hell-bent on consumption and fragmentation. In the absence of a transcendent *telos* nations have turned to nationalism to preserve unity; persons have turned to mind-numbing media to quell their desire for God. The mobility and efficiency of modern travel has in part led to the breakdown of communities. Where once there was hospitality and stability, there is now anonymity and vulnerability. Although it is easier to connect and to communicate than ever before, many are perpetually connected and yet ever alone. Thus, the most "modern" countries in the world, the most successful and affluent, also exhibit startlingly high rates of murder, drug use, and suicide. A world without "the opiate of the masses" has literally turned to opium instead.[4] Aldous Huxley's *Brave New World* was not far off the mark.[5]

1. Ratzinger, *Church, Ecumenism, and Politics*, 232.
2. Ratzinger, *Church, Ecumenism, and Politics*, 232.
3. For example, "I think we run up against the limits of this approach when we try to make sense of the mall . . . the genius of mall religion is that actually it operates with a more holistic, affective, embodied anthropology . . . than the Christian church tends to assume! . . . In order to recognize the religious power and formative force of the mall, we need to adopt a paradigm of cultural critique and discernment that think even deeper that beliefs or worldviews and takes seriously the central role of formative practices" (Smith, *Desiring the Kingdom*, 24).
4. Ratzinger, *Dogma and Preaching*, 225.
5. Huxley, *Brave New World*.

At this point one may be tempted to argue that Ratzinger's sacramentalism—his eucharistically framed ecclesiology and missiology—offers a profound answer to secularism when concretely lived out, but that would be an argument of which Ratzinger would not approve,[6] for it would be a reduction of the Gospel to a means to a sociological or political end. Rather, Ratzinger might say that a church formed by the Eucharist and living eucharistically, offering life as λογική λατρεία, is a model from which Christian communities can receive the tools for engaging men and women in the modern age precisely because it conforms to the truth. For Ratzinger, because God is triune, reality is metaphysically grounded in relation, in trinitarian communion. Jesus reveals the transcendence and depth of communion and love and offers to women and men participation in his body. For Ratzinger, this is the truth of reality. Secularism is nothing but a powerful, pervasive, and seductive lie. Counteracting both the reduction of truth to the makeable and the flattening of reality to the nominal requires a recognition of the sacred. Ecclesial life that eloquently bears witness to the transcendent, to the sacred, to the triune, can counter secularism at the root, not because it is good politics or good sociology, but because it conforms to the reality created by the triune God.

8.2 Communion and Mission Embodied in the Movements

In response to the isolation and materialism of the modern world and in view of his own call for creative minorities, Ratzinger recognizes that in the church today "a principal need is for a reconstruction of the existential context of the Catechumenate . . . the common experience of the Spirit that can thus become also a foundation of realistic reflection."[7] Those being evangelized ought to be able to experience the *communio* of the church, and by being inserted into this horizontal *communio* ought to perceive the church's communion with the Father through Son and in the Spirit.

This bearing witness and being a space where the presence of Christ can be experienced is essential to the church's mission. Because today, "only with great difficulty can the faith touch the hearts of people by means of simple or moral speeches . . . simply proclaiming the message does not penetrate to the depths of people's hearts, it does not touch their freedom, it does

---

6. See Ratzinger, *Church, Ecumenism, and Politics*, 143–277, esp. 216. For example, where he asks, "How can Christianity become a positive force for the political world without becoming turned into a political instrument and without on the other hand grabbing the political world for itself?"

7. Ratzinger, *Principles*, 26.

not change their lives. What attracts is, above all, the encounter with believing persons who, through their faith, draw others to the grace of Christ by bearing witness to him."[8] Instead of ignoring the concrete human element of the church, Ratzinger's ecclesiology demands that Christian communities become places where Christianity takes on its nature as encounter, such that our communion becomes the sacrament of an encounter with the Lord.

Where can such a concretely human and sacramental experience of God be felt? Ratzinger places hope in the "newly formed communities [which] offer themselves, communities that have sprung directly out of the sharing of believers and give this the freshness of immediate experience."[9] In 2010, Pope Benedict explained to a group of bishops his own encounter with these modern movements not long after the council:

> I confess to you the pleasant surprise that I had in making contact with the movements and the new ecclesial communities. Watching them, I had the joy and the grace to see how, at a moment of weariness in the Church, at a time when we were hearing about "the winter of the Church," the Holy Spirit was creating a new springtime, awakening in young people and adults alike the joy of being Christian, of living in the Church, which is the living Body of Christ. Thanks to their charisms, the radicality of the Gospel, the objective contents of the faith, the living flow of her tradition, are all being communicated in a persuasive way and welcomed as a personal experience, as adherence in freedom to the present event of Christ.[10]

These ecclesial communities presuppose "a deep, personal encounter with Christ. . . . Only when the person is struck and penetrated by Christ to the depths of his or her being, can others too be touched in their innermost being."[11] They are where "faith becomes a form of lived experience, the joy of setting out on a journey and of participating in the mystery of the leaven that permeates the whole mass from within and renews it."[12] These communities can offer spheres in which real communion can exist and be experienced as communion, which shapes the entirety of one's life, and can then be shared with a world craving it.

---

8. Benedict XVI, "Address to the Bishops of Portugal."
9. Ratzinger, *Yes of Jesus Christ*, 37.
10. Benedict XVI, "Address to the Bishops of Portugal," in Leahy, *Ecclesial Movements and Communities*, 69–70.
11. Ratzinger, *New Outpourings of the Spirit*, 49.
12. Ratzinger, *Introduction to Christianity*, 19.

In fact, Ratzinger sees precedent in tradition for recognizing these new movements as "irruptions of the Spirit."[13] At the May 1998 gathering of movements at St. Peter's, then Cardinal Ratzinger talked at length about the movements' place in the church. He rejected several popular dichotomies. For example, institution-charism is misleading because the institutional dimension contains a charismatic element within it (e.g., vocations to the priesthood are called by the Holy Spirit). Likewise, the charismatic dimension contains an institutional element, including movements' internal organization and approved statutes.[14] No charismatic movement can ultimately be successful in evangelizing the world if it lacks a sacramental foundation. He also rejected the proposed dichotomy between the christological and the pneumatological, often connected with the institution-charism split, because neither can be taken in isolation from the other.[15] Finally, he rejected the dichotomy between hierarchy and prophecy because there is no scriptural basis for it.[16]

Instead, he found an historical approach to be most fruitful.[17] The apostles' divinely mandated mission was universal. Subsequent itinerant missionaries also sought to spread the good news throughout the world, forming the local leadership to continue to oversee the particular community. As the Gospel spread through the known world, these itinerant protégés of the apostles disappeared, and the remaining local leadership assumed the apostles' prophetic, sanctifying, and governing role. Nevertheless, apostolic succession can here be seen to refer to "the familiar idea that the bishops guarantee the continuity and unity of faith—in a continuity we call sacramental,"[18] while at the same time maintaining that to which the first apostles were sent.

In response to the church's assimilation into the world after the Roman persecution, Anthony fled to the desert to implement radically the Gospel. The ensuing monastic lifestyle was encouraged by the popes who recognized its importance for the church's universal mission.[19] Tracing the church's subsequent history from Anthony through the charisms of Benedict, Francis, Dominic, Ignatius, and the nineteenth-century missionary orders, Ratzinger identified twentieth-century charisms with this same tradition, and

---

13. Ratzinger, "Theological Locus," 481–504.
14. Ratzinger, "Theological Locus," 482–85.
15. Ratzinger, "Theological Locus," 485–87.
16. Ratzinger, "Theological Locus," 487–88.
17. Ratzinger, "Theological Locus," 488–91.
18. Ratzinger, "Theological Locus," 491.
19. Ratzinger, "Theological Locus," 492.

drew some conclusions from the commonalities of their distinct histories.[20] "So much is clear: the monastic movement creates a new center of life that does not abolish the local ecclesial structure of the post-apostolic Church, yet does not completely coincide with it, but is active within it as a vitalizing force. This center also functions as a reservoir from which the local church can draw a truly spiritual clergy [*geistliche-Geistliche*] that constantly renews the fusion of institution and charism."[21]

More concretely, each new movement, each new body of persons inspired by a charism, radically lived the Gospel. Their life overflowed the bounds of the local church. From Ratzinger's historical survey of the "waves" of "movements," which followed early monasticism, emerge elements he identifies as constitutive of authentic movements. First, Ratzinger credits Gregory the Great (590–604) for having "recognized monasticism's missionary potential,"[22] as exemplified by Augustine of Canterbury, but also by Patrick, Cyril, and Methodius. From this Ratzinger learns that "the papacy did not create the movements, but it did become their principal reference-point in the structure of the Church, their ecclesial support."[23] In other words, creative minorities will likely not be initiatives of the hierarchy but will grow from "irruptions of the Spirit" as manifested in charismatic leaders. Additionally, the examples of Augustine of Canterbury, Patrick, and others reveal that "the poverty and freedom of the evangelical life are conditions for a service to the gospel that goes beyond one's own homeland and its community."[24] Thus, while "creative minorities" will immediately have an impact on their local communities, the evangelical life tends to overflow into the universal mission of the church. In fact, it was usually the pope who encouraged and protected these new buds in the church. The classic example is the thirteenth-century tension between the recently-born mendicant orders—the Franciscans and Dominicans—and the so-called seculars.[25] Contra the "seculars," Ratzinger turns to Thomas Aquinas who "emphasized that Christ himself is the model and, on the basis of this model, defended the superiority of the apostolic life over a purely contemplative form of life" to which the seculars wished to constrict religious movements.[26] Aquinas argued, "The active life that brings to others the truths attained through

20. Ratzinger, "Theological Locus," 493.
21. Ratzinger, "Theological Locus," 493.
22. Ratzinger, "Theological Locus," 494.
23. Ratzinger, "Theological Locus," 494.
24. Ratzinger, "Theological Locus," 494.
25. Ratzinger, "Theological Locus," 497.
26. Ratzinger, "Theological Locus," 496.

preaching and contemplation is more perfect than the exclusively contemplative life."[27] For Ratzinger, Aquinas's fundamental insight is to have recognized Jesus's missionary discourse of Matthew 10 as "the rule of life and mission that the Lord gave to the apostles [and] is itself the permanent rule of the apostolic life, which the Church always needs. It is this rule that justifies the new movement of evangelization."[28] I add that Aquinas, in calling attention to the missionary aspect of the apostolic life, takes for granted the presence of a contemplative life, of a time and process of formation within the community. This immersion into the liturgical life of the church is ordered toward an immersion into the rest of society, to share the fruits of the retreat with the world. Lived communion and formation in the church, in its sacramental life understood concretely *and* spiritually, is a prerequisite for mission. In this framework, Ratzinger envisions a wider understanding of apostolic succession to encompass not only the bishops, but also the charisms given by the Holy Spirit over the centuries, because they correspond to the apostles' universal mission which included and exceeded the bounds of the local church.

From all of this, Ratzinger concludes that these movements, which renew and revitalize the church, "generally come from a charismatic leader and they take shape in concrete communities that live the whole gospel anew from this origin and recognize the Church without hesitation as the ground of their life, without which they could not exist."[29] When it comes to the needed reform and re-invigoration of the church, Ratzinger has no illusions of changing things from the top. His ecclesiology cannot be said to be monarchical in this sense. Rather, any *aggiornamento* that breathes new life in the church will come from the *anawim*, the remnant, the saints. As Ratzinger explains:

> All of this presupposes—and the source is usually the flame of the initial charism—a deep personal encounter with Christ. The formation and upbuilding of community does not exclude the personal element, but calls for it. Only when the person is struck and opened up by Christ in his inmost depth can the other also be inwardly touched, can there be reconciliation in the Holy Spirit, can true community grow. Within this basic Christological-pneumatological and existential structure, there can be a great diversity of accents and emphases, in which Christianity

---

27. Ratzinger, "Theological Locus," 496, quoting Aquinas, *Summa Theologiae*, III.40.1–2.

28. Ratzinger, "Theological Locus," 497.

29. Ratzinger, "Theological Locus," 501.

is a perpetually new event and the Spirit unceasingly renews the Church.[30]

Thus, around a charismatic leader dedicated to life in Christ through the Spirit can be gathered a community dedicated to the *vita evangelica*, to the proclamation of the good news in word and deed, to λογική λατρεία. "After all, this proclamation never happens through words alone; love, which is its inner center, at one and the same time the center of its truth and of its action, must be lived and in this way be proclamation."[31]

And so, in answer to his own question as to "Where, beyond its official teaching and its sacramental order, will I be able to experience [the Church] as what it is?"[32] a question which he admits can strike us with distressing urgency, he points to those ecclesial movements. These new ecclesial communities are the irruptions of the Spirit. They are movements "where the Church can be experienced and thus [are] a place of access to fellowship with Jesus, to sharing in his vision."[33]

8.3 The Example of the Focolare

Let us now turn to one of these communities to exemplify Ratzinger's existential ecclesiality. First, a brief introduction to Chiara Lubich, foundress of the Work of Mary, also called the Focolare,[34] sets the background for understanding why the spirituality and life of this movement qualifies as one possible way of concretely embodying Ratzinger's ecclesiology. Finally, the successful reputation of the young movement offers evidence of the potential efficacy of Ratzinger's notion of creative minorities.

8.3.1 Chiara Lubich and the Focolare: Concrete Unity

Chiara Lubich was born in 1920 in Trent. At the age of nineteen, upon returning from a Catholic Action retreat in Loreto she reported to her spiritual director she had discovered God's direction for her life. "He asked was it to be a religious sister, or in marriage, or as a consecrated virgin living in the world. She answered that it was none of these vocations, but another

---

30. Ratzinger, "Theological Locus," 502.
31. Ratzinger, "Theological Locus," 502.
32. Ratzinger, *Yes of Jesus Christ*, 37.
33. Ratzinger, *Yes of Jesus Christ*, 37.
34. For more on the life of Chiara Lubich, see Robertson, *Chiara*; Gallagher, *Woman's Work*.

way, inspired by the life of Mary at Nazareth: to be given completely to God; to live in a family; to live in the world. It was a 'fourth way' combining all of these vocations into one."³⁵ While she consecrated herself as a "bride of God" in 1943, this vocation took shape shortly later, in the midst of the heavy bombings under which Trent suffered during World War II. There, Chiara and a few other young women, her "first companions," gathered in bomb shelters, read the Gospel, and returned to the war-torn city to put that Word into practice. They read "Love your neighbor as yourself" (Matt 19:19) and, without pausing to ask what this meant, they sought to aid those in need. Chiara later explained, "each time we were filled with God's gifts: bread, powdered milk, marmalade . . . which we took to those who needed [them]."³⁶

This first community came to be known as a "*focolare*," which translates as "hearth" or "fireside." A couple of Jesus's *logia* became programmatic for them. When they read "Love one another as I have loved you" (John 15:13), understanding Jesus's passion as the form of his love, they subsequently made a pact to love like him. As a result, they learned to love each other concretely by sharing everything and being willing to sacrifice unto death for each other. Amid this mutual love, the Lord further made his presence known among them.

> We saw our lives take a qualitative leap forward. Someone came into our group, silently, an invisible Friend, giving us security, a more experiential joy, a new peace, a fullness of life, an inextinguishable light. Jesus was fulfilling his promise to us: "Where two or three are gathered in my name, I am there among them" (Matt 18:20).³⁷

Thus, one cardinal point of Focolare spirituality is "Jesus in our midst." Chiara explains this more distinctly in a recording from 1969: "I discovered him [Jesus in our midst] because he was there. In loving one another, we had established his presence . . . he enlightened us, he led us to understand the gospel 'where two or three are united, I am there,' that is, it was he who revealed himself."³⁸

On another occasion they opened, read, and lived "Father, may they all be one" (John 17:21). Lubich later recounted, "One thing was clear in our hearts: what God wanted for us was unity. We lived for the sole aim of being one with him, one with each other, and one with everyone. This marvelous

---

35. Purcell, "Focolare Movement," 161.
36. Lubich, *Essential Writings*, 4.
37. Lubich, *Essential Writings*, 6.
38. Lubich, May 10, 1969, Loppiano, Italty, in Povilus, *United in His Name*, 42.

vocation linked us to heaven and immersed in the one human family. What purpose in life could be greater?"[39] And so, "Unity" has become characteristic of the Focolare charism, a fundamental aspect of the concrete life lived and shared in a variety of contexts by Focolarini from all walks of life, vocations in the church, and places in the world.

This pattern—of gathering around the Gospel, changing their relationships with God and each other, and then bringing those new relationships to others—transformed their little corner of the world. "In this way, the Word generated the community. After only two months, in Trent five hundred people of different ages, vocations, and social classes lived this extraordinary experience together."[40] This movement for unity in and with Jesus has spread to all parts of the world and across denominations. It is as if more than twenty years before "communion" became a theme of Vatican II, the Holy Spirit was preparing a hearth around which to bring the experience of communion to the world. In fact, Chiara recognized the church had grown dark and cold in places and needed the light and warmth of Christ. It needed this concrete experience as well. In 1959 she wrote:

> In this world we are all brothers and sisters and yet we pass each other as if we were strangers. And this happens even among baptized Christians. The Communion of Saints, the Mystical Body exists. But this Body is like a network of darkened tunnels. The power to illuminate them exists; in many individuals there is the light of grace, but Jesus did not want only this when he turned to the Father, calling upon him. He wanted a heaven on earth: the unity of all with God and with one another; the network of tunnels to be illuminated; the presence of Jesus to be in every relationship with others, as well as in the soul of each. This is his final testament, the most precious desire of a God who gave his life for us.[41]

Before exploring more closely how the Focolare have been fire-starters, instruments of the Spirit in the world, let us examine how Chiara's spirituality relates to Ratzinger's ecclesiology.

---

39. Lubich, *Essential Writings*, 99.
40. Purcell, "Focolare Movement," 162.
41. Lubich, *Essential Writings*, 17.

8.3.2 Lubich and Ratzinger: Jesus in the Midst as Concrete Communion for Mission

Unity Modeled After the Trinity

In chapter 3, I argued that Ratzinger's notion of ecclesial communion finds its ground in the divine *communio personarum*. Trinitarian unity is christologically mediated to humanity in the Spirit. This is affected sacramentally and made concrete in the church. Though Lubich uses different terminology, her meaning is fundamentally the same.

As early as 1946, only three years after the first gathering that became the Focolare, in a text entitled "Unity," Chiara explains,

> Unity requires souls who are ready to lose their own personalities, entirely. It is because unity is God, and God is *one and triune*.
>
> Because of their very same nature, which is love, the three live unifying themselves (by emptying themselves) and in doing so they each re-find themselves.[42]

Lubich here foreshadows Ratzinger's notion of person as relation defined in reference to the Trinity. Later in 1949, Lubich returned to the same topic, explaining in her own terms the christological mediation of unity and the manner in which it images the Trinity:

> For him to be present [Jesus in our midst], this is how we must live [love one another as Christ loved us]. But . . . loving in this way means being "other Christs." . . .
>
> When he is among us, we are one and we are three, each equal to the one . . .
>
> What happens between you and me is similar to what happens between the persons of the Trinity . . .
>
> The Holy Spirit is third, after the Father and the Son. He proceeds from both.
>
> Yet he is eternal with the two.
>
> In fact, how can we imagine a Father who generates and loves the Son, if Love is not in him? And how can we imagine a Son who loves if Love is not in him? Yet, [Love] proceeds from the other two and is third (so to speak).
>
> In our own terms we would say that each one of the three is at the same time before and after the other two.

---

42. Lubich, unpublished writing, December 2, 1946, in Povilus, *United in His Name*, 59–60.

> This happens when two are united in the name of Jesus. They must be Jesus in order to have him among them, but they are Jesus when they have him among them...
>
> When we are united, and he is present, we are no longer two, but *one*.
>
> His is a mystical presence among us. He is in the Father; therefore, in him, the two of us are in the Father and we participate in the life of the Trinity.
>
> The trinitarian life flows freely in us, and as we love the others as He has loved us, we bring them to participate in this treasure of divine life.
>
> Or better, they experience in themselves the treasure they had already received when they were engrafted into God through Jesus by way of baptism and the other sacraments.[43]

Christians can experience communion, or unity as Lubich prefers to express it, only if Jesus is actively present in their midst. When Christians are living this unity, they are mirroring and living in some real albeit imperfect way the trinitarian life. After all, "Unity only exists between God and God."[44] In content, Lubich is here quite close to Ratzinger for whom "Trinitarian faith and faith in the Incarnation guide the idea of communion.... Communio first must be understood theologically. Only then can one draw implications for a sacramental notion of communio, and only after that for an ecclesiological notion."[45] Yet let us note a subtle difference in emphasis. For Ratzinger faith in the Trinity and the Incarnation "guide the *idea* of communion," which is to be "understood theologically." For Lubich however, all the theological articulations and spiritual reflections have grown out of the concrete experience of unity and of Jesus in the midst. This unity with Jesus and with others in Jesus is for the Focolare a real existential experience through which they perceive their own participation in the life of the Trinity.

For Ratzinger the theological understanding of communion leads to ecclesiological communion. How does the concrete life of the Focolare relate to ecclesiology?

The Ecclesiological Dimension of Jesus in Our Midst

Now we consider how Lubich's notion of unity maps onto life in the church. As is her way, Lubich explains her understanding based on her experience

---

43. Lubich, unpublished writing, 1949, in Povilus, *United in His Name*, 60-61.
44. Lubich, "Dialogo aperto," 33, in Povilus, *United in His Name*, 138n10.
45. Ratzinger, "Communio," 444, 446.

with the Lord, who "reopened the mystery of the Church for us . . . that is he led us to understand what it means to be Church and to live it with greater awareness. He unveiled a spirituality, which is the spirituality of the mystical body, the spirituality of the Church."[46] For Chiara, as for Ratzinger, no community, charism, or spirituality can be truly legitimate outside of the visible church.[47] Therefore, this spirituality can only exist in communion with the whole church. Or as Ratzinger might say, it can only receive its ecclesiality sacramentally through recognition and acceptance of apostolic succession. For Chiara, the church must recognize not only the spirituality, but, in a certain sense, the love that animates the charism verifies the church. For, if "Jesus in the midst is lacking" among the faithful, then "[those faithful] are [only] potentially in the full beauty of the Church; they are the Church, but they are like this room with the lights out. The room is here, but you cannot see it. So too, the Church is present, but you cannot see it."[48]

A careful observer might here object, where is the Eucharist in all this? Is it not the Eucharist that makes the church and that is the origin of mission in Ratzinger's theology? For Chiara, the Eucharist and Jesus in our midst mutually depend upon and enrich each other. On the one hand, "Jesus in the eucharist is a function of Jesus in our midst,"[49] and on the other hand, the Eucharist is the "means for having Jesus in our midst."[50] However, for Lubich, there is no tension between these statements. She admits that "We cannot understand unity without the sacrament of unity, the one thing that makes everybody one, one single body,"[51] and further clarifies the relationship between the Eucharist and Jesus in our midst as follows: "Jesus in our midst does not substitute for Jesus in the eucharist, but is nourished by him. . . . Generally, unity for us is unthinkable without Jesus in the eucharist, he is the bond of unity."[52] Thus, for Lubich as for Ratzinger, the Eucharist makes the church. Jesus in the Eucharist effects ecclesial communion. The

---

46. Lubich, July 7, 1962, Grottaferrata, Italy, in Povilus, *United in His Name*, 81.

47. "Only Jesus among us was our master, father and guide . . . yet not even him would we have wanted had the church not approved of this life of ours. For this reason the light that came from the presence of Jesus among us was subjected to the one who represented the Church to us. For us there was no Christ without the Church" (Lubich, December 8, 1971, Rocca di Papa, Italy, in Povilus, *United in His Name*, 80).

48. Lubich, October 20, 1975, Rocca di Papa, Italy, in Povilus, *United in His Name*, 82.

49. Lubich, October 20, 1975, Rocca di Papa, Italy, in Povilus, *United in His Name*, 85.

50. Lubich, March 17, 1975, Frascati, Italy, in Povilus, *United in His Name*, 85.

51. Lubich, unpublished writing, 1950, 19, in Povilus, *United in His Name*, 85.

52. Lubich, *Diary*, 116, in Povilus, *United in His Name*, 85.

difference between the two lies primarily in the contrast between Lubich's more concrete and experiential context and Ratzinger's rather academic theological style.

Yet, despite the apparent profound agreement between the two, one may still question the compatibility of their thought. From what has been said thus far, Chiara seems heavily focused on Jesus in *our* midst, on unity within the community, perhaps to the neglect of evangelization and mission. Thus, now I consider how the Focolare's life of unity can evangelize the world.

Jesus in Our Midst and the Mission of the Church

For Ratzinger, Jesus instituted the new and true worship, in which Christians participate through the Eucharist. Proper reception of the Eucharist, which is right worship, worship in accord with the *logos*, means becoming Eucharist. True and right worship is in itself a credible witness of the presence of God in the world. However, Ratzinger's liturgical sensibilities are not so narrow as to be concerned only with what happens during Mass properly speaking. Rather, "the Christian liturgy . . . in a certain sense is more realistically celebrated in everyday life than in the ritual execution of it."[53] This was the view of the fathers, for whom "the everyday practice of charity is an essential part of the eucharistic event, and furthermore only in this way is the status of Christians as the Body of Christ fully achieved."[54] This is also Ratzinger's view, and it is not far from that of Lubich.

Like Ratzinger, Lubich recognizes that the world is deeply troubled and diseased—in need of the divine physician who alone can cure it. "The world needs to be enlightened, healed, and cleansed by a solid block of Christians among whom lives Christ, the only one capable of creating a *new world*. This is what we want."[55] Christ heals in and through the church. Ratzinger calls for creative minorities to do this work. Chiara speaks of "local action cells," "which are like little fires that are enkindled where Christ is in the midst of laborers, clerical workers, government officials, etc."[56] If these cells can manage to keep Jesus in their midst, to bring Jesus into the midst of their little portion of the world, then the reign of God, the civilization of love, will

---

53. Ratzinger, *Das neue Volk Gottes*, 22, in Heim, *Joseph Ratzinger*, 246.

54. Ratzinger, *Das neue Volk Gottes*, 22, in Heim, *Joseph Ratzinger*, 246.

55. Lubich, "Carissimi volontari," March 6, 1976, Rocca di Papa, Italy, in Povilus, *United in His Name*, 97.

56. Lubich, June 8, 1965, Rocca di Papa, Italy, in Povilus, *United in His Name*, 98.

begin to take root more fully. She explains that if Jesus is in our midst at all times in all places,

> there will be an upsurge of vibrant cells in the Church which, in time, will be able to animate the society that surrounds them until the whole mass is penetrated. This mass, then, informed by the spirit of Christ, will be better able to fulfill God's plan for the world, and give a decisive thrust to a peaceful, irresistible social revolution bearing consequences we never dared hope for.
>
> If the historical Christ healed and satisfied the hunger of souls and bodies, Christ mystically present among his followers today knows how to do just the same. If the historical Christ asked his Father, before dying, for oneness among his disciples, Christ mystically present among Christians knows how to bring this about.[57]

In fact, not only is this some happy side effect or secondary goal of the Focolare. Rather, it is the purpose of Jesus in the midst. After all, "In today's de-christianized and materialistic society, Christians, wherever they are, must build among themselves a spiritual cloister. If they themselves would be the columns, living water would flow in their midst for the use of many."[58] And since the historical Christ came for the sick and sinners some 2000 years ago, so he comes in our midst for the same today:

> "People who are healthy do not need a doctor; sick people do. ... It is mercy I desire and not sacrifice. I have come to call not the self-righteous, but sinners" (Matt 9:12–13). This is the vocation of the historical Jesus.
> It is the mission of *Jesus in the midst of us*.[59]

So, just as the Eucharist is the origin of mission and communion is ordered to mission in Ratzinger's thought, so here Jesus in the midst, the center of Focolare life and spirituality, has the healing of the sick and sinner as its *telos*. Unity leads to mission. This should come as no surprise since one of the other sayings of Jesus foundational for the Focolare is his prayer, "*ut unum sint*." Jesus himself makes the connection between communion and mission, praying, "that they may all be one; even as you, Father, are in me, and I in you, that they also may be in us, so that the world may believe that you have sent me" (John 17:21).

---

57. Lubich, *Yes, Yes, No, No*, 89–90, in Povilus, *United in His Name*, 98.
58. Lubich, *Scritti Spirituali*, 227, in Povilus, *United in His Name*, 99.
59. Lubich, *Diary*, 168, in Povilus, *United in His Name*, 99.

One question remains. All of this might sound good on paper. It is nice to talk about as a spirituality. But, is it practical? Is it effective? Can love, communion, unity change the world?

8.3.3 The Concrete Effects of a Mission that Flows from Unity

It is difficult to examine the evangelical or missional effects of life in communion.[60] Such effects are not always verifiable, nor should apparent "successes" be attributed simplistically to one cause or another. Nevertheless, in the case of the movements in general and the Focolare in particular, there are some concrete examples to which to point.

Recognition of the Evangelical Effectiveness of Unity in the Movements

First, as referenced in Pope Benedict's post-synodal apostolic letter, *Verbum Domini*, the 2008 synod on the Word of God in the life and mission of the church "recognized with gratitude that the ecclesial movements and the new communities are a great force for evangelization in our times and an incentive to the development of new ways of proclaiming the Gospel."[61] Thus, the fruit born of the work of the Focolare and the other new communities has been recognized officially and magisterially and synodally. Two years later Pope Benedict expanded on the manner in which the modern age might be moved to encounter the Lord. In an already quoted address to the bishops of Portugal, he explained:

> In fact, when, in the view of many people, the Catholic faith is no longer the common patrimony of society and, often, seen as threatened and obscured by the "gods" and masters of this world, only with great difficulty can the faith touch the hearts of people by means of simple speeches or moral appeals, and even less by a general appeal to Christian values. The courageous and integral appeal to principles is essential and indispensable; yet simply proclaiming the message does not penetrate to the depths of people's hearts, it does not touch their freedom, it does not change their lives. What attracts is, above all, the encounter

---

60. Bishop Julius Porteous explains, "To attempt to catalogue the ways in which this work of evangelization is being realized [in the movements] is impossible. They are legion" (Porteous, *New Wine and Fresh Skins*, 107–8).

61. Benedict XVI, *Verbum domini* 94.

> with believing persons who, through their faith, draw others to the grace of Christ by bearing witness to him.[62]

This is precisely the mode of Christ-encounter offered by the Focolare, whose purpose and joy is to love each other such that Jesus is in their midst and in so loving to prepare the hearts of others to also encounter Christ in their midst. In his book *Ecclesial Movements and Communities*, Brendan Leahy, the bishop of Limerick, Ireland and a member of the Focolare, takes up Ratzinger's and Toynbee's term to describe how the movements function in the world. Leahy writes, "As creative minorities the movements respond to the recognition that to mend 'the Christian fabric of society' the Church also needs to 'remake the Christian fabric of the ecclesial community itself.'"[63] Leahy refers to the comments of Medard Kehl, who highlights the importance of the particular form of mission effected by a life of unity. Kehl explains that the movements "represent an authentically Christian response to the challenge of the contemporary cultural situation in proportion as they try expressly to live ecclesial 'communio' in conditions of modern individualization."[64] Kehl proceeds to draw attention to the manner in which concrete unity offered by the Focolare moves

> the existential core of man in his relation of faith with God and love for his neighbor. The conscious decision to embrace the faith, the experience of its beauty and reciprocal support make such Christians capable of conforming their concrete mode of life to the spirit of the Gospel and thus acting in a missionary sense within our society. It is surprising that, even among the ranks of those "far from the Church," many feel attracted by these communities: here the Church is undoubtedly presented to them in a surprising humanity and immediately.[65]

As Leahy follows the argument, Kehl concludes with an emphatic statement, important for our topic. He claims the movements "may be the most authentically and (from a practical point of view) effective Christian response to many religious and quasi-religious needs of people in our society; a response which the highly institutionalized churches are no longer thought

---

62. Benedict XVI, "Address to the Bishops of Portugal," in Leahy, *Ecclesial Movements*, 113–14.

63. Leahy, *Ecclesial Movements*, 114, quoting John Paul II, *Christifidelis laici*, 34.

64. Leahy, *Ecclesial Movements*, 116, quoting Kehl, *Wohin geht die Kirche*, 153–57.

65. Leahy, *Ecclesial Movements*, 116, quoting Kehl, *Wohin geht die Kirche*, 153–57.

capable of giving, and which is therefore being sought in large part in the most varied mystic-natural currents."⁶⁶

Kehl puts his finger on the pulse of the argument: Ratzinger calls for creative minorities who, through their eucharistic life of communion, can bring Christ to the world by being Eucharist for the world. Ratzinger sees the new movements as fonts of hope for the Spirit's movement within and renewal of the church and the world. Kehl claims these same movements may be the most authentic and effective form of evangelizing the modern age, precisely because their mission is communal and their communion is missionary.

λογική λατρεία *and the Cry of Jesus Crucified and Forsaken*

The above offers convincing reasons for hope in the movements as creative minorities, which can re-invigorate the church for performing its task as the universal sacrament of salvation. However, if the movements are recognized so broadly and internationally for their evangelical effectiveness,⁶⁷ why focus on the Focolare? What makes Ratzinger's contribution noteworthy?

For Ratzinger, the new worship which is right worship demands that Christians offer themselves, their lives, as Eucharist. True worship is not limited to ritual sacrifices but demands submission of one's whole life to God.⁶⁸ Participation in the Mass that is not preceded and followed by a life offered to God, a life of love, of self-offering, is dangerously close to becoming an empty ritual and a dead letter.⁶⁹ In this sense, true worship is found only in the Eucharist where Jesus offers his historical and his ecclesial body to the Father, and is accomplished where the church in her members become Eucharist "for the life of the world," when Christians "offer [their] bodies as a living sacrifice, holy and pleasing to God, [their] spiritual worship," λογική λατρεία (Rom 12:1).

Another cardinal point in the spirituality of the Focolare, which approximates Ratzinger's eucharistic and liturgical view of mission, is Chiara's devotion to Jesus crucified and forsaken. In an address given to the World Council of Churches,⁷⁰ Lubich offers the Focolare's "spirituality of unity"

---

66. Leahy, *Ecclesial Movements*, 116, quoting Kehl, *Wohin geht die Kirche*, 153–57.

67. This is true; however, it is also true that US bishops have been slower to adopt and welcome the movements than bishops in Europe, Asia, Africa, and South America.

68. See Ratzinger, *Pilgrim Fellowship of Faith*, 117.

69. See Ratzinger, *Pilgrim Fellowship of Faith*, 120.

70. Lubich, "Unity and Jesus Crucified," 87–95. The address was originally given at the Ecumenical Centre in Geneva, October 29, 2002.

as a foundation for ecumenical dialogue[71] and describes unity and Jesus forsaken[72] as the two main principles of their spirituality.[73] She narrates a sequence of events in which the Holy Spirit revealed to them "the precious 'key' for accomplishing unity. It is Jesus crucified who cried out: 'My God, my God, why have you forsaken me?' (Matt 27:46)."[74] In articulating the import of Jesus's cry of abandonment she turns to John of the Cross who explains the moment of Jesus's cry as "the most extreme forsakenness, sensitively, that [Jesus] had suffered in his life."[75] For Lubich, Jesus offers to Christians his forsakenness "as the model to imitate in all trials, and especially—we must say at once—in the sufferings of disunity,"[76] because in his cry from the cross, Jesus offers a mirror image of any physical, moral, or spiritual suffering which people can undergo.[77] Therefore,

> In all of these sufferings, which we can experience personally, we can recognize him. But we can see him also in every brother and sister who suffers. We see him in the situations of poverty we encounter.
>
> And what happens when we encounter these living images of Jesus forsaken?
>
> In approaching those who resemble him, we can openly speak to them of him. For all who recognize their similarity to him and accept a share in his fate, this is how he turns out to be: speech for the mute, the answer for the ignorant, light for the blind, a voice for the deaf, rest for the weary, hope for the despairing, satisfaction for the hungry, reality for the deceived, victory for the failure, daring for the timid, joy for the sorrowful, certainty for the uncertain, normality for the strange, company

---

71. She notes that on January 6, 2001, Pope John Paul II had formally suggested this "spirituality of communion" to the whole Church in his Apostolic Letter, *Novo millennio ineunte*, 25–27.

72. Lubich explains, "We like to understand [Jesus' cry of abandonment] this way: is not God after all One, distinct in three Persons, contemporaneously One and Three, in a time so to speak outside time, where Love lives, where the Father is perennially generating the Word, and the Holy Spirit perennially proceeds as a divine Person himself too, simultaneously uniting and distinguishing the Father and the Son, so that they are One and they are Three?" (Lubich, *Cry*, 25).

73. Lubich, "Unity and Jesus Crucified," 87.

74. Lubich, "Unity and Jesus Crucified," 88.

75. John of the Cross, *Collected Works*, 124, in Lubich, "Unity and Jesus Crucified," 89.

76. Lubich, "Unity and Jesus Crucified," 89.

77. Lubich, "Unity and Jesus Crucified," 90.

for the lonely, unity for the separated, that which is uniquely useful for the useless.[78]

Not only is Jesus forsaken to be recognized in the sufferings of others, but he is also the model for how we can respond to our own sufferings.

> What is the best way to overcome every personal or collective disunity?
>
> In both cases, I must say this: "If he has taken upon himself every suffering, every division and trauma, I can think that wherever I see suffering, I also see him. This suffering reminds me of him; it's a presence of his, a countenance of his." And like him, we too must not stop in the cracks of division. If Jesus re-abandoned himself to the Father who was abandoning him, in like manner we must go beyond and overcome the trial saying: "In this suffering, I love you, Jesus forsaken, I want you, I embrace you"!
>
> And if we are thus willing, generous and attentive to continue loving what God wants from us in the following moment, our experience is that, more often than not, the suffering disappears as if by a divine alchemy. This is because love calls forth the gifts of the Spirit—joy, light, peace—and the risen Lord in us takes the place of the forsaken one.[79]

For Lubich, Jesus crucified and forsaken is the personal image by which all impediments to unity and love can be overcome. Whenever Christians are tempted to ignore or to run from the suffering of others or to use their own suffering, hurt, or fear as an excuse to fail to love, Jesus forsaken can strengthen them to abandon themselves to God, and so to love.

But how is this related to Ratzinger's notion of true worship and the eucharistic origin of mission? For Chiara, Jesus crucified and forsaken is not merely a model to be imitated; he "is himself the sacrifice."[80] In the physical (blood) sacrifice of Jesus's body on the cross, Lubich sees Jesus's cry of forsakenness as his spiritual sacrifice because in that moment the Son experiences the concealment of the Father's presence and yet "re-abandons himself to the Father, reuniting himself to him."[81] By taking on sinful humanity's perception of having been abandoned by the Father, Jesus's cry "brought about the reconciliation and union of the human race with God

---

78. Lubich, "Unity and Jesus Crucified," 90.
79. Lubich, "Unity and Jesus Crucified," 91.
80. Lubich, *Cry*, 22.
81. Lubich, *Cry*, 27.

through grace,"⁸² and thus was the church born. For these reasons—the birth of the church and the reuniting (in a certain sense) of Father and Son effected by the cry—the Focolare believe that "Love for Jesus crucified and forsaken—leads to that external, and especially internal, detachment which is needed for the realization of all supernatural unity."⁸³ So for Lubich and the Focolare both the Eucharist and love for Jesus forsaken are roots of unity, communion.

For Lubich, as one might expect, this is all very concrete, not merely theoretical or academic. She explains that this love for Jesus forsaken commands action. Like Christ, "we too have been given a body by God, which we are to use to obey him . . . [which] means fulfilling God's will. This allows us, too, to make a sacrifice of our own lives."⁸⁴ In the immediate context of the above she turns to the same quote from which Ratzinger takes the term "λογική λατρεία." She continues, "Paul expressed himself as follows: 'I urge you, there, brothers, by the mercies of God, to offer your bodies as a living sacrifice, holy and pleasing to God, your spiritual worship' (Rom 12:1)."⁸⁵ And if Christians are to offer themselves with Jesus forsaken as a sacrifice to God, then "every Christian is truly a priest. Since unity is now restored, access to God is no longer reserved once a year to the high priest, as in the Old Testament, but too all the baptized who have become 'a chosen race, a kingdom of priests' (1 Pet 2:9)."⁸⁶ She ventures to proclaim that this spiritual worship, these "spiritual sacrifices" offered by the Focolare, might be the providential design of God. "Perhaps God raised up our Movement also for this purpose: to contribute to the revival of the priestly character of the Christian people, as Vatican II desires, after the manner of the early Christians."⁸⁷ Furthermore, if the self-offerings of these "local action cells," of these creative minorities, enacted out of love for Jesus forsaken and out of submission to the will of the Father, qualify as priestly sacrifices, they certainly qualify as "profound act[s] of worship."⁸⁸ Lubich sums up the manner in which concrete love for Jesus forsaken is really eucharistic, is really λογική λατρεία and is therefore missionary:

> In preaching the gospel, the apostle does God's will and offers himself as a victim. In preaching the gospel, the apostle also

---

82. John of the Cross, *Collected Works*, 124, in Lubich, *Cry*, 28.
83. Opera di Maria, *Statuti generali* 8, 14, in Lubich, *Cry*, 29.
84. Lubich, *Cry*, 32.
85. Lubich, *Cry*, 32.
86. Lubich, *Cry*, 33.
87. Lubich, *Cry*, 33. Lubich refers to LG 10, 34.
88. Lubich, *Cry*, 33.

performs a real sacrifice, offering God his converts, who appear like victims transformed by the Holy Spirit from what is "carnal" into what is "spiritual" (cf. Rom 15:16). They were often called "firstfruits" (a term generally used in connection with worship: "But we must always give thanks to God for you, brothers and sisters beloved by the Lord, because God chose you as the firstfruits." (2 Thess 2:13, NRSV).

Is this not also what characterizes the worship our Movement offers to God? Basically our work is nothing but being converted and reconverted to God, and converted and reconverting many, many others. We too, in our own selves and in many others, have spiritual victims and firstfruits to offer to God all over the world.

Let's be delighted that our whole life, lived according to the guidelines given us by God and blessed by the Church (and so are God's will for us) is a continuous worship offered to God; a genuine expression of the royal priesthood that clothes us all.[89]

For Lubich, as for Ratzinger, the most effective means of communicating Christ to the world is for the church, for small communities of Christians, to be sacraments of the divine *communio personarum*. As Lubich explains, "A people that is united in the name of the Father, the Son, and the Holy Spirit" makes Christ known "through the reciprocal love among its members ... through the unity it creates."[90] She elaborates, "The greatest witness to the existence of God that we can give the world is that of living in such a way as to have his presence in our midst. In this way, he bears witness to himself. ... God also wanted to be testified through a community that carried his presence in its midst. It is a return to the spirit of the early Christians, who themselves bore witness to unity."[91] After all, "The life we must try to imitate is the life of the Holy Trinity, by loving each other, with the grace of God, in the way the persons of the Holy Trinity love one another. Living in this manner gives the world the strongest witness of God."[92] All of this is priestly, eucharistic; it is spiritual worship. As we have seen, Ratzinger believes that a eucharistic ecclesiology not only speaks to the formal structures of the church but also has concrete implications for the lives and the ethos of Christian communities. Eucharist is not some *thing* to be received

---

89. Lubich, *Cry*, 34.

90. Lubich, "Dialoge aperto," 35, in Povilus, *United in His Name*, 43.

91. Lubich, September 17, 1961, Grottaferrata, Italty, in Povilus, *United in His Name*, 43.

92. Lubich, "Sintesi della spiritualità," 75, in Povilus, *United in His Name*, 65–66.

or adored. Christians are to become Eucharist, to become other Christs, as Lubich states.

The Focolare's insights into "Jesus in the midst" and love for "Jesus crucified and forsaken" are quite similar to Ratzinger's notion of the faithful becoming Eucharist, to the ethos of his ecclesiology. After all, "Jesus does not want to remain only within the tabernacle. He desires to be present among human beings. To share their thoughts their plans, their concerns, their joys."[93] Ratzinger's eucharistic ecclesiology and communion missiology, like the life shared by the Focolare, is thoroughly concrete, existential. At the same time, the practical insight of Lubich's charism and of Ratzinger's ecclesiology is no ethical code or moralism. Rather, as Lubich explains, "it is the mysticism of those who love one another as he loved us; the mysticism of a unity of souls who are a reflection, here on earth, of the Trinity above: here on earth, because here below we bear witness to the God-man and here below is the Church."[94]

This mysticism is the mysticism of the church as the mystical body. It is the "mystical life of the Church." It indicates part of the uniqueness of Chiara's insight, part of what makes the charism worthy of its own ecclesial designation and not merely some new derivation of Franciscanism, Dominicanism, etc. This mysticism, like the challenge of Ratzinger's eucharistic ecclesiology, is not some vague otherworldly ideal, but is a question of living the life of the church to the full, of moving out of pious Pelagianism and lukewarm passivity into lives offered as eucharistic sacrifices to the Father. For the Focolare, Jesus in the midst is the demand and the confirmation of true ecclesial life. In Ratzinger's ecclesiology, saying "amen" to the Eucharist requires that we cultivate Jesus in our midst. Or, as Augustine says, that we begin more fully to be what we see and to receive what we are.

The ecclesial movements in general—and the Focolare in particular—exemplify well how creative minorities like those envisioned by Joseph Ratzinger can fulfil the mission of the church to be the universal sacrament of salvation through their communal worship, both in the liturgy and in their lives.

---

93. Lubich, unpublished writing, December 25, 1974, in Povilus, *United in His Name*, 47.

94. Lubich, unpublished writing, September 29, 1950, in Povilus, *United in His Name*, 66–67.

9

Conclusion

RECALL THAT RATZINGER BELIEVES that "we need men like Benedict of Nursia, who, in an age of dissipation and decadence, immersed himself in the uttermost solitude. Then, after all the purification he had to undergo, he succeeded in rising again to the light . . . where he assembled the forces from which a new world was formed."[1] St. Benedict found something true, good, and beautiful, and built it up. Thus, Ratzinger calls for creative minorities that can offer stability and fellowship in a time of mobility and anonymity,[2] which, in their withdrawal to, and lived worship of God, can bear witness to God's presence in the world concretely and eloquently.

One may perceive in this Benedictinism the image of withdrawal, which is then often equated with escapism and quietism—in a word, with giving up on the world. However, perhaps there is something about the image of Benedictine "withdrawal" that can help us to think better about formation and witness today. Perhaps the aspect of Benedictine life that might be characterized negatively as withdrawal contains within it something that is important for our times. After all, St. Benedict did not actually withdraw from the world for the sake of doing so, he ran to the Father in single-minded devotion. Indeed, many of these monastic communities did not head to the land to hide from "the world"; rather, they built their monastery upon a hill, a beacon to the stranger and sojourner. Their hospitality initiated relationships in which Christ could be encountered, in which the "others" could experience the joy of the Gospel. Perhaps this different form of physical presence-in-withdrawal can be a helpful analogy for the tasks of the New Evangelization.

Furthermore, in light of the power of the modern hegemony, Ratzinger's Bonaventurean view, which emphasizes that grace does not merely perfect nature but converts and heals it, demands a willingness to admit

1. Ratzinger, *God and the World*, 392.
2. Ratzinger, *Dogma and Preaching*, 210–21, esp. 213–17.

that one is sick and to go to the divine physician in search of a cure. Indeed, withdrawal to the physician to be cured *for* mission seems an apt response. In this context, one might fairly conceive of secular liberalism as a societal riptide that grabs persons and pulls them out into the deep. One cannot swim against the tide. The message is simply too hegemonic, the tide too strong. One would either be swept away or become exhausted and drown. Rather than directly opposing it, the proper response to encountering a riptide is to swim perpendicular to the tide, to withdraw from it in order to rest, gather one's strength, and only then to return to the mission. This notion of withdrawal is not an example of defeatism, quietism, or escapism. It is withdrawal ordered to mission.

Jesus's first public action after his baptism is withdrawal to the desert, retreat. Just as Elijah retreats to Horeb to find the silence in which God can be heard, and Jesus retreats into the desert to gather the strength and focus necessary for his mission, so the church retreats during Lent to prepare to accompany the Lord on that mission on the way to Calvary. Can we not admit that in this modern era—when so many cradle Catholics and baptized Christians remain unconvinced of their responsibility to evangelize, when so many of our imaginations are more formed by super-hero movies and commercials than by the saints and the Gospels, and when so many of us can more aptly be described as "moralistic therapeutic deists"[3] than as disciples or evangelizers—communities desperately need to be formed together. Only thus can they hear effectively God's call, receive God's grace, and store up strength to fulfill God's mission: to glorify him in their bodies.

Even in the military a retreat is not a rout. A retreat is pulling back in order to regroup. Retreat always has a purpose. For St. Benedict, for Ratzinger, for creative minorities today, withdrawal means withdrawal for proper formation. Just as Chiara Lubich and her first companions first gathered around the Gospel to receive Jesus in the midst before bringing his presence to war-torn Trent, so women and men living in this modern age must escape from the hegemonic riptide to prepare the way for the Lord, in order to change their own minds, hearts, and lives so that they may then change the world.

Humans have a limited amount of mental, emotional, and spiritual power. As our minds and energies are dispersed among distractions, we ultimately run out of energy, lose focus, are drained of our strength to convert, to change, to evangelize. So, it is a practical necessity, an act of humility, to recognize the need to withdraw precisely to gather strength, to undergo conversion and formation, to build up communion for the sake of mission.

---

3. Smith and Denton, *Soul Searching*, 162.

When this occurs, the person and the community can coil itself like a spring, until the mind, emotions, and will are clarified and focused, ready to bound with joy and perseverance out of the desert and into the world. People and communities simply will not significantly change the world, will not bring Christ to the world if they do not first retreat. They must welcome Jesus in their own midst first before they can bring him to the world.

For Ratzinger, this retreat is a eucharistic retreat. It is a retreat into re-formation, into the remembering (*anamnesis*) and re-membering that makes the church. The church will fulfill the mission of Christ only to the degree that Christian persons and communities are more closely conformed to Christ. It is only from, through, and in the Eucharist that the church can efficaciously be His flesh for the life of the world.

Ratzinger's Benedictine articulation of Toynbee's "creative minorities" calls for small, intentional communities of Christians in whom Christ can be encountered, through whom persons can enter into the universal body of Christ, with whom they can become "creative" evangelizers in the modern world. Moreover, Ratzinger's notion of creative minorities—when read through the lens of his thoroughly eucharistic ecclesiology and his communion of mission and as exemplified in the Focolare—cannot be interpreted as escapism. Rather it provides an effective model for communicating the life of Christ present in a community performing the life of love in the city of God to persons still wandering in the city of man, still seeking truth, goodness, and beauty in the midst of the static noise propagated by the secular liturgies.

Although Ratzinger's ecclesiological writings have left him vulnerable to criticisms, nevertheless, upon an examination of his linking of liturgy and mission, those criticisms lose their footing. One perceives that for Ratzinger the church is also quite incarnate. His is an embodied ecclesiology whereby the church is called to express in its ethos what it celebrates in worship. Members of the body are to manifest this communion "through the Body," in love and reconciliation. Their lives are to be a priestly offering of glory to God (*doxa*), expressed in *lived communion*. In this way through embodied signs of *caritas*, the church as sacrament of salvation to the world can be beheld and encountered. This encounter already takes place in the ecclesial movements, which for Ratzinger are signs of authentic ecclesial existence made fruitful by the Spirit. They are "concrete places of Revelation," which testify that we come to know God through the "other," and in community. Ratzinger explains that through the movements the church can be "experienced and thus [be] a place of access to fellowship with Jesus, to sharing in his vision."[4] This is not to idealize the concrete experience of communion that the new ecclesial movements embody. However, fifty years after the Second Vatican Council, through the gift of the renewed outpouring of the Holy Spirit on the church, they provide a tangible, necessary testimony to the ecclesiology of communion as a living reality. After all, "the universal Church becomes abstract and unreal if it is not presented here and now, in this place and in this time, in an actual community as a living thing."[5] Thus creative minorities, if they "live out a true and profound catholicity in their individual communities, whatever form they may take . . . then they become fruitful and become themselves the Church, the place where faith is born and place of rebirth into the truth"[6] and into love. In other words, in these creative minorities one can encounter a contextualized type of Ratzinger's existential ecclesiality, which offers an effective, and attractive model for realizing the reality of communion in a manner capable of speaking to the men and women of the twenty-first century. In them, Ratzinger's eucharistic ecclesiology is being put into practice. In them one can often experience Jesus in the midst.

---

4. Ratzinger, *Yes of Jesus Christ*, 37.
5. Ratzinger, *Yes of Jesus Christ*, 38.
6. Ratzinger, *Yes of Jesus Christ*, 38.

Bibliography

Alberigo, Giuseppe, and Joseph Komonchak, eds. *History of Vatican II*. 5 vols. Maryknoll, NY: Orbis, 1995–2006.

Aquinas, Thomas. *Knowing and Naming God (1a. 12–13)*. Vol. 3 of *Summa Theologiae*. Translated by Herbert McCabe. Cambridge: Cambridge University Press, 2006.

Augustine. *City of God (De Civitate Dei)*. Part I. Vol. 6 of *The Works of Saint Augustine: A Translation for the Twenty-First Century*. Translated by William Babcock. Notes by Boniface Ramsey. Hyde Park, NY: New City, 2012.

Balthasar, Hans Urs von. "Gotteserfahrung biblisch und patristisch." *IKZ* (1976) 497–509.

———. *Razing the Bastions: On the Church in This Age*. San Francisco: Communio, 1993.

———. *Theology of Karl Barth*. Translated by Edward Oakes. San Francisco: Ignatius, 1992.

Balthasar, Hans Urs von, and Joseph Ratzinger. *Two Say Why*. Translated by John Griffiths. London: Search, 1971.

Bauerschmidt, Frederick Christian. "Augustine and Aquinas." In *T&T Clark Companion to Augustine and Modern Theology*, edited by C. C. Pecknold and Tarmo Toom, 113–30. London: Bloomsbury, 2013.

Benedict. *The Rule of Saint Benedict*. Edited by Timothy Fry. New York: Vintage, 1998.

Benedict XVI. "Address to Bishops of Portugal, Fatima." Speech. May 13, 2010. Online. http://www.vatican.va/holy_father/benedict_xvi/speeches/2010/may/documents/ hf_ben-xvi_spe_20100513_vescovi-portogallo_en.html.

———. *Caritas in veritate*. Encyclical Letter. San Francisco: Ignatius, 2009.

———. *Deus caritas est*. Encyclical Letter San Francisco: Ignatius, 2006.

———. "Faith, Reason, and the University: Memories and Reflections: Aula Magna of the University of Regensburg." Speech. September 12, 2006. Online. http://www.vatican.va/holy_father/benedict_xvi/speeches/2006/september/documents/ hf_benxvi_spe_20060912_university-regensburg_en.html.

———. "General Audience." April 27, 2005. Online. http://www.vatican.va/content/benedict-xvi/en/audiences/2005/documents/hf_ben-xvi_aud_20050427.html.

———. *Spe salvi*. Encyclical Letter. San Francisco: Ignatius, 2008.

———. "Verbum domini." Apostolic Exhortation. September 30, 2010. Online. http://w2.vatican.va/content/benedict-xvi/en/apost_ exhortations/documents/hf_ben-xvi_exh_20100930_verbum-domini.html.

BIBLIOGRAPHY

Betz, John. "After Barth: A New Introduction to Erich Przywara's *Analogia Entis*." In *Analogy of Being: Invention of the Anti-Christ or the Wisdom of God?*, edited by Thomas Joseph White, 35–87. Grand Rapids: Eerdmans, 2011.

———. "Beyond the Sublime: The Aesthetics of the Analogy of Being (Part Two)." *Modern Theology* 22.1 (2006) 1–50.

Bonagura, David. "Logos to Son in the Christology of Joseph Ratzinger/Benedict XVI." *New Blackfriars* 93.1046 (2012) 475–88.

Bonaventure. *Disputed Questions on the Mystery of the Trinity*. Translated by Zachary Hayes. St. Bonaventure, NY: Franciscan Institute, St. Bonaventure University Press, 1979.

Cavanaugh, William T. *Migrations of the Holy: God, State, and the Political Meaning of the Church*. Grand Rapids: Eerdmans, 2011.

———. *Torture and Eucharist: Theology, Politics, and the Body of Christ*. Malden, MA: Blackwell, 1998.

Chenu, M. D. "The Signs of the Times." In *The Church Today: Commentaries on the Pastoral Constitution on the Church in the Modern World*, edited by Group 2000, 43–54. Westminster, MD: Newman, 1968.

Colombo, Giueppe. "La teologia della chiesa locale." In *La teologia della chiesa locale*, edited by Andrea Tessarolo, 17–38. Bologna: Dehoniane, 1969.

Congar, Yves. *I Believe in the Holy Spirit*. Translated by David Smith. 3 vols. New York: Crossroad, 1997.

Congregation for the Doctrine of the Faith (CDF). *Communionis notio*. Vatican: Libreria Editrice Vaticana, 1994.

Day, Dorothy. "On Pilgrimage." *Catholic Worker*, September 1956. Online. http://dorothyday.catholicworker.org/articles/710.html.

Del Colle, Ralph. "Communion and the Trinity: The Free Church Ecclesiology of Miroslav Volf—A Catholic Response." *Pneuma: The Journal of the Society for Pentecostal Studies* 22.2 (2000) 303–327.

Dianich, Serverino. *Chiesa in missione: Per una ecclesiologia dinamica*. Rome: Ed. Paoline, 1985.

———. *De caritate ecclesiae: Il principio "amore" e la Chiesa*. Padua: Messaggero, 1987.

Doyle, Dennis. *Communion Ecclesiology: Vision and Versions*. Maryknoll, NY: Orbis, 2000.

Dreher, Rod. *The Benedict Option: A Strategy for Christians in a Post-Christian Nation*. New York: Sentinel, 2018.

Ehle, Mary. "A Trinitarian Ecclesiology of Communion and the Mission of the Church: Beyond the Debate between Joseph Cardinal Ratzinger and Leonardo Boff; The Contribution of Bernd Jochen Hilberath." PhD diss., Marquette University, 2002.

Extraordinary Synod of Bishops (ESB). "Final Report: The Church, in the Word of God, Celebrates the Mysteries of Christ for the Salvation of the World." Translated by Vatican. Irondale, AL: EWTN, 1985.

Francis. "Lumen fidei." Encyclical Letter. June 29, 2013. Online. http://w2.vatican.va/content/francesco/en/encyclicals/documents/papa-francesco_20130629_enciclica-lumen-fidei.html.

Gallagher, James. *A Woman's Work*. Hyde Park, NY: New City, 1997.

Gilson, Étienne. *The Philosophy of St. Bonaventure*. Paterson, NJ: St. Anthony Guild, 1983.

Giono, Jean. *Les vraies richesses*. Paris: Grasset, 1936.

Haight, Roger. "Critical Witness: The Question of Method." In *Faithful Witness: Foundations of Theology for Today's Church*, edited by Leo O'Donovan and T. Howland Sanks, 185–204. New York: Crossroad, 1989.

Heim, Maximilian Heinrich. *Joseph Ratzinger: Life in the Church and Living Theology; Fundamentals of Ecclesiology with Reference to Lumen Gentium*. Translated by Michael Miller. San Francisco: Ignatius, 2007.

Hitchcock, James. *Catholicism and Modernity: Confrontation or Capitulation?* New York: Seabury, 1979.

Huxley, Aldous. *Brave New World*. New York: HarperPerennial, 1998.

International Theological Commission (ITC). "Select Themes of Ecclesiology on the Occasion of the Twentieth Anniversary of the Closing of the Second Vatican Council." 1984. Online. http://www.vatican.va/roman_curia/congregations/cfaith/cti_documents/rc_cti_1984_ecclesiologia_en.html.

John XXIII. "Humanae salutis." In *The Encyclicals and Other Messages of John XXIII*, edited by the staff of *Pope Speaks* magazine, 386–97. Translated by Austin Vaughn. Washington, DC: TPS, 1964.

John Paul II. "Christifidelis laici." Apostolic Exhortation. December 30, 1998. Online. http://w2.vatican.va/content/john-paul-ii/en/apost_exhortations/documents/hf_jp-ii_exh_30121988_christifideles-laici.html.

———. "Novo millennio ineunte." Apostolic Letter. January 6, 2001. Online. http://w2.vatican.va/content/john-paul-ii/en/apost_letters/2001/documents/hf_jp-ii_apl_20010106_novo-millennio-ineunte.html.

———. "Redemptoris missio." Encyclical Letter. July 12, 1990. Online. http://w2.vatican.va/content/john-paul-ii/en/encyclicals/documents/hf_jp-ii_enc_07121990_redemptoris-missio.html.

Kasper, Walter. "On the Church: A Friendly Reply to Cardinal Ratzinger." *America* 184 (2001) 8–14.

Kehl, Medard. *Wohin geht die Kirche? Eine zeitdiagnose*. Freiburg: Herder, 1996.

Kerr, Fergus. "Recent Thomistica IV." *New Blackfriars* 87 (2006) 651–59.

Komonchak, Joseph. "A propos de la priorité de l'Eglise universelle: analyse et questions." In *Nouveaux apprentissages pour l'Église: mélanges offerts à Hervé Legrand*, edited by Gilles Routhier and Laurent Villemin, 245–68. Paris: Cerf, 2006.

———. "The Church: God's Gift and Our Task." *Origins* 16.2 (1987) 735–41.

———. "The Epistemology of Reception." *The Jurist* 57 (1997) 180–203.

———. *Foundations in Ecclesiology*. Edited by Fred Lawrence. Supplementary Issue of *Lonergan Workshop* 11. Boston: Lonergan Workshop, 1995.

———. "The Local Church and the Church Catholic: The Contemporary Theological Problematic." *The Jurist* 52 (1992) 416–47.

———. "Ministry and the Local Church." *Proceedings of the Catholic Theological Society of America* 36 (1981) 56–82.

———. "Modernity and the Construction of Roman Catholicism." *Cristianismo nella storia* 18 (1997) 353–85.

———. "The Redaction and Reception of Gaudium et Spes: Tensions within the Majority at Vatican II." Originally published as "Le valutazioni sulla Gaudium et spes: Chenu, Dossetti, Ratzinger." In *Volti di fine Concilio: Studi di storia e teologia sulla conclusione del Vaticano II*, edited by Joseph Doré and Alberto Melloni, 115–53. Bologna: Il Mulino, 2000. Online. http://jakomonchak.files.wordpress.com/2013/04/jak-views-of-gaudium-et-spes.pdf.

———. "Towards a Theology of the Local Church." *Federation of Asian Bishops' Conferences Papers* 42 (1986) 1–41.

———. *Who Are the Church?* Milwaukee: Marquette University Press, 2008.

Kucer, Peter Samuel. *Truth and Politics: A Theological Comparison of Joseph Ratzinger and John Milbank.* Minneapolis: Fortress, 2014.

Lamb, Matthew, and Matthew Levering, eds. *Vatican II: Renewal within Tradition.* New York: Oxford University Press, 2008.

Latourelle, Rene, ed. *Vatican II: Assessment and Perspectives.* 3 vols. New York: Paulist, 1988.

Leahy, Brendan. *Ecclesial Movements and Communities: Origins, Significance, and Issues.* Hyde Park, NY: New City, 2011.

Lohaus, Gerd. "Das Verhaltnis von Ortskirche und Universalkirche bei Joseph Ratzinger: Ein beitrag zum nachkonziliaren streit um die universale und partikulare Kirche." *Pastoralblatt fur die Diozesen Aachen, Berlin, Essen, Hamburg, Hildesheim, Koln, Osnabruck* 45.8 (1993) 234–45.

Lohfink, Gerhard. *Does God Need the Church? Toward a Theology of the People of God.* Translated by Samuel Moore. Collegeville, MN: Liturgical, 1999.

Lonergan, Bernard. *Method in Theology.* Toronto: University of Toronto Press, 1999.

Lubac, Henri de. *Catholicism: Christ and the Common Destiny of Man.* Translated by Lancelot C. Sheppard and Elizabeth Englund. San Francisco: Ignatius, 1988.

———. *La foi chretienne: Essai sur la structure du symbole des apotres.* 2nd ed. Paris: Aubier-Montaigne, 1970.

———. *Meditation sur L'Eglise.* Paris: Aubier, 1953.

———. *The Splendor of the Church.* Translated by Michael Mason. San Francisco: Ignatius, 1999.

Lubich, Chiara. *The Cry: Jesus Crucified and Forsaken in the History and Life of the Focolare Movement, from Its Birth in 1943, until the Dawn of the Third Millennium.* Hyde Park, NY: New City, 2001.

———. "Dialogo aperto: Solitudine e unità." *Città Nuova* 19.22 (1975) 33.

———. *Diary 1964/65.* Hyde Park, NY: New City, 1987.

———. *Essential Writings: Spirituality, Dialogue, Culture.* Hyde Park, NY: New City, 2007.

———. *Scritti Spirituali.* Vol. 1 of *L'attrattiva del tempo moderno.* Rome: Città Nuova, 1978.

———. "Unity and Jesus Crucified and Forsaken: Foundation of a Spirituality of Communion." *The Ecumenical Review* 55.1 (2003) 87–95.

———. *Yes, Yes, No, No.* London: New City, 1977.

MacIntyre, Alasdair. *After Virtue: A Study in Moral Theory.* Notre Dame: University of Notre Dame Press, 2007.

Madar, Martin. "The Contribution of Joseph A. Komonchak to the Theology of the Local Church in Light of Lumen Gentium." PhD diss., Catholic University of America, 2014.

Manning, Henry Edward. "On Progress." In vol. 1 of *Miscellanies*, by Henry Edward Manning, 293–324. London: Burns and Oates, 1877.

Mannion, Gerard. *Ecclesiology and Postmodernity: Questions for the Church in Our Time.* Collegeville, MN: Liturgical, 2007.

Massa, James. "The Communion Theme in the Writings of Joseph Ratzinger: Unity in the Church and in the World through Sacramental Encounter." PhD diss., Fordham University, 1996.

McGregor, Peter John. *Heart to Heart: The Spiritual Christology of Joseph Ratzinger.* Eugene, OR: Pickwick, 2016.

———. "The 'Spiritual Christology' of Joseph Ratzinger/Pope Benedict XVI: An Exposition and Analysis of its Principles." *Radical Orthodoxy: Theology, Philosophy, Politics* 2.1 (2014) 51–89.

Milet, Jean. *God or Christ? The Excesses of Christocentricity.* New York: Crossroad, 1981.

Neuner, Josef, and Jacques Dupuis, eds. *The Christian Faith in the Doctrinal Pronouncements of the Catholic Church.* 7th ed. New York: Alba, 2001.

Newman, John Henry. *Historical Sketches II.* London: Longmans, Green, 1906.

———. "The Infidelity of the Future." In *Faith and Prejudice, and Other Unpublished Sermons.* New York: Sheed & Ward, 1956.

Nichols, Aidan. *The Thought of Pope Benedict XVI: An Introduction to the Theology of Joseph Ratzinger.* London: Burns & Oates, 2007.

Norris, Thomas. *Fractured Relationship: Faith and the Crisis of Culture.* Hyde Park, NY: New City, 2010.

Oakes, Kenneth. "The Cross and the *Analogia Entis* in Erich Przywara." In *Analogy of Being: Invention of the Anti-Christ or the Wisdom of God?*, edited by Thomas Joseph White, 147–71. Grand Rapids: Eerdmans, 2011.

———. "Nature and Grace in Barth." *Modern Theology* 23.4 (2007) 604–5.

O'Malley, John W. *What Happened at Vatican II.* Cambridge, MA: Belknap Press of Harvard University Press, 2008.

Paul VI. "Evangelii nuntiandi." Apostolic Exhortation. December 8, 1975. Online. http://w2.vatican.va/content/paul-vi/en/apost_exhortations/documents/hf_p-vi_exh_19751208_evangelii-nuntiandi.html.

Paul VI, and Floyd Anderson. *Council Daybook: Vatican II, Session 3.* Washington, DC: National Catholic Welfare Conference, 1965.

Pinckaers, Servais. *Morality: The Catholic View.* Translated by Michael Sherwin. South Bend, IN: St. Augustine's, 2001.

Porteous, Julius. *New Wine and Fresh Skins: Ecclesial Movements in the Church.* Ballan, Victoria, Australia: Modotti, 2010.

Povilus, Judith M. *Gesú in mezzo: Jesus nel pensiero di Chiara Lubich.* Rome: Città Nuova, 1981.

———. *United in His Name: Jesus in Our Midst in the Experience and Thought of Chiara Lubich.* Translated by Jerry Hearne. Hyde Park, NY: New City, 1992.

Przywara, Erich. *Analogia Entis: Metaphysics: Original Structure and Universal Rhythm.* Translated by John Betz and David Bentley Hart. Grand Rapids: Eerdmans, 2014.

———. *Gottgeheimnis der welt: drei vorträge über die geistige krisis der gegenwart.* München: Theatiner-Verlag, 1923.

———. *Schriften.* 3 vols. Einsiedeln: Johannes, 1962.

Purcell, Brendan. "The Focolare Movement." *The Australasian Catholic Record* 89.2 (2012) 161–73.

Ratzinger, Joseph. *Behold the Pierced One: An Approach to a Spiritual Christology.* San Francisco: Ignatius, 1986. Originally published as *Schauen auf den Durchborten.* Einsiedeln: Johannes, 1984.

———. *Called to Communion: Understanding the Church Today*. Translated by Adrian Walker. San Francisco: Ignatius, 1996. Originally published as *Zur gemeinschaft gerufen Kirche heute verstehen*. Freiburg im Breisgau: Herder, 1991.

———. "Catholicism after the Council." *The Furrow* 18 (1967) 3–23.

———. *Christianity and the Crisis of Cultures*. Translated by Brian McNeil. San Francisco: Ignatius, 2006. Originally published as *L'Europa di Benedetto nella crisi delle culture*. Roma: Cantagalli, 2005.

———. *Church, Ecumenism, and Politics: New Essays in Ecclesiology*. Translated by Robert Lowell and Dame Frideswide Sandemann. New York: Crossroad, 1988. Originally published as *Kirche, ökumene und politik: Neue versuche zur ekklesiologie*. Einsiedeln: Johannes, 1987.

———. "Communio: A Program." Translated by Peter Casarella. *International Catholic Review: Communio* 19.3 (1992) 436–49.

———. "Concerning the Notion of Person in Theology." Translated by Michael Waldstein. *International Catholic Review: Communio* 17.3 (1990) 439–54.

———. *Das neue volk Gottes: Entwürfe zur ekklesiologie*. Düsseldorf: Patmos, 1977.

———. *Dogma and Preaching: Applying Christian Doctrine to Daily Life*. Translated by Michael J. Miller. San Francisco: Ignatius, 2011. Originally published as *Dogma und Verkündigung*. Munich: E. Wewel, 1973.

———. "Eschatology and Utopia." In *Church, Ecumenism, and Politics: New Essays in Ecclesiology*, by Joseph Ratzinger, 223–38. New York: Crossroad, 1988.

———. *Eschatology: Death and Eternal Life*. Translated by Michael Waldstein and Aidan Nichols. Washington, DC: Catholic University of America Press, 2007. Original published as *Eschatologie—tod und ewiges leben*. 6th ed. Regensburg: F. Pustet, 2007.

———. *God and the World: A Conversation with Peter Seewald*. San Francisco: Ignatius, 2002. Originally published as *Gott und die welt: Glauben und leben in unserer zeit. Ein gespräch mit Peter Seewald*. Munich: Knaur Taschenbuch, 2005.

———. *God Is Near Us: The Eucharist, the Heart of Life*. Translated by Henry Taylor. San Francisco: Ignatius, 2003. Originally published as *Eucharistie: Mitte der Kirche*. Munich: E. Wewel, 1978.

———. *The God of Jesus Christ: Meditations on the Triune God*. San Francisco: Ignatius, 2008. Originally Published as *Der Gott Jesus Christi: Betrachtungen über den dreieinigen Gott*. Munich: Kösel, 1976.

———. "*Gratia praesupponit naturam*: Erwägungen über Sinn und Grenze eines scholastischen Axioms." In *Einsicht und Glaube: Festschrift G. Söhngen zum 70. Geburtstag*, edited by Joseph Ratzinger and Heinrich Fries, 135–49. Freiburg: Herder, 1962.

———. *Images of Hope: Meditations on Major Feasts*. San Francisco: Ignatius, 2006. Originally published as *Bilder der hoffnung: wanderungen im kirchenjahr*. Freiburg: Herder, 1997.

———. *In the Beginning: A Catholic Understanding of the Story of Creation and the Fall*. Translated by Boniface Ramsey. Grand Rapids: Eerdmans, 1995. Originally published as *Im anfang schuf Gott*. Munich: E. Wewel, 1986.

———. *Introduction to Christianity*. Translated by J. R. Foster. San Francisco: Ignatius, 2004. Originally published as *Einführung in das Christentum: Vorlesungen über das apostolische glaubensbekenntnis*. Munich: Kösel, 1968.

———. "Introduzione." In Lettera "Communionis notio" su alcuini aspetti della Chiesa intesa come comunione (28 maggio 1952): Testo e commenti, edited by the Congregation for the Doctrine of the Faith, 7–10. Vatican City: Libreria Editrice Vaticana, 1994.

———. Jesus of Nazareth: Part One. From the Baptism in the Jordan to the Transfiguration. Translated by Adrian J. Walker. New York: Doubleday, 2007. Simultaneously published in German as Jesus von Nazareth: Erster Teil. Von der Taufe im Jordan bis zur Verklärung. Freiburg im Breisgau: Herder, 2007.

———. Jesus of Nazareth: Part Two. Holy Week. Translated by Philip J. Whitmore. San Francisco: Ignatius, 2011. Simultaneously published in German as Jesus von Nazareth: Zweiter Teil. Vom einzug in Jerusalem bis zur Auferstehung. Vatican: Liberia Editrice Vaticana, 2011.

———. "Kirche als Tempel." In Vom wiederauffinden der mitte: Grundorientierungen: Texte aus vier jarhzehnten, edited by S. O. Horn, et al., 148–57. Freiburg: Herder, 1997.

———. The Meaning of Christian Brotherhood. San Francisco: Ignatius, 1993. Originally published as Die Christliche Brüderlichkeit. Munich: Kösel, 1960.

———. Milestones: Memoirs 1927–1977. Translated by Erasmo Leiva-Merikakis. San Francisco: Ignatius, 1998.

———. The Nature and Mission of Theology: Approaches to Understanding Its Role in the Light of Present Controversy. San Francisco: Ignatius, 1995. Originally published as Wesen und auftrag der Theologie: versuche zu ihrer ortsbestimmung im disput der gegenwart. Einsiedeln: Johannes, 1993.

———. New Outpourings of the Spirit: Movements in the Church. San Francisco: Ignatius, 2007.

———. A New Song for the Lord: Faith in Christ and Liturgy Today. New York: Crossroad, 1996. Originally published as Ein neues lied für den Herrn: Christusglaube und liturgie in der gegenwart. Freiburg: Herder, 1995.

———. "Part I: The Church and Man's Calling—Introductory Article and Chapter 1—The Dignity of the Human Person—Pastoral Constitution on the Church in the Modern World." In vol. 5 of Commentary on the Documents of Vatican II, translated by W. J. O'Hara, edited by Herbert Vorgrimler, 115–63. New York: Herder and Herder, 1969.

———. Pilgrim Fellowship of Faith: The Church as Communion. Translated by Henry Taylor. San Francisco: Ignatius, 2005. Originally published as Weggemeinschaft des glaubens: Kirche als communio. Edited by S. O. Horn and V. Pfnur. Augsburg: Sankt Ulrich, 2002.

———. Principles of Catholic Theology: Building Stones for a Fundamental Theology. Translated by Mary Frances McCarthy. San Francisco: Ignatius, 1987. Originally published as Theologiesche prinzipienlehre: Bausteine zur fundamentaltheologie. Munich: E. Wewel, 1982.

———. "Pro Eligendo Romano Pontifice." Homily for Mass. April 18, 2005. Online. http://www.vatican.edu/gpII/documents/homily-pro-eligendo-pontifice_20050418_en.html.

———. "Probleme von Glaubens und Sittenlehre im europäischen Kontext." In Zu grundfragen der theologie heute, by Joseph Ratzinger, 7–17. Paderborn: Bonifatius, 1992.

———. *Salt of the Earth: Christianity and the Catholic Church at the End of the Millennium. An Interview with Peter Seewald*. Translated by Adrian Walker. San Francisco: Ignatius, 1997. Originally published as *Salz der erde: Christentum und katholische Kirche an der jahrtausendwende*. Stuttgart: Deutsche, 1996.

———. *Seeking God's Face*. Chicago: Franciscan Herald, 1982.

———. *The Spirit of the Liturgy*. Translated by John Saward. San Francisco, CA: Ignatius, 2000. Originally published as *Der geist der liturgie: eine einführung*. Freiburg: Herder, 2001.

———. *Theological Highlights of Vatican II*. New York: Paulist, 1966.

———. "The Theological Locus of Ecclesial Movements." *Communio* 25 (1998) 481–504.

———. *Theologie der liturgie: die sakramentale begründung christlicher existenz*. Meitingen and Freising: Kyrios, 1967.

———. *The Theology of History in Bonaventure*. Translated by Zachary Hayes. Chicago: Franciscan Herald, 1971. Originally published as *Die geschichtstheologie des heiligen Bonaventura*. Munich: Schnell und Steiner, 1959.

———. "Theology of the Liturgy." In *Looking Again at the Question of the Liturgy with Cardinal Ratzinger: Proceedings of the July 2001 Fontgombault Liturgical Conference*, edited by Alcuin Reid, 18–31. Farmborough: St. Michael's Abbey, 2003.

———. *Truth and Tolerance: Christian Belief and World Religions*. Translated by Henry Taylor. San Francisco: Ignatius, 2004. Originally published as *Fede—verità—tolleranza: il cristianesimo e le religioni del mondo*. Siena: Edizioni Cantagalli, 2010.

———. *Volk und haus Gottes in Augustins lehre von der Kirche*. Vol. 1 of *Gesammelte Schriften*. Freiburg: Herder, 2011.

———. "We Experienced That There God Dwells with Men." *Inside the Vatican*, January 1998. 43–47.

———. *What It Means to Be a Christian: Three Sermons*. Translated by Henry Taylor. San Francisco: Ignatius, 2006. Originally published as *Vom Sinn des Christseins*. Munich: Kösel, 1966.

———. *The Yes of Jesus Christ: Exercises in Faith, Hope, and Love*. Translated by Robert Nowell. New York: Crossroad, 2005. Originally published as *Aus Christus shauen: Einubung in glaube, hoffnung, liebe*. Freiburg: Herder, 1989.

Ratzinger, Joseph, with Vittorio Messori. *The Ratzinger Report: An Exclusive Interview on the State of the Church*. Translated by Salvator Attanasio and Graham Harrison. San Francisco: Ignatius, 1985.

Ratzinger, Joseph, and Marcello Pera. *Without Roots: The West, Relativism, Christianity, Islam*. Translated by Michael F. Moore. New York: Basic, 2006.

Robertson, Edwin. *Chiara*. Belfast: Christian Journals, 1978.

Rush, Ormond. *Still Interpreting Vatican II: Some Hermeneutical Principles*. New York: Paulist, 2004.

Schenk, Richard. "Analogy as the *discrimen naturae et gratiae*: Thomism and Ecumenical Learning." In *The Analogy of Being: Invention of the Antichrist or the Wisdom of God?*, edited by Thomas Joseph White, 172–91. Grand Rapids: Eerdmans, 2011.

———. "Bonaventura als klassiker der analogia fidei: Zur rezeption der theologischen programmatik Gottlieb Söhngens im frühwerk Joseph Ratzingers." In *Offenbarung und heilsgeschichte: Joseph Ratzingers Bonaventura-studien unter theologiegeschichtlichen und systematischen aspekten.* Edited by Marianne Schlosser und Franz Xaver Heibl. Regensburg: Friedrich Pustet, 2011.

———. "Epilogue: Analogy of Being—Invention of the Antichrist or the Wisdom of God? Looking Back, Looking Forward." In *The Analogy of Being: Invention of the Antichrist or the Wisdom of God?*, edited by Thomas Joseph White, 411–16. Grand Rapids: Eerdmans, 2011.

———. "The Unsundered Net: Benedict XVI and the Prospects of Ecumenism." *Dialog: A Journal of Theology* 44.3 (2005) 292–96.

Second Vatican Council. "Gaudium et Spes." Pastoral Constitution on the Church in the Modern World. December 7, 1965. Online. http://www.vatican.va/archive/hist_councils/ii_vatican_council/documents/vat-ii_const_19651207_gaudium-et-spes_en.html.

———. "Lumen Gentium." Dogmatic Constitution on the Church. November 21, 1964. Online. http://www.vatican.va/archive/hist_councils/ii_vatican_council/documents/vat-ii_const_19641121_lumen-gentium_en.html.

Smith, Christian, with Melinda Lundquist Denton. *Soul Searching: The Religious and Spiritual Lives of American Teenagers*. London: Oxford University Press, 2005.

Smith, James K. A. *Desiring the Kingdom: Worship, Worldview, and Cultural Formation.* Grand Rapids: Baker Academic, 2009.

Söhngen, Gottlieb. "The Analogy of Faith: Unity in the Science of Faith." *Pro Ecclesia* 21.2 (2012) 169–94 Originally published as "Analogia fidei." *Catholica* 3 (1934) 198–200.

———. *Mysterium Salutis*. Cologne: Benziger, 1965.

———. "Wesen und akt in der scholastischen Lehre von der participatio und analogia entis." *Studium Generale* 8 (1955) 649–62.

Starnes, Colin. *Augustine's Conversion: A Guide to the Argument of "Confessions" I–IX.* Waterloo, ON: W. Laurier, 1990.

Strauss, Leo. "Progress or Return? The Contemporary Crisis in Western Civilization." In *An Introduction to Political Philosophy: Ten Essays*, edited by Hilail Gildin, 249–310. Detroit: Wayne State University Press, 1989.

Taylor, Charles. *A Secular Age*. Cambridge, MA: Belknap Press of Harvard University Press, 2007.

Toynbee, Arnold Joseph. *A Study of History: Abridgement of Volumes I–VI.* Edited by D. C. Somervell. New York: Oxford University Press, 1987.

Valentini, Donato. *Il nuovo popoli di Dio in cammino: Punti nodali per una ecclesiologia attuale*. Rome: LAS, 1984.

Volf, Miroslav. *After Our Likeness: The Church as the Image of the Trinity*. Grand Rapids: Eerdmans, 1998.

Wainwright, Geoffrey. "The 'New Worship' in Joseph Ratzinger's *Jesus of Nazareth*." *Nova et Vetera* (English Edition) 10.4 (2012) 993–1013.

White, Thomas Joseph. "'Through Him All Things Were Made' (John 1:3): The Analogy of the Word Incarnate according to St. Thomas Aquinas and Its Ontological Presuppositions." In *The Analogy of Being: Invention of the Antichrist or the Wisdom of God?*, edited by Thomas Joseph White, 246–79. Grand Rapids: Eerdmans, 2011.

Index

analogy of being, 29, 30, 32, 34–36, 50, 51
analogia entis, 8, 29–36, 40, 50–54, 56
analogy of faith, 30, 35, 36, 50, 51
analogia fidei, 30, 34–37, 50, 51, 53
Anselm, Saint, 36
Anthony, Saint, 162
Aristotle, 38, 39, 124, 144
Arnold Toynbee, 5
Augustine, Saint, 28, 29, 36, 51, 63, 67–70, 77, 81, 82, 97, 98, 142, 151, 152, 155, 163, 180, 185
Augustinian, 28, 29, 37, 67, 82

Balthasar, Hans urs von, 31, 34, 44, 55, 133
Barth, Karl, 29, 32–37, 39–42, 46, 51
Bauerschmidt, Frederick, 28
Benedict, Saint, 2–8, 56, 106, 137, 162, 174, 181, 182
Benedict Option, 3
Benedict XVI, Pope. *See* Ratzinger, Joseph
Betz, John, 29, 32, 33, 35, 36, 50, 51
Boethius, 69, 71
Boff, Leonardo, 126, 132, 133, 156
Bonagura, David, 64
Bonaventure, Saint, 30, 34, 36–43, 45, 48, 51–54, 56, 63, 142, 146
Bouyer, Louis, 127

Caritas in veritate, 53, 185
Cavanaugh, William, 151
Chenu, M. D., 27, 28, 34, 36

Christ, 2, 4–8, 14, 17, 20–24, 36–38, 41, 44, 46, 49, 51–53, 55, 56, 61–63, 65–68, 70–72, 74–76, 78–94, 98–101, 103–6, 108–13, 117, 119–26, 128, 132–37, 139–43, 145, 146, 148, 150–53, 155, 160, 161, 163–65, 167, 168, 170–72, 174, 175, 178, 179, 181, 183, 184
Christology, 49, 52, 54, 55, 62, 64–69, 71, 74, 75, 78, 81, 83, 101, 111, 137, 140–42, 148, 150–52
  Logos Christology, 52, 54
  spiritual Christology, 64, 66, 69, 74, 75, 83, 101, 137, 140, 141, 148, 150–52
Chrysostom, Saint John, 151
communio, 29, 62, 63, 65, 68, 71, 75–77, 80, 85, 86, 88, 90, 109, 141, 148, 160, 168, 169, 174, 179, 185
communion and mission, 1, 3, 8, 9, 77, 87, 90, 92, 93, 98, 105, 136, 138, 158, 160, 172
  communion missiology, 43, 115, 134, 150, 180
communion ecclesiology, 2, 8, 59, 67, 71, 113, 135, 136
  communio ecclesiology, 76, 77, 87
  communion, ecclesial, 63, 86, 94, 113, 118, 119, 151, 168, 170
Communionis notio, 130
communio personarum, 62, 63, 71, 75, 141, 168, 179
Congar, Yves, 135

195

INDEX

creative minorities, 5–9, 13, 17, 43, 56, 57, 77, 89, 109, 110, 115, 137, 143, 148, 150, 153, 157, 158, 160, 163, 165, 171, 174, 175, 178, 180–84
Cyprian, Saint, 61, 76, 151
Cyril, Saint, 163

Day, Dorothy, 156
Dei Verbum, 53
Del Colle, Ralph, 138, 139, 142
Dianich, Severino, 126, 128
Didache, 99, 103
Dominic, Saint, 162, 163, 180
Donatist, 68, 110
Doyle, Dennis, 67, 71
Dreher, Rod, 3

ecclesial communities, 8, 94, 126, 161, 165, 174
ecclesial movements, 9, 150, 158, 161, 165, 173–75, 180, 183, 184
ecclesiology and missiology, 40, 69, 134, 136, 153, 160
ecclesiology of communion, 8, 37, 59, 61, 75, 115, 118, 132–36, 150, 153, 184
Ehle, Mary, 9, 118, 131–38, 150, 151, 153–56
eschatology, 30, 40, 46, 54, 57, 103, 104
eucharist, 59, 75, 77, 79–82, 85–91, 94, 98–102, 104–9, 112, 113, 125, 127, 131, 133, 134, 143, 148, 151–53, 160, 170–72, 175, 178–80, 183
eucharistic ecclesiology, 3, 8, 9, 43, 89, 108, 111, 137, 151, 153, 179, 180, 183, 184
Evangelii nuntiandi, 1, 93, 94
evangelization, 2, 4, 27, 42, 45, 48, 50, 53, 90, 93, 94, 110, 111, 124, 131, 143, 144, 151, 153, 164, 171, 173, 181

Focolare, 115, 158, 165–69, 171–75, 178, 180, 183
Francis, Pope, 17, 21

Francis of Assisi, Saint, 162
Franciscan, 36, 38, 48, 163, 180

Gaudium et Spes, 21, 23, 24, 26–30, 34, 37, 39, 41–43, 45, 55, 56, 76
Gilson, Etienne, 38
Gregory the Great, Pope Saint, 163

Haight, Roger, 123
Heim, Maximilian Heinrich, 20, 44, 45, 67, 68, 78, 79, 82, 86, 105, 111, 112, 117, 171
Huxley, Aldous, 159
hypostatic union, 65, 71, 73, 74, 123

Ignatius of Antioch, Saint, 109, 162
Ignatius of Loyola, Saint, 162
incarnation, 19, 23, 41, 53, 62–65, 71, 78, 83, 84, 94, 103, 108, 140, 146, 151, 169
Irenaeus, Saint, 95

Jesus, 14, 19, 20, 49, 55, 62–67, 70–76, 78–80, 82–85, 88–91, 93, 98–105, 108, 109, 111, 120, 128, 139, 140, 142, 146, 147, 152, 154, 160, 161, 164–72, 174–78, 180, 182–84
John Paul II, Pope Saint, 1, 2, 92–94, 174, 176
John XXIII, Pope Saint, 1, 8, 27, 45, 56
Julian the Apostate, 3, 50

Kasper, Walter Cardinal, 35
Kehl, Medard, 174, 175
Kolbe, Saint Maximilian, 141
Komonchak, Joseph, 9, 13, 18, 19, 28, 43, 118, 122–32, 135–38, 143, 144, 147, 148, 150, 151, 185
Kucer, Peter Samuel, 48, 51

Lamb, Matthew, 13
Latourelle, Rene, 13
Leahy, Brendan, 161, 174, 175
Legrand, Hervé, 127, 129
Levering, Matthew, 13

INDEX

liturgy, 8, 30, 43, 56, 59, 85, 92, 94–98, 100, 101, 103–9, 112, 171, 180, 183
   liturgy and mission, 94, 183
local church, 56, 88, 89, 108, 122–31, 135, 136, 143, 144, 146–51, 153, 163, 164
Lohaus, Gerd, 86
Lohfink, Gerhard, 47, 77, 90, 91
Lonergan, Bernard, 122, 124, 125
Lubac, Henri de, 20, 62, 76, 77, 127
Lubich, Chiara, 115, 158, 165–72, 175–80, 182
Lumen fidei, 17, 21
Lumen Gentium, 21–23, 27, 76, 91, 106

MacIntyre, Alasdair, 2, 3
Madar, Martin, 123, 124
Manning, Henry Cardinal, 19
Mannion, Gerard, 118
Marx, Karl, 46, 155
marxism, 16, 39, 42, 45–47, 78, 133
Massa, James, 81, 85, 86
McGregor, Peter John, 64
missiology, 8, 40, 43, 69, 90, 115, 131, 132, 134–37, 150, 153, 156, 160, 180
mission, 1–3, 7–9, 21–23, 25, 26, 29, 43, 52, 55, 59, 68, 69, 77, 81, 82, 87, 90–94, 98, 104–6, 111–13, 117, 118, 125, 128, 131–38, 144, 148, 150, 151, 153–58, 160, 162–64, 168, 170–75, 177, 180, 182, 183

nature and grace, 28, 29, 33, 34, 36, 39, 40, 146
neo-scholastic, 21, 25, 27, 34, 41, 43, 122
neo-Thomism, 36, 38–40, 42
Newman, Saint John Henry, 7, 14, 16, 122
new worship, 90, 98–104, 113, 152, 175
Nichols, Aidan, 80–82
Norris, Thomas, 47, 50

Oakes, Kenneth, 36, 51
O'Connor, Flannery, 49
O'Malley, John, 13

particular church, 126, 128, 130, 131, 147
Patrick, Saint, 163
Paul, Saint, 36, 41, 51, 66, 82, 85, 107, 108, 146, 178
Paul VI, Pope Saint, 1, 21, 22, 93, 94
people of God, 23, 49, 61, 78, 79, 86, 91, 94, 95, 105, 124, 125, 128, 145, 146, 151
Pinckaers, Servais, 141
pneumatology, 67–69, 81, 83, 117, 132, 152, 162
Polycarp, Saint, 109, 141
Przywara, Erich, 29–34, 36, 37, 48, 51–53, 56
Purcell, Brendan, 166, 167

Ratzinger, Joseph, 3–9, 13–17, 19–23, 26–31, 34, 35, 37–57, 59, 61–91, 94–113, 115, 117–26, 129–65, 167–72, 174, 175, 177–85
   ecclesiology, 3, 8, 9, 59, 75, 77, 81, 86, 89, 94, 111, 115, 117–19, 123, 129–32, 134, 136, 142, 144, 148, 150–53, 158, 161, 165, 167, 180, 184
   existential ecclesiality, 118, 165, 184
   missiology, 131, 132, 134, 136, 150, 156
   Regensburg address, 52, 147
   spiritual Christology, 66, 75, 101, 140, 141, 148, 151, 152
   spiritual mission, 118, 133–35, 150, 151
   trinitarian theology, 69, 76, 119, 132, 135, 136, 141, 142
Redemptoris missio, 1, 92, 94
Richard of Saint Victor, 71
Romero, Saint Oscar, 156

Schenk, Richard, 32, 34, 36, 37, 42, 51
Second Vatican Council. *See* Vatican II, Council of)
Smith, Christian, 182

Smith, James K. A., 159
Söhngen, Gottlieb, 30, 32, 34–37, 39, 42, 45, 51, 52, 54, 56
Spe salvi, 20, 46, 185
Starnes, Colin, 77

Taylor, Charles, 3
Tertullian, 151
Third Council of Constantinople, 65, 83, 140
Thomas Aquinas, Saint, 28, 29, 31, 32, 34–37, 39, 69, 139, 163, 164, 185
Toynbee, Arnold, 5, 6, 174, 183
Trent, Council of, 21, 84, 165–67, 182
Trinity, 8, 53, 61–63, 67, 69, 73, 76, 77, 80, 87, 118–20, 132, 136, 138, 139, 141, 142, 168, 169, 179, 180
  Father, 33, 52, 55, 59, 61–68, 70, 72–79, 81, 84, 89–94, 98, 102, 104, 109, 111, 120, 121, 132, 135, 140, 141, 152, 160, 166–69, 172, 175–81
  Holy Spirit, 4, 8, 15, 22, 33, 61, 62, 66–68, 72–77, 81, 84, 87, 89, 92, 93, 102, 109, 112, 120, 123, 125, 128, 129, 132, 135, 140, 141, 147, 150–53, 158, 160–65, 167, 168, 176, 177, 179, 183, 184
  Son, 20, 33, 61–68, 71, 72, 75–77, 79, 81, 83, 84, 92–94, 101, 109, 113, 120, 121, 132, 133, 135, 140, 146, 160, 168, 176–79

trinitarian communion, 59, 63, 75, 76, 87, 118, 133, 134, 136, 141, 160
trinitarian ecclesiology, 62, 118, 132–36, 150, 153

union, 65, 71, 73, 74, 123
universal church, 76, 89, 118, 123, 125–27, 129–31, 135, 143, 147–49, 151, 184
universal mission, 22, 91, 162–64
universal sacrament of salvation, 1, 8, 29, 38, 56, 126, 175, 180

Valentini, Donato, 131, 143
Vatican I, Council of, 21
Vatican II, Council of, 1, 13, 20–27, 43, 45, 61, 78, 79, 84, 106, 122, 147, 167, 178, 184, 185
Verbum domini, 173, 185
Vico, Giambattista, 14–16, 26
Volf, Miroslav, 9, 118–22, 132, 135, 136, 138–42, 150
Vorgrimler, Herbert, 13, 43

Wainwright, Geoffrey, 98–103

Zizioulas, John, 118

λογική λατρεία, 57, 89, 107–10, 112, 113, 137, 152, 157, 160, 165, 175, 178
  spiritual worship, 57, 109, 113, 175, 178, 179

www.ingramcontent.com/pod-product-compliance
Lightning Source LLC
Chambersburg PA
CBHW051739230426
43670CB00012B/2090